Stuart Hall

*In fond memory of my friend, Ioan Davies (1936–2000),
Professor of Social and Political Thought, York University
Toronto, who was there in Yorkville, Pittsburgh, Madrid,
Berlin, Shinjuku, and 'Black's', London, when it started*

Stuart Hall

Chris Rojek

polity

First published in 2003 by Polity Press in association with Blackwell Publishing Ltd

Editorial office:
Polity Press
65 Bridge Street
Cambridge CB2 1UR, UK

Marketing and production:
Blackwell Publishing Ltd
108 Cowley Road
Oxford OX4 1JF, UK

Distributed in the USA by
Blackwell Publishing Inc.
350 Main Street
Malden, MA 02148, USA

ISBN 0-7456-2480-4
ISBN 0-7456-2481-2 (pbk)

A catalogue record for this book is available from the British Library and has been applied for from the Library of Congress.

Typeset in 10½ on 12 pt Palatino
by SNP Best-set Typesetter Ltd., Hong Kong
Printed and bound in Great Britain by MPG Books, Bodmin, Cornwall

For further information on Polity, visit our website: http://www.polity.co.uk

Key Contemporary Thinkers

Published

Wes Sharrock and Rupert Read, *Kuhn: Philosopher of Scientific Revolution*
David Silverman, *Harvey Sacks: Social Science and Conversation Analysis*
Dennis Smith, *Zygmunt Bauman: Prophet of Postmodernity*
Nicholas H. Smith, *Charles Taylor: Meaning, Morals and Modernity*
Geoffrey Stokes, *Popper: Philosophy, Politics and Scientific Method*
Georgia Warnke, *Gadamer: Hermeneutics, Tradition and Reason*
James Williams, *Lyotard: Towards a Postmodern Philosophy*
Jonathan Wolff, *Robert Nozick: Property, Justice and the Minimal State*

Forthcoming

Maria Baghramian, *Hilary Putnam*
Sara Beardsworth, *Kristeva*
James Carey, *Innis and McLuhan*
George Crowder, *Isaiah Berlin: Liberty, Pluralism and Liberalism*
Thomas D'Andrea, *Alasdair MacIntyre*
Maximilian de Gaynesford, *John McDowell*
Reidar Andreas Due, *Deleuze*
Eric Dunning, *Norbert Elias*
Jocelyn Dunphy, *Paul Ricoeur*
Matthew Elton, *Daniel Dennett*
Chris Fleming, *René Girard: Violence and Mimesis*
Nigel Gibson, *Frantz Fanon: The Postcolonial Imagination*
Sarah Kay, *Žižek: A Critical Introduction*
Paul Kelly, *Ronald Dworkin*
Carl Levy, *Antonio Gramsci*
Moya Lloyd, *Judith Butler*
Dermot Moran, *Edmund Husserl*
Jim Murray, *C. L. R. James: Ideas in Social Movement*
James O'Shea, *Wilfrid Sellars*
Kari Palonen, *Quentin Skinner: History, Politics, Rhetoric*
Nicholas Walker, *Heidegger*

Contents

Acknowledgements

Stuart Hall once remarked that he did not seek to appropriate the thought of his foremost intellectual mentor Antonio Gramsci. Rather he positioned and repositioned it according to the circumstances of his time. Hall's Gramsci is *his* Gramsci, indelibly marked with all of the contradictions of the various 'conjunctures' in which he found himself to be situated and about which he wrote with such distinction. It is a good precedent to emulate. The Stuart Hall that emerges in these pages is *my* Hall, full of the partialities of perspective that one brings to the task of engaging with the work of a still living writer, whose capacity to surprise appears to be undimmed.

I thought it a task worth undertaking for two reasons. First, rather surprisingly, this is the first full-length solo-authored book on Hall and his work. Given his contribution to intellectual and political life along many fronts, some kind of critical assessment is now due. Second, with only a handful of exceptions, the secondary literature on Hall is a product of the Birmingham diaspora: the students and associates he worked with during his years in the Birmingham Centre for Contemporary Cultural Studies. This is the first full-length study to appear outside of the circle. In general, the Birmingham Circle has maintained a fierce sense of loyalty to Hall and the foundational ambitions of the Centre. For most graduates who enrolled in the extraordinary collaborative experiment of Birmingham in its heyday it was, one might venture, the decisive experience in their intellectual lives. Arguably, this results in an unhealthy degree of protectionism about Hall and the contemporary meaning of the Centre. Certainly, in researching the book with some Birmingham graduates I encountered a depressingly defensive reaction that boiled down to the presupposition that if you weren't there (in the 1960s and 1970s) you can't know what it was like. In any event, while there are obvious dangers in an outsider exploring Hall's work, I maintain there may also be significant advantages in being free of the understandable emotional attachments that being a Birmingham student in the 1960s and 1970s entails.

I have tried to give an honest and useful account of Hall in these pages. But I have no doubt that much of what I say will be challenged, especially by Birmingham alumni, for this book is no *hommage à Hall*, but an attempt to critically interrogate his ideas and evaluate his cultural and political influence. To write critically about Hall is to enter the lion's den. For many academics, not merely those with Birmingham credentials, Hall is a role model of what an intellectual should be: politically engaged, eloquent and fearless in his opposition of humbug and authoritarianism. Throughout, I was aware of writing not merely about a considerable intellectual, but about a cultural icon who arouses deep and conflicting passions. I tried to achieve and maintain the appropriate level of sang-froid, while conveying the respect I hold for Hall's intellectual ambition and cultural contribution. It is for others to judge whether or not I have been successful in this regard.

This book is not an *intellectual* biography of Hall. It deals with his printed ideas and their influence. Except for some well-documented material concerning his background in Jamaica, I do not comment on his private life. For example, the complex stratification structure in Jamaica during Hall's youth was, I believe, a factor that predisposed him to assign a central role to hybridity and respect for difference in his later work. The book should be judged as a critical engagement with Hall's published work. It is in no sense a biography of him.

Many thanks are due to those who have allowed me to make this book the *hallmark* of my recent research. At Nottingham Trent, Roger Bromley, Deborah Chambers, Stephen Chan, Mike Featherstone, Sandra Harris, Ali Mohammadi, John Tomlinson and Patrick Williams provided me with generous support and fellowship without which no academic work can flourish. Nik Smith was simply the best librarian one could hope for – a particularly important asset in Hall's case because so many of his writings take the form of obscure journal articles, uncollected conference presentations and interviews. My faculty awarded me a sabbatical in the second semester of the 2000–1 academic year. This was invaluable in bringing my work to fruition on time.

Outside Nottingham, Don Robotham in New York made some crucial observations about Jamaican politics and class relations in the 1930s and 1940s that helped me gain a better appreciation of Hall's milieu before coming to the UK. Amanda Root provided me with photocopies of some obscure occasional papers and the 1979 Director's Report in Birmingham, and engaged in fruitful email correspondence that contributed immensely to my understanding of what the Birmingham Centre was like under Hall's directorship. Peter Beilharz, Alan Bryman, Ellis Cashmore, Eric Dunning, Adrian Franklin, David Frisby, Peter Hamilton, Maggie O'Neill, Elspeth Probyn, George Ritzer, Barry Smart, Ros Spry, Keith Tester, Bryan Turner, Paul Willis and Elizabeth Wilson provided me with good company and comradeship – necessary qualities to maintain sanity and perspective in these times of Teaching Quality Assessments and Research Assessment Exercises. I am particularly indebted to Roger Bromley, David Harris, Jim McGuigan, Amanda Root and Patrick Williams for reading the whole of the first draft and supplying me with indispensable feedback.

My own view is that events, relations, structures do have conditions of existence and real effects, outside the sphere of the discursive; but that only within the discursive, and subject to its specific conditions, limits and modalities, do they have or can they be constructed within meaning. Thus, while not wanting to expand the territorial claims of the discursive infinitely, how things are represented and the 'machineries' and regimes of representation in a culture do play a constitutive, and not merely a reflexive, after-the-event, role. This gives questions of culture and ideology, and the scenarios of representation – subjectivity, identity, politics – a formative, not merely an expressive, place in the constitution of social and political life.

Stuart Hall (1992)

This does not make it any easier to conceive of how a politics can be constructed which works with and through difference, which is able to build those forms of solidarity and identification which make common struggle and resistance possible but without suppressing the real heterogeneity of interests and identities, and which can effectively draw the political boundary lines without which political contestation is impossible, without fixing those boundaries for eternity.

Stuart Hall (1992)

Introduction

Stuart Hall is the pre-eminent figure in Cultural Studies today.
Nobody else enjoys the same prestige. This derives as much from
his charisma as from his writings. Hall's leadership of the influential Centre for Contemporary Cultural Studies in Birmingham in
the 1970s, and his oratorical role as a public intellectual, contributed
immensely to the ascent of Cultural Studies. I do not mean this to
be taken as a slight on his published work. On the contrary, I hold
that there are contributions in Hall's writings that are seminal for
the study of popular culture. Yet as Hall would surely be the first
to acknowledge, he can hardly be classed as an original theorist.
His forte is to synthesize, clarify, popularize, and sometimes to
provoke.

These are qualities of elucidation. In his refreshing book on intellectuals, Edward Said defends the Socratic ideal of the intellectual
as the unparalleled agent of independent social criticism in civil
society (1994: 17). On this reading, the job of the intellectual is to
aggravate cliché, combat dogma and delineate a space that does not
answer to power. In as much as this is so, Said identifies the intellectual as an agent who intervenes in the public sphere, expressing
issues of public conscience, injustice and the misuse of power. Said,
in fact, rejects the traditional conservative ideal of the intellectual
as the avatar of taste, hygienically insulated from the public by
virtue of superior knowledge and greater cultural capital. For Said,
the independent intellectual is the highest form of public man,
ready to enunciate truths and perspectives which, when circumstances demand, disturb convention and intimidate power.

Perhaps Hall would recognize his reflection in Said's description. The Cultural Studies tradition that Hall embodies does not endorse a donatory view of cultural analysis. It does not posit fountainheads of knowledge or support a 'great man' view of history. To do so would be inconsistent with Hall's view of culture and knowledge, which is that identity, history, agency and practice are not fixed entities but parts of a system of representation which is permanently *in process*. Note that this position does not privilege society over the individual. Hall is an unstinting critic of sociologism, the doctrine which, following Durkheim (1895), maintains that society is the ultimate 'social fact', exerting priority, externality and constraint over the individual. Nor does Hall seek to foist his view of culture on others or to define what is integral or of superior worth in culture. Questions of aesthetic judgement are not at the heart of his approach, although latterly he has written more about visual culture, especially black photography. Rather, he has been richly dismissive of donatory perspectives, which he associates justly with elitism. Instead Hall's approach favours widening access, establishing dialogic relationships and exploring the shifting relationships between hegemony, power and articulation.

To these ends, Hall has ploughed an independent furrow. He is not, and never has been, a mouthpiece of government, party, media or business. Although he has played a prominent role in the public sphere, most notably through his journalism, television appearances and public lectures, he remains 'incorrigibly independent, answering to no one', a condition which Russell Jacoby (1987) identified as the *sine qua non* of the intellectual.

In a television debate during the 1980s, Hall (1985d) concurred with Umberto Eco that one of the pivotal functions of the intellectual is to construct uncomfortable arguments that, under certain conditions, articulate contradictions in the body politic which are conducive to social change. In Hall's case, of course, social change is a phenomenon that he wishes to see develop in a socialist direction. However, he is careful to insist that this must only be attempted from a position of intellectual strength, in which the arguments have been tempered with knowledge and responsibility. For Hall, intellectual strength means producing better arguments than one's opponents and using them responsibly to make constructive interventions into culture and society. 'It has to do, in part,' he writes, 'with how to construct the social imaginary in ways which enable us to see ourselves transformed in the mirror of politics, and thus to become its "new subjects"' (1988a: 13). For Hall, then, the distinctive space occupied by the intellectual explores the limitations, elisions and double-think of power and deploys the knowledge gained from this process responsibly to intervene in the public sphere.

This view rejects the model of the traditional intellectual as someone who pursues ideas for their own sake. It binds intellectual labour to political and cultural intervention. For Hall, intellectual labour is always political. However, although his work has political implications and is frequently of interest to the media, Hall does not regard himself as a politician or media pundit. The space he inhabits, his 'terrain' as he would say, is the realm of ideas. The balance between intellectual work and politics is subtle and changes in complex ways. Hall insists that 'there is all the difference in the world between understanding the politics of intellectual work and substituting intellectual work for politics' (1992f: 286).

This has frequently placed Hall in conflict with his 'natural' allies. For example, his 'New Times' thesis (Hall and Jacques 1989) was scornful of many sacred cows in traditional socialist thought. Written in the midst of the long Thatcherite adventure of resurgent neoliberalism, it discounted the conviction of many on the Left that, *après* Thatcher, the postwar neo-Keynesian settlement could be reinstated at a 'higher' level. Instead Hall insisted that enhanced globalization, the increased mobility of capital, the mechanization of work, and the growth of the service class constitute a new problematic. Thatcherism recognized this, but was unsatisfactory in two respects. First, the deregulation of the market could not succeed because it failed to address the need to modernize the economic and political infrastructure, and therefore precipitated social unrest. Second, the revival of nationalism ignored the growing cultural and economic effects of globalization. Neither neoliberal rhetoric nor cultural insularity were sustainable in the face of globalization, multiculturalism and the challenges that each posed to nationalism and identity thinking.

The 'New Times' thesis proposed that the traditional postwar divisions between Left and Right, nation and 'the rest' are obsolete. Hall called on the Left to rethink solidarity and agency afresh, through a new politics: a politics that he terms 'the politics of difference'.

Significantly, in these 'New Times' the state apparatus is still privileged as the central instrument of change. As we shall see later, Hall retains a strong commitment to the centrality of the state in socialist transformation and the importance of local politics in social and cultural intervention. Even so, New Times and the politics of difference went much deeper than a mere shift in emphasis. It envisaged a fundamental revision in the conception of political space, transformative practice, the conception of identity and the meaning of solidarity. Whereas the traditional Left repeated the mantra of class identity and socialist transformation, Hall now spoke of 'multi-accented identity', 'new ethnicities' which cross-cut proletarian consciousness, and the collapse of the 'binary oppositions' that were the foundations of the Western *episteme*. Among Hall's contemporaries and confrères on the Left, the 'New Times' thesis represented an attack on left-wing dogma. It outraged many traditionalists, who alleged that Hall had been seduced by postmodernist rhetoric (Callinicos 1989: 135).

Prima facie, Hall had certainly shifted ground. Between the 1960s and the mid-1980s, it was relatively clear where he stood. His identification of the centrality of class and ideology in capitalist hegemony (1977a; 1978b), his designation of the ethnic metropolitan diaspora as the 'sub-proletariat', and his influential analysis of Thatcherism as 'authoritarian populism' (1988a; 1989a), located him firmly in the left-wing tradition of social criticism and political agency. The work of the Marxist black Caribbean scholar C. L. R James (1932; 1938) clearly inspired him, not least because James hailed from the same geographic region, and overcame similar barriers of racial condescension from the established white intelligentsia. He acknowledged the significance of James in revealing the importance of slavery in the ascent of capitalism as a system of world domination (Hall 1998c) and he praised the strong sense of global history that James's work imparts. Yet interestingly, Hall maintains that he was never a Marxist, in the orthodox Jamesian sense of the term (1995c: 667). He attests to long-standing reservations about the adequacy of the Marxist perspective on imperialism, and he dismisses the base–superstructure dichotomy for producing an unsatisfactory, reductive position on culture. Unlike many others of his generation, he never attributed theological significance to Marxism.

Nonetheless, the attempt to marry aspects of Althusser's structuralism with Gramscianism was widely perceived to be at the heart of intellectual labour conducted at the Birmingham Centre in the 1970s. Hall is on record as noting that the failure of British culturalism to build a dialogic relationship with Marxism was a catalyst in the distinctive forms of intellectual craftsmanship developed in the Birmingham Centre (Hall 1976: 2). The collection on 'the living tradition of Marxism' that he edited with Paul Walton laments the insularity of the British Left in the 1950s and 1960s (Walton and Hall 1973). It avows that Marxist revisionism is a vital resource in both intellectual reconstruction and the development of a relevant approach to the study of culture. Further, his paper on Marxism and culture (1978e) identifies Marxism as the engine behind the revival of radical thought in postwar Britain. If Hall was never an orthodox Marxist, he evidently found much in the Marxist tradition to be formative and congenial to his outlook.

But from the mid-1980s, the picture changes. The formulation of the 'New Times' thesis urges the Left not to bury its head in the sand regarding the intellectual challenges of globalization and postmodernism. Hall now declares himself in favour of a Marxism 'without guarantees' (1986c), an awkward formulation which apparently signals both a retreat from mainstream Marxism and a desire to remain faithful to selected tenets of the tradition. Hall is too much of a left-wing loyalist to embrace the extremes of postmodern nihilism. For example, he insists on the continuing relevance of hegemony, representation and signification, and therefore politics, in cultural analysis. Yet he is also too much of a postmodern revisionist to dismiss the discursive reconfiguration on questions of identity, solidarity and strategy prompted by the postmodern 'moment'. So he now speaks of 'the politics of difference', 'interrupted' and 'hyphenated identity' and, courtesy of Derrida, the 'logic of *différance*'.

Emancipatory politics

Hall is still recognizably a man of the Left. However, his political allegiance is now primarily devoted to what might be called emancipatory politics. This reflects the profound reassessment that he undertook after the-mid 1980s into the nature of political space, collectivism and agency. As we shall see in greater detail later, Hall maintains that the Western *episteme* was founded on a series of binary oppositions, the most important of which is the opposition between identity and other. As a result of a combination of developments, most notably globalization, postcolonialism and multiculturalism, Hall believes that these oppositions have capsized, creating new spaces for the articulation of belonging, and social and cultural intervention. In as much as the class dialectic is one of these epistemic categories, Hall's later work breaks with the Marxist tradition by decentring class. Class, he argues, can no longer be seen as the rock on which socialist transformation is founded. This is because it presupposes a form of collective identity that is no longer tenable. Hall's appropriation of postmodernism and postcolonialism may be selective, but it concludes that agency and politics need to be conceptualized anew.

Hall's attachment to emancipatory politics is situated on three interrelated levels. First, it endorses the postcolonial coupling of nation with narration, which countermands notions of national integrity and racial purity. Second, it absorbs Benedict Anderson's thesis of the imagined nature of community (Anderson 1991) and, by extension, collectivity, and so reinforces the pre-eminence of representation and signification in the reproduction of order, and the necessity of an active reflexive consciousness in positing belonging and difference. Third, it reveals a predilection for Bhabha's 'third space' politics (1990; 1994), which privileges indeterminacy, relationalism, contingency, hybridity and emergence, in subjective and intersubjective relations.

The combined effect of all three levels is to replace 'identity thinking', saturated with connotations of fixity, solidity and boundaries, with an approach that seeks to encapsulate the interstitial, diasporic, translational and unfinished aspects of practice and representation. The foundational binary couplets of the Western *episteme* are repudiated as false conceptual dichotomies of the Enlightenment formation (Hall 1992b). In particular, the binary opposition between identity and other is attacked on a number of levels, notably in relation to race, nation and agency.

Yet he also appreciates the paradox of anti-binarism, or, as he has expressed it elsewhere, borrowing again from Derrida, 'thinking at the limit':

> Having refused the binarism which is intrinsic to essentialism, you have to remind yourself that binaries persist. You've questioned them theoretically, but you haven't removed their historical efficacy. Just because you say there is no absolute distinction between black and white doesn't mean that there aren't situations in which everything is being mobilized to make an intractable difference between black and white ... The binary is the form of the operation of power, the attempt at closure: power suturing language. It draws frontiers: *you* are inside, but *you* are out. There is a certain theoreticism from the standpoint of which, having made a critique of essentialism, that is enough. It isn't enough. (Hall 1997a: 35; emphasis in the original)

This is an especially revealing and important passage in Hall's writings on the politics of difference and the promises and dilemmas inherent in hybrid, 'non-identity' thinking. It recognizes that identity is a contingent 'point of enunciation', and is therefore positioned in and through hegemony, signification and representation. However, in acknowledging that identity is also 'a point of agency', Hall refuses to deny the political significance of reflexivity and identity thinking in contemporary culture.

How can one both reject the validity of essentialism and continue to negotiate the binary oppositions that dwell in everyday subjective and intersubjective relations? Hall's reply is to relate to 'the binary' as always, and already, 'under erasure' (1996b; 1997a: 35). The move reveals Hall's indebtedness to linguistic models of culture, which became prominent in his work after the mid-1980s. It is unsatisfactory because, having demolished essentialism at the level of theory, politics and identity, he smuggles in what he unwisely calls 'a little "strategic essentialism"' (1997a: 35) at the level of life-politics. Hall thus endeavours, at one and the same time, to pursue the structuralist thesis that meaning is arbitrary, and to defend the orthodox position of the Left, that some meanings are more important than others. For Hall's critics it is a taxing position, which seems to suggest that Hall wants to have his cake and eat it. The questions are, how can Hall simultaneously defend and repudiate essentialism? What kind of politics can be extrapolated and practised from a theoretical position that recognizes one is simultaneously 'in' and 'out' of the 'suturing' effect of binary oppositions? Is 'the limit' the correct 'terrain' to occupy in transformative politics?

The problem of slippage

Slippage is arguably the most serious criticism made of Hall's work. The move from a relatively conventional, albeit semi-detached, adherence to Marxism to a more general alignment with emancipatory politics has already been mentioned. In his defence Hall might claim that his adhesion to Marxism was always overstated in the secondary literature and that it is the intellectual's right to shift positions when circumstances demand. From this perspective the turn away from Marxism to hybridity and hyphenated identity in the late 1980s was less a case of slippage than a considered reformulation of perspective. But allegations of slippage are more entrenched and general, and, in some circles, have raised doubts about the validity of his contribution. Thus, Hall has been variously criticized for conceptual imprecision, analytical inconsistency, sophistry and political naivety (Harris 1992; Jessop et al. 1989; Callinicos 1989; Eagleton 1996; Mahmood 1996; Wood 1998; Mulgan 1998; Tudor 1999; Giddens 2000). Some of this criticism is addled and confused. For example, Saba Mahmood's (1996) attempt to paint Hall as an apologist for Western supremacism is very peculiar, and Hall (1996c) was right to defend himself in what, by his lights, were decidedly liverish terms. However, as we shall see, other critics are less easily swept aside, particularly those who make the general charge that Hall is in key respects an inconsistent thinker.

Parenthetically, one should note that criticizing Hall is not something to be done rashly. There are two reasons for this. Firstly, Hall is a prolific and versatile thinker who has practised his intellectual vocation over a remarkably wide, interdisciplinary space. His work is expansive and generous, in the best sense of the terms. In as much as it is in the nature of criticism to foreclose these qualities in favour of expounding faults and weaknesses, there has been some reluctance, especially among his colleagues in the Birmingham circle, to mobilize a genuine critical assessment.

The second point relates back to Hall's charisma. Few contemporary figures in the British academic Left command as much popular attention and respect as Hall. Among his former students in Birmingham he is generally regarded as an inspirational figure, as the 'father' of Cultural Studies. Actually, Richard Hoggart, not Hall, established the Centre, with a small educational bequest made by the publisher Sir Allen Lane, of Penguin Books. Moreover, the British culturalist tradition, embodied in the principal writings of Raymond Williams, Edward Thompson and Hoggart himself, initially constituted the axis of intellectual inspiration in Birmingham. Hall was appointed as Hoggart's right-hand man, and certainly played the decisive role in establishing the field of research and pedagogy and supervising the first cohorts of students. After Hoggart's departure, he staunchly defended the Centre against attacks from a hostile cabal within the university administration grown fearful of what they took to be a radical genie in their midst. He also battled against the condescension of established intellectuals, located notably in the departments of English and Sociology, who poohpoohed the attempt to create a new 'mongrel' discipline on campus (Hall 1989b).

By all accounts, as a teacher Hall was a superb enabler, helping students make intellectual connections and find their own voice. For dozens of students who were unable to be inspired by the traditional divisions between academic disciplines, or who rejected them for being out of touch, the Centre was the hub of a momentous paradigm shift. Paul Willis, who enrolled at the Centre in 1968, remembers feeling exhilarated by abandoning the 'practical criticism' and 'close reading' techniques of his Cambridge training, in favour of the Birmingham approach that restored culture to its 'social connections' (2001: ix–x). Others who came to the Centre from an orthodox Marxist background must have felt the same uplift in entering a milieu in which the base–superstructure couplet was unapologetically overturned and economic reductionism spurned. Nobody encapsulated the zeitgeist of the Centre more potently than Hall. Yet he was also the leading voice in defending the ethic of collective work in the Centre.

Participation between staff and students in research and publishing was encouraged. Interestingly, although after the 1980s Hall became perhaps the leading celebrity in the Anglo-American tradition of Cultural Studies, he has always been a relatively diffident figure, ill-disposed to the ceremonies of academic pantheon-building. Richard Hoggart comments of Hall in the Birmingham years, that 'his intellectual energy went into ideas, not self-presentation . . . and establishing the Centre and its area of work' (1992: 91).

In Birmingham relations of positive collaboration between staff and students were constructed which were perhaps unprecedented in the British system of higher education. The creation of specialized subgroups as a central pedagogic device fostered intellectual exchange between staff and students. Hall is on record as approving the 'dismantling' of the 'authorially integrated "I"' at the centre of the Western *episteme* (1985a: 1996a), which he regards as an accomplishment of the work of Saussure, Lévi-Strauss, Althusser and structuralist linguistics. As he declares, structuralism demonstrates that 'there is no essential, unitary "I" – only the fragmentary, contradictory subject' (1985a: 109). Consistent with his view of intellectual craftsmanship is the proposition that it is not enough to formally recognize this, one must also apply it to the levels of culture and politics. One way in which this was attempted in Birmingham was the deliberate disestablishment of the 'individualistic, highly possessive' tradition of intellectual practice 'dominant' in the humanities and social sciences in favour of more

collaborative work between faculty and students. Hall's justifica-
tion for this was partly pragmatic. 'We did not think', recalls Hall,
'that what had to be done was clear-cut from the first day we
opened. Gradually, it emerged that we had to have working seminars in which the theory itself was actually developed' (1989b: 17).

Neither the university, nor the state Department of Education
designated Cultural Studies as a growth area. It therefore struggled
to attract adequate funding. The initial complement of full-time staff
was two. Never, in Hall's time, did it exceed three. Hall became
acting director in 1968 when Hoggart left to become Assistant
Director-General for the Humanities, Arts and Social Sciences
at UNESCO in Paris. Eventually, Michael Green from English and
Richard Johnson from History joined Hall to teach in the Centre
(Davies 1995: 36). The full-time staff complement was therefore
never adequate to cover the range of supervision, research and
labour-intensive teaching that the Birmingham project required.
The achievements in critical pedagogy and research were therefore
all the more a tribute to the astounding energy and dedication of
Hall and his colleagues.

In seeking to pin down what one might call the peculiar resonance that Hall's reputation has among the Left, it is also perhaps
worth noting that his career coincided with the erosion of the traditional white, middle-class, insular establishment in Britain. Hall's
twenties were stamped with a decisive cultural shift in which the
time-worn institutions of nation and Empire came under sustained
fire from postwar youth culture and the economic and political realities of the world economy. By the time Hall entered Oxford, in 1951,
the welfare state was outwardly established as the progressive, revisionist compact for social and economic reconstruction. *Prima facie*,
Britain was now governed by a new centrist-nationalist welfare
settlement in which class prejudice and inequality were relegated
to the dustbin of history. It was a picture that Hall instinctively
recognized as false. The fiasco of the British and French invasion of
the Suez Canal zone, and the Soviet invasion of Hungary in 1956
politicized Hall dramatically, and compounded his critical estrangement from 'the two systems', capitalist imperialism and communism. As a black scholar who was openly critical of elitism and
white racism, Hall symbolized deeper transformations in British
society. He was 'accepted' into British society, but only on condition
of acknowledging himself to be an 'alien'. For someone of his background, schooled as a boy in one of Jamaica's leading secondary
schools to revere British parliamentarianism and the tradition of fair

play, this naive native reaction was perhaps unexpected. It was undeniably wounding. In his editorial work at the *New Left Review*, and throughout his academic career, Hall was an unusual, often solitary, black presence, reminding white radicals of the limitations of the welfarist 'solution' to inequality and justice. However, one consequence of all of this is that critics tend to be defensive about Hall's work. Even Colin Sparks, who has a forensic grasp of some of the central tensions in Hall's thought, is cloying in the respectful tenor of his remarks (Sparks 1996).

Axiomatic to Hall's conception and practice of intellectual labour is the proposition that criticism is part of the intellectual vocation. Criticizing others and being critically reflexive about one's own work are necessary. Doubtless Hall was touched by what is, in effect, a *festschrift* for him, edited by Gilroy, Grossberg and McRobbie (2000), but perhaps he also squirmed at the relentlessly anodyne tone of the collection. Arguably, the editors were too close to Hall, personally, professionally, as well as in terms of intellectual genealogy, to evaluate his work with sufficient critical distance. 'Saint Stuart' is an epithet from which Hall would recoil. Yet because of Hall's historical and cultural position in the division of academic labour, most treatments of his work since the late 1970s to date have been automatically reverential rather than genuinely critical.

Anti-essentialism

I hold that the defining characteristic of Hall's social thought is anti-essentialism. As this study seeks to demonstrate, he has explored it inexhaustibly and variously. It is the main reason why critics task him with slippage. It accounts for the unquestionable imprecision in his analysis of hegemony, articulation, race and identity. It underlies his vague, unsatisfying views of the kind of culture and society that he wishes to see. From his earliest publications, Hall resolutely refused to be cabined or confined by any tradition or school of thought. One reason why he found concepts like *différance*, hybridity and diaspora to be so congenial in his later work is that they exploit and develop interdisciplinarity, and resist exclusivity and closure.

In mitigation, it should be observed that Hall is not an indiscriminate thinker, but a voracious one. The content of the first taught MA in Birmingham extended well beyond Marx and Lukács to embrace Lévi-Strauss, Durkheim, Weber, Garfinkel and Sartre. His receptivity to new ideas and his readiness to think again, from first principles if necessary, are commendable. Yet one consequence of anti-essentialism is that it privileges mobility over consistency, and inclines towards pragmatism in theory.

Thus Hall enrolled at Oxford as a quasi-Leavisite certainly in as much as he acknowledged Leavis's project to be 'serious', although he was also obviously critical of many of Leavis's assumptions, judgements and political positions. Through the work of Richard Hoggart, Edward Thompson and particularly Raymond Williams, and his friendships with fellow students like Alan Hall (no relation), Raphael Samuel and Charles Taylor, he glimpsed 'another Britain', less preoccupied with hierarchy and rank, but at one with Leavis in taking culture seriously. Hall correctly regarded British culturalism to be too parochial. In privileging experience, struggle and agency, it was unable to go beyond 'naive humanism' (Hall 1980a). Structuralism was enlisted as a resource to situate cultural practice in a determinate context of totality. In addition, totality underlined the ubiquitous place of ideology in practices of representation and signification. Hall always appreciated the tendency of structuralism to elicit a mechanistic, overdeterministic reading of culture. He sought to retain the centrality of agency, consciousness, struggle and intervention in cultural studies. Indeed, he notes that Gramsci and Althusser became significant in the intellectual labour conducted in Birmingham during the 1970s precisely because they appeared to present ways of analysing culture that avoided reductionism (1997a: 26).

Interestingly, when he fought to resist the tendency towards closure in structuralism during the late 1970s and 1980s, he did not attempt to revive culturalism. Instead, he turned to poststructuralism and postcolonialism, notably by recruiting the concepts of dissemination, *différance*, diaspora and hybridity. What emerges most powerfully is the restless, questing nature of Hall's mind. His is not the sociology of the last word. He has always eschewed purism at the level of theory, in favour of an approach that is conducive to understanding culture cogently and, as he would have it, 'correctly', and he has made a virtue of a chequered intellectual pedigree.

Another point to make in response to the charge of slippage is that Hall's approach to culture, like that of Gramsci, regards history to be composed of many conjunctural shifts. In Gramscian sociology the term 'conjuncture' refers to the historically specific balance of ideology, class consciousness, class interests and economic contradictions, which either elicits or inhibits social change. The elements that constitute a conjuncture are always 'overdetermined', or condensed, in a 'moment' that is not repeatable, and under conditions which are unique. Thus history is perceived as a collection of interlinked 'moments' in which decisive shifts in social and cultural patterns may, or may not, occur. Given the changing concatenation of factors that constitute a given conjuncture, a degree of 'slippage' or flexibility in interpretation is unavoidable. It is therefore, unreasonable to expect strict consistency from this approach since it recognizes contingency in historical patterns and modes of analysis. In Hall's own words, 'the search for an "essential, true, original meaning" is an illusion' (1984d: 2). Yet this merely reinforces his anti-essentialism. The question is what remains from an intellectual perspective that is so pragmatic in interpreting the course of human history? And, following from this, if meaning and identity are contingent, why is the labour of the organic intellectual more valuable than that of anyone else? These are methodological questions and the subject of methodology is massively neglected in Hall's writings.

The lacuna of methodology

In the 1960s Hall became a genuinely eclectic thinker. In reminiscing about the Birmingham years, he recalls the sheer range of intellectual resources that were enlisted as he, and his associates, struggled to 'invent' cultural studies (1989b; 1995c; 1996e). At the beginning, he observes, the Centre was 'reading practically everything' (1997a: 26). Looking back, from a sociological standpoint, the early influences were quite orthodox. The work of Mannheim, Weber, Parsons and Goldman figured prominently in the initial agenda of study. Surprisingly, it was not until the 1970s that the Marxist inflection became pronounced. The ideas of Marx, Gramsci, Althusser, Volosinov, Bakhtin, Benjamin, Fanon, Brecht, Marcuse and Lukács were explored and debated, and efforts were launched to synthesize them. This reflects the importance of the Marxist tradition in shaping intellectual labour in Birmingham during the crucial decade of the 1970s, in which most of the work that established the Centre's reputation was published.

But it is inadmissible to pair the Birmingham approach with Marxism. In the 1970s Hall began to recruit arguments and propositions from French structuralist and poststructuralist schools. The work of Saussure, Lévi-Strauss, Foucault, Derrida, Barthes, Kristeva and Lacan entered the Birmingham melting pot, and remained influences in Hall's thought after 1979, when he moved to the Chair of Sociology at the Open University.

Hall's later work retained an arterial connection to Marxism, albeit now 'without guarantees'. Among contemporary writers in the Marxist tradition, Laclau and Mouffe, in particular, have been significant influences. Hall boldly incorporated aspects of Derridean textual deconstructionism, Foucaultian discourse analysis and post-feminism. Lately, over the last decade, postcolonialism has become significant in his work, particularly the ideas of Bhabha, Said, Spivak and Gilroy.

Although he took a benign view about the importance of ethnography during his directorship of the Birmingham Centre and his years at the Open University, Hall was no clipboard sociologist or kitchen-sink researcher. His most important methodological contribution to Cultural Studies was arguably the famous paper on encoding and decoding (1973a) which is now regarded as a key paper in narrative analysis (Denzin and Lincoln 2001). However, this is best classed as a contribution to *Marxisant* semiotics, rather than an innovation in nuts and bolts methodology. On the subjects of how to conduct interviews, how to construct a detached relationship from qualitative data, and how to avoid naturalistic fallacies in qualitative research, Hall remains relatively silent. The survey in *Culture, Media, Language* (Hall et al. 1980) of the achievements and current research themes in Birmingham identified ethnography, media studies, language studies and English studies as the principal areas of activity. Yet aside from the outstanding reflexive fieldwork of Paul Willis (1977; 1978; 2001), no detailed attempt to rationalize the methodology of Cultural Studies emerged. True, the writings of Hebdige (1979; 1988), Morley (1980; 1986; 1992), McRobbie (1978) and Hobson (1982) extend the encoding/decoding model, and the practice of ethnography developed in Birmingham in interesting and significant ways. Yet none of them are strictly speaking reflections on methodology. Arguably, all compound the epistemological problem of failing to advance a tenable basis for extrapolating 'preferred readings' from the play of infinite semiosis. Indeed, some critics hold that Cultural Studies has avoided the question of epistemology altogether (Tudor 1999: 191).

Arguably, with respect to Hall's work, this criticism is unfair, since Hall's account of representation (1985a; 1993e; 1996a) constantly poses questions of epistemology. Nonetheless, there is some merit in Tudor's complaint that Cultural Studies has never subjected epistemology to the same critical interrogation achieved by sociology. There is no parallel in Cultural Studies to the *methoden-streit* dispute between Neo-Kantians and naturalists in late nineteenth-century German philosophy and sociology. The former asserted that the natural and social sciences are intrinsically different and therefore require the development of distinctive methodologies, while the latter held that a uniform methodology was applicable to both. Hermeneutics and the method of *Verstehen* emerged from this conflict, as did the centrality of value judgements in the assessment of sociological analysis and explanation.[1]

In practice, Cultural Studies has favoured the qualitative research tradition, without, however, clearly articulating the presuppositions behind this option. This has produced tension between textual readings of agency which ultimately privilege structure, and ethnographic 'rich descriptions' (Geertz 1973), seeking to remain true to the intentions and knowledge of the actor, which ultimately privilege agency over structure. For example, Morley's work on the television audience (1980; 1986; 1992) fails to satisfactorily resolve the division between regarding the viewer as a social subject and as a social agent. The familiar dilemma in sociology between analysis that prioritizes agency over structure, or vice versa, is therefore substantially replayed. For many critics this is a general weakness in Cultural Studies, invalidating its claim to go beyond established academic disciplines (Tudor 1999: 194).

Yet Cultural Studies has been much bolder in cross-fertilizing different research traditions. This is evident in Hall's own thought that mixes Marxism, poststructuralism, feminism, Derrida, Lacanianism, semiotics, discourse theory and postmodernism into a heady analytical brew. One should note that Hall received no formal training in sociology as an undergraduate. Had he sat through sociology, one, two and three, in the 1950s, he might have been suffocated by the Parsonian model of structural functionalism or the methodology of the empiricist sociology that dominated the discipline. True, C. Wright Mills mounted an effective *sortie* against what he pejoratively called 'grand theory' and 'abstracted empiricism' from within sociology (1959). Interestingly, Mills's work was manifestly gravitating towards cultural questions in a way that might have supported the secession of a critical sociology of culture from orthodox sociology.[2] But Mills died young and, in any case, he was probably perceived as too much of a maverick to inspire a field, still less to be the figurehead for a new discipline.

The positive consequence of Hall's non-sociological background is that it endows his work with extraordinary fluency. A formally trained contemporary sociologist of his generation could never have roamed so freely or widely across interdisciplinary boundaries to bring together the analytic tools that would constitute an innovative, alternative approach to culture. The negative consequence is, arguably, that Hall has been too cavalier about questions of methodology. Hall has tended to use his commitment to the Gramscian ideal of the 'organic intellectual' as *carte blanche* for ignoring the complex questions of 'fact 'and 'value' and 'involvement' and 'detachment' posed in the *Methodenstreit.*

Syncretic narrative fusion

The concept of the organic intellectual is pivotal in reaching an accurate understanding of Hall's perception of intellectual labour. For this reason it needs to be considered at length later in the study (see pp. 76–80). Here it suffices to make a preliminary note that the concept requires the intellectual labourer to be both at the forefront of knowledge, and to act as a transmission belt linking intellectual labour with the community. Although reflexivity is integral to the concept, it also assumes, a priori, identification with the aspirations and interests of the proletariat. Hence, Hall's lifelong conviction that intellectual labour is always suspect if it remains aloof from the politics relating to the activities and lifeworld of ordinary culture. Of course, it does not follow from this that Hall's work is methodologically unsatisfactory; merely that his methodology is undertheorized. In as much as this is so, Hall almost invites others to fill in the gap in methodology for him.

I propose to describe his methodology as *syncretic narrative fusion.* By this term, I mean the welding of interdisciplinary components from dispersed and, in some cases, mutually incommensurate intellectual traditions.

The method of syncretic narrative fusion, I hold, does not always result in intellectual cohesion, a point of view that I share with Terry Eagleton (1996), who has wondered if the varous bits and bobs from Marx, Gramsci, Althusser, Volosinov, Bakhtin, Lacan, Derrida, Foucault, Laclau and Mouffe brought together in Hall's work cohere. For me the best example of the tension embedded in Hall's eclecticism is his attempt in the 1960s and 1970s to weld elements of Gramsci's interpretive approach with Althusser's structuralism. This culminated in arguably the single most important study produced in the Birmingham years, *Policing the Crisis* (Hall et al. 1978). However, friction between Gramsci's approach and that of Althusser is rife in the book. Similarly, Hall's attempts to join elements of poststructuralist and postmodern theory with a politics of cultural intervention have not been convincing. The advocacy of non-identity thinking and the politics of difference operate most persuasively at a heuristic level. They reveal the 'violence' of essentialism, but fail to articulate practical, tenable foundations for the reconstruction of solidarity and effective agency, based around the principles of equality, cohesion and difference advocated in the Parekh Report (2000). Syncretic narrative fusion reinforces Hall's predilection for pragmatism in the analysis of culture. As he puts it, 'I am inclined to prefer being "right but not rigorous" to being "rigorous but wrong"' (1985a: 94).

In his defence, Hall might respond that he has always regarded his work as being in the business of challenging boundaries. Trial and error are part and parcel of this process. The attempt to fuse together elements in the Gramscian and Althusserian traditions may have been abandoned, but the process was conducive in opening up new problematics and rethinking the 'conjunctural' nature of history and power. Similarly, the project of operating theory and politics 'under erasure' is unquestionably tricky and contradictory. Hall recognizes that it does not bring quick or easy solutions. On the other hand, it flags the obsolescence of foundational concepts in the Western *episteme*. In lieu of wholly new concepts to replace them, there is, he writes, 'nothing to do but to continue to think with them – albeit now in their detotalized or deconstructed forms, and no longer operating within the paradigm in which they were originally generated' (Hall 1996a: 1).

One of the considerable appeals of Hall's work is that it conveys a sense of mobile involvement with unfolding social and cultural processes. If syncretic narrative fusion has been unsuccessful in some cases, it has also achieved some notable breakthroughs. For example, the integration of Gramsci's concept of hegemony with the poststructuralist semiotics of signification was inspired. It produced a more sophisticated approach to the politics of representation, manipulation and control. Analogously, Hall's revisionist reading of Gramsci's proposition of the 'national-popular' as the terrain of cultural and hegemonic struggle through Volosinov's (1973) 'multi-accentual' analysis of communication has elicited a more flexible and useful approach to ideological contestation and the organization of subjectivity. Hall is much too modest and level-headed to claim that his work has moved us into a 'post-essentialist' mode. As he notes elsewhere (1978a: 118), the Achilles heel of anti-essentialism is that it is, in effect, a disguised 'essentialist critique', which allows for no kind of agency or reconstruction built around the notion of the collective subject. Yet arguably this is precisely the position that Hall, especially in his later work, drifts towards. For what kind of solidarity can be constructed around a politics of 'erasure'? If one recognizes hybridity, diaspora and the endless play of *différance*, at what point is it legitimate to halt deconstruction, and what resources might be enlisted to engage in transformative action? How can a politics of difference revive socialism?

These are difficult questions and it would be unfair to drag Hall over the coals for not providing satisfactory answers to them. After all, he has never set himself up as a cultural commissar. He does not see his task as propounding cultural solutions and managing administrative systems to achieve them. To repeat, his distinctive terrain is the realm of ideas. From Hall's standpoint, if unravelling certain key dichotomies in the Western *episteme*, notably the identity–other couplet, fails to elicit viable forms of 'post-identity' agency, it is a secondary matter. The primary object is to expose the brutal limitations of identity thinking, the insufferable condescension that automatically proposes superiority on the basis of race, class and gender, and the complex constellations of power that contribute to the governance of subjectivity. This reinforces Hall's premise that, in certain circumstances, it is legitimate for intellectual labour to be expended in the articulation of crisis, as a catalyst for the transformation of social consciousness and conditions.

The problem of 'modishness'

Anti-essentialism often goes hand-in-hand with a mercurial and quixotic orientation to social and cultural analysis. This was certainly the criticism made of some prominent postmodernists at the zenith of postmodernism. Indeed, Hall himself complained that Baudrillard and Lyotard in their 'celebratory modes' had gone 'through the sound barrier' in terms of the extremity of some of their central propositions (1986a: 45). Among other things, he meant by this that it was hard to extract a serviceable form of politics from their arguments on the implosion of the masses, the collapse of grand narratives and the recognition of pluralism and galloping fragmentation. As he remarked elsewhere, 'the politics of infinite dispersal is the politics of no action at all' (1993d: 137). Ironically, traditional left-wing critics attacked Hall's later work (1996a; 1996b; 1998b) on the same grounds, especially in respect of his 'New Times' thesis and postulate of the 'politics of difference'. The first was attacked for appearing to dilute solidarity with pluralism and contingency, while the second intimated the rise of what was sometimes scornfully dismissed as 'designer socialism', that is, an implausible appeal to solidarity on the basis of profound material and cultural difference.

Terry Eagleton extended the criticism in an outwardly respectful but really rather waspish piece that alleged root and branch 'modishness', reflected in the 'frenetic recycling of theories', in Hall's work. Eagleton is a more dyed-in-the-wool Marxist than Hall. While he commends Hall's 'impeccable' anti-essentialism, anti-reductionism, anti-naturalism and non-teleological principles (1996: 3), he does so with the stripe of a critic who suspects that Hall does not quite live in the real world. For Eagleton, Hall is a professor who is neither coherent nor transparent in what he professes.

What is identified as a weakness by Eagleton is presented as a strength by others. For example, Larry Grossberg commends Hall's openness to new theories and his readiness to identify new struggles, new contexts and new questions (Grossberg 1993). The point is partly made to underline Hall's semi-detachment from the Marxist tradition. According to Grossberg, Marxism was a seminal influence on Hall's thought, but he always saw himself working simultaneously with and against the tradition in developing his approach to culture.

There is no doubt that Hall's capacity to mix elements from different theoretical traditions, such as Marxism, Gramscianism, Althusserianism, structuralism, deconstructionism, feminism, semiotics, Lacanianism, Fanonism, postcolonialism and postmodernism, on the same palette frequently leaves readers bewildered. It is not simply that the theories are of different types, so that the attribution of consistency becomes an act of authorial fiat, producing a strained eclecticism. It is also the suspicion that intellectual fashion may play an unduly large part in his work. In the words of Eagleton, Hall frequently confuses being *'au fait'* with being *'à la mode'* (Eagleton 1996).

To some extent Eagleton's criticism is playful. He wants to puncture the uncritical devotion with which Hall's pronouncements are received in some quarters. For example, Hall's former student and chief envoy of the Birmingham approach in the US, Larry Grossberg, arguably replicates a 'celebratory mode' in respect of

Hall's own writings which refuses to 'accept the necessity of either correspondence or non-correspondence, either the simple unity or absolute complexity of the social formation' (1997: 179). The refusal to admit either 'correspondence or non-correspondence', 'simple unity or absolute complexity' produces a level of generosity in social analysis which is so extreme as to be rejected as untenable. To be fair, Hall has remarked on the 'fictional necessity' of assigning 'arbitrary closure' as a precondition of agency in politics and cultural analysis (1993d: 137). But he has left the matter of attributing the criteria of fictional necessity and invoking arbitrary closure as a question of critical taste and political judgement.

To some degree the concern with fashion, contingency and overturning tradition goes with the field. Part of the original appeal of Cultural Studies was that it is capable of engaging with concrete, topical matters more rapidly and flexibly than sociology, because the latter is generally obliged to bring the heavy guns of the great classical tradition to bear on topical issues. Cultural Studies established itsef as a critique of common sense using specificity and complexity as part of its methodology. But this freedom often made a convenient virtue of eclecticism. Ferguson and Golding are not alone in finding 'imprecision' and an 'indigestible mix' in the interdisciplinary, hybrid Birmingham approach to Cultural Studies, and, by extension, in Hall himself:

> Such concepts as 'terrain', 'site of struggle', 'problematic' (as a noun), 'configuration', 'articulation', 'moment', 'project', 'turn', all lost any focus with which they had been endowed in the literatures from which they were borrowed, and became merely the calling card of the cognoscenti . . . Endless appeals to an unexplicated 'complexity' remind the reader that nothing is as it seems, that the cultural studies text signals, but cannot for the moment deliver, a limitless elaboration of what had previously seemed self-evident. (Ferguson and Golding 1997: xxi–xxii)

One is reminded of Grossberg's recollection that Hall once commented to him that the more 'obvious' a statement, the more 'ideological' it is (2000: 148). This is a peculiar remark. Even if one allows that it was probably made in the 1970s when Hall was under the full sway of Althusserianism, it suggests that anti-essentialism cannot go beyond the perimeter of ideologically impregnated language. For if everything is impregnated with ideology, on what basis does critique function? Ferguson and Golding's impatience with the circularity of major aspects of Birmingham eclecticism and theoretical hybridity rings true.

Nonetheless, their bromide about 'endless appeals to unexplicated complexity' perhaps overstates the case. One does not have to agree with everything in Hall et al's *Policing the Crisis* (1978) to acknowledge that the study is a considerable interpretation of the crisis in the British state formation process in the 1970s.

Like Eagleton, Ferguson and Golding badly misjudge the ethos of the New Left and British Cultural Studies. It was an ethos that permeated significant sections of the British university system in the 1960s and 1970s and, to boot, was indispensable in Hall's intellectual development. As Hall himself reminds us (1989f: 23), the New Left saw themselves as 'modernizers' refuting both the bogus consensus politics of the national-centre and old socialist dogma. The New Left stood for what they regarded as an innovative form of intellectual life in Britain based in a serious engagement with all levels of politics and culture. Although this ideological formation is generally regarded as having arisen in Britain, it developed strong international links, notably with the Commonwealth countries and the United States. The sociologist C. Wright Mills was a prominent partner in the US. After his premature death in 1962 a proposal for a book about the emerging critical political consciousness in America with the working title 'The New Left' was found among his papers (Mills 2000: 7).

The New Left rejected the stereotype of the detached academic rigorously sifting through the data to produce a balanced picture. Instead they favoured a model of intellectual labour as culturally and politically engaged with the concrete issues of the day, and as committed to elucidating them in theoretically informed ways. Balance and rigour were not cast aside, but they were applied within a framework attached to breaking with the shackles of the past and promoting socialist change. Perhaps this necessarily saddled them with the appearance of 'modishness', since they were very deliberately opening doors in the Academy that had been bolted for a long time and were using new theoretical influences from continental Europe and concrete, changing economic, cultural and political circumstances as their warrant. They certainly deployed methods of presentation that conveyed the impression that their approach was more relevant than established standpoints, sometimes at the price of producing unintentionally selective readings of these positions.

The New Left was an enormously energizing and fruitful intervention into politics and culture in the 1950s and 1960s. Its emphasis on independence widened the narrow, institutionally demarcated notion of 'the political'. Interestingly, Hall singles out two identifying characteristics of the New Left (1989h: 151–3). First, its realism, unblinkered by ties to party loyalty or tradition. The New Left, writes Hall, was

> profoundly rooted in the realities of the present. Gramsci said: 'Turn your face violently towards things as they exist now.' Not as you'd like them to be, not as you think they were ten years ago, not as they're written about in the sacred texts, but as they really are: the contradictory, stony ground of the present conjuncture. (1989h: 151)

Critics may object that the New Left was never sufficiently reflexive about the epistemological niceties and ontological dilemmas of its articulation of 'the stony ground of the present conjuncture'. But there can be no quibble with the New Left's lack of pomposity, abhorrence of rank and detestation of cant and humbug.

The second identifying characteristic nominated by Hall is the New Left's utopianism. This may seem surprising given the emphasis placed on realism. However, for the New Left, articulating an image of a social order based on the mutual benefit of equal participants was an indispensable component of its realism. Hall expresses this very well:

> The New Left was not a socialism of the will, but it was a socialism of what I call 'the social imaginary'. Raphael Samuel talked about the libertarian element, and I would talk about the utopian element, in the New Left. I don't see a socialist politics of any kind arising in this country which cannot capture the 'social imaginary', which is unable to talk about transcendence, about the political, social and cultural realities towards which people are moving. If we remain locked into the language of the present, the left will become a footnote in the onward march of modernity. (1989h: 153)

However, there were always doubts in some quarters about the basis on which these non-elected representatives could speak on behalf of 'society', and about the ambiguous relationship between the New Left and the organized labour movement. The board of the *New Left Review* (*NLR*) was very centrally involved in politics, but generally as independent intellectuals rather than fully committed members of social movements. True, Edward Thompson was an important figure in the Campaign for Nuclear Disarmament. Many others on the *NLR* board supported him. But this highly public political action was the exception to the rule. Although the *NLR* regarded itself as a socialist organization, it put down no strong roots with the labour movement. Nor did its members cultivate a strong organizational culture. Of course, by the debates that it initiated in public meetings and through its columns, the *NLR* was a vital switchboard for New Left thought. But as a vanguard activist grouping its influence was symbolic, propagandist and strategic rather than instrumental and policy oriented.

Hall shrewdly recounts Peter Sedgwick's telling observation that the New Left was always more of a milieu than a movement (Hall 1989f: 30). Its characteristics were a self-conscious break with the past, a disdain for the traditions of limpid insularity and empiricism in British intellectual life, and the espousal of the cultural value of independent thought. It opened the floodgates for continental Marxism, phenomenology, critical psychoanalysis and other 'foreign' traditions of thought to come into Britain.

Significantly, their 'modernizing' influence in intellectual life coincided with the Labour government's belated modernization of the university sector in the 1960s. The Wilson government's espousal of the 'white hot technological revolution' required expanded numbers working in the technocracy and knowledge and communication sectors. This led to increased investment in the established university sector, the foundation of new greenfield universities, the establishment of the polytechnic system and the creation of the Open University, which Hall eventually joined as Professor of Sociology in 1979. A new stratum of intellectual workers, largely drawn from the middle and lower middle classes, was created outside the traditional university system. Very few were actually from the working class and scarcely any hailed from ethnic minorities. They challenged the traditional curriculum and established pedagogic methods.

Critical disciplines long spurned by Oxbridge were enthusiastically embraced. For example, academic sociology in England put down roots in unfashionable provincial universities like Leeds, Durham, Hull and Leicester and rapidly flourished. Cultural Studies was first institutionalized at Birmingham University under the leadership of Hoggart and Hall. It was duly subjected to derision from some members of the campus establishment who questioned its status as a discipline. But it progressed to make major innovations in theory, method and pedagogy that spread like wildfire through the university system in the West during the 1980s and 1990s. Perhaps only feminism rivalled the New Left in signifying

the sea-change in British academic life during the 1960s. The New
Left was the catalyst for the creation of networks (History Workshop, *Screen*, *Radical Philosophy*, *m/f*) that undermined the pillars of
establishment knowledge. It was a significant radicalizing influence
in British intellectual and cultural life in the 1960s and 1970s. But it
never became a vanguard of political and cultural transformation.
This raises questions about the coherence and integration of the
New Left intelligentsia.

The problem of the radical intelligentsia in England

Bryan Turner, in an important and oddly neglected contribution to
the history of ideas (1992), submits that a radical intelligentsia is
generally the product of a cultural crisis in which the structural
social, political, economic and religious foundations of society are
challenged. England experienced its cultural crisis sooner than most
of Western Europe and America. The Civil War and the execution
of Charles I in the seventeenth century subjected all levels of the
economy, society and culture to radical scrutiny. But it was a revolt
of the middle class and lower middle class rather than the peasantry. It arose from anger and disquiet with the dereliction of the
role of the monarch rather than from a coherent radical programme
for fundamental social change. The Parliamentarian repression of
the Levellers and Diggers revealed the conservative grain of Oliver
Cromwell's revolution (Hill 1975; Coward 1991). The Restoration
symbolized the preference in the state formation process in England
for gradualism and piecemeal change. While this contributed immensely to the stability of civil society, it also resulted in the
emergence of a pragmatic tradition in English intellectual life.
Turner maintains that the English were not required to theorize an
alternative social system or to seriously defend liberal bourgeois
democracy against either proletarian revolution or fascist takeover
(1992: 197). The result is the intellectual pre-eminence of pragmatism and empiricism, enthroned, for example, in Bentham and
Mill's utilitarianism, Locke's political philosophy, David Hume's
liberal scepticism and the middle-class idealism of T. H. Green.

   Socialist radicalism in Britain owed much to Methodism and
the secular tradition of dissent and nonconformity. While Marxist
ideas infiltrated the labour movement by the 1870s, they operated
in a *modus vivendi* of mutual suspicion with the co-operativist and

workers' guild traditions. Although Chartism in the 1830s and 1840s, the new unionism of the 1880s and 1890s and the General Strike of 1926 all threatened bourgeois liberal democracy, what emerges most powerfully is the extraordinary capacity of the parliamentary system to weather any storm (Corrigan and Sayer 1985). Hall himself portrayed the period between 1880 and 1930 in Gramscian terms as a classic 'war of position and manoeuvre' in which the ruling power bloc adroitly wove alliances and brokered concessions with labour without ceding the fundamentals of power (1984c; Hall and Schwarz 1985).

The Great Depression and the Second World War are usually presented as the climacteric of this state of affairs. They represented a decade and a half in which the ruling power bloc was forced to concede on key aspects of rule, notably in the creation of the mixed economy and the welfare state. Indeed the war was popularly regarded not only as a campaign against fascism, but as a struggle to dismantle the old established order and build a welfare state society in which there was no place for traditional aristocratic privilege. But there are dangers in portraying the Labour government of 1945 as a break or rupture with the former order of liberal bourgeois democracy. The Attlee government was in many ways a *continuation* of the policy and strategy adopted by the coalition government of the war years. The Beveridge Report of 1942 and the national commitment to introduce the National Health Service and full employment were *wartime* accomplishments. During the war Attlee and his foremost colleagues participated in the programme of economic and political management on the home front. The institutions and state personnel that managed the war effort remained to implement the welfare state after 1945. The electoral rout of Churchill's Conservative Party and the staunch application of nationalization programmes were significant. But Hall et al. are surely right to assert that the Labour government of 1945–51 was actually 'the end of something rather than the beginning: everything that had matured during the extraordinary conditions of a popular war, was even then, even in its heyday, beginning to pass away' (1978: 227–8).

Hemmed in by a continuing need to maintain austerity in postwar reconstruction, plunged into massive devaluation in 1949 by the inflation of the Korean war, and openly siding with the US in the burgeoning Cold War with the Soviets, the Labour government capitulated to the requirements of global capitalism. Most radical intellectuals were co-opted into the welfare settlement and became employed by the state apparatus in universities, government think-tanks and the community and welfare system. A managed national-centrist consensus was imposed on the country and the liberal bourgeois solution to the struggle for hegemony remained basically intact.

This was the historic conjuncture from which the New Left emerged in the 1950s. It constituted the postwar origins of the crisis in culture, economy and civil society that climaxed in Thatcherism and the shift away from consensus to coercion. It was a malaise of hegemony in which the national interest and the centre ground were interpellated to marginalize real social frictions and divisions of class. It was a malaise because it required strong economic growth to support the welfare state. This became more elusive in Britain after the long global consumer boom of the 1950s. In the 1960s and 1970s labour unrest, the repeated balance of payments crises, inflation, the decline of empire, the rise of the counterculture and the emergence of new ethnicities in Britain's cities exposed the structural limitations of national-centrist ideology. These limitations were not simply recognized by critics on the Left. On the contrary, the New Right became a stern critic of national-centrist 'drift' and the 'failures' of the welfare state. To be sure, Hall's campaign for socialist renewal under Thatcherism was based on the predicate that the New Right in the 1970s and early 1980s was more adroit in identifying the structural changes in the economy, politics and civil society and better at postulating opportunities for intervention than the Left (Hall 1988a).

Perry Anderson (1990) proposes that Thatcherism may be regarded as a radical conjuncture in the British state formation process out of which a radical intelligentsia emerged. But this exaggerates the coherence and integration of the opposition to authoritarian populism. There is not a radical intelligentsia in England if we mean by the term a disciplined movement, attached to a systematic programme of political, economic and cultural transformation, with strong roots in the organized labour movement. English radicals tend to be *declassé* and strongly individualist. Modishness is part of the job. To some extent, Anderson concedes this by identifying in England 'the liveliest republic of letters in European socialism' (1990: 44). Anderson has in mind the writings of Williams, Hall, Samuel, Tom Nairn, Bhabha, Hobsbawm, Laclau and Mouffe and the flourishing network of home-based journals, such as *Marxism Today*, *Screen* (1969), *Radical Philosophy* (1972), *Economy and Society* (1972), *Critique* (1973), *Critique of Anthropology*

(1974), *History Workshop* (1976), *Social History* (1976), *Capital and Class* (1977), *Cambridge Journal of Economics* (1977) and *Feminist Review* (1979). But in making the case he illustrates the profound depth of the New Left's didactic, textual and discursive solution to radical intervention. In Communist Russia, Hungary, Poland and the Palestine Liberation Organization, a radical intelligentsia engaged in direct political activity with a coherent programme based in part on organized violence and a disciplined party organization. There is no real equivalent in English intellectual life.

In Gramscian terms, the New Left emerged as the result of a protracted disarticulation of hegemony, an accumulation of contradictions in which the whole basis of political and cultural leadership was exposed and contested. The New Left constituted an intellectual milieu in which criticism of social democratic hegemony, the rise of the consumer society and the apparent incorporation of the working class around a national-centrist agenda was openly articulated. Among the central themes it debated were the deformations of state bureaucracy, the Cold War, the failure of Labour to encapsulate the popular roots of ordinary culture, the anti-intellectualism of national life, and a whole range of specific issues relating to literature, theatre, cinema, modern architecture, town planning, housing and youth subcultures. The institutional axis of this milieu was the *New Left Review*, founded in 1960. Like-minded, collegial and joined in the spirit of critical change, the New Left never became a power bloc.[3] It was too reflexive and rooted in the English tradition of radical nonconformity to achieve this status. But it did grow into an extraordinarily stimulating movement that struck very precisely at critical positions in hegemonic culture and the 'common sense' of the ruling power bloc. The *NLR* under Hall pursued an editorial line of humanist anti-Stalinism emphasizing building socialism 'from below' and acting rather than succumbing to Adornoesque 'resignation'. By 1968 this was regarded as too naive and soft by the 'Trotskyite' vanguard on the editorial board (Schwarz and Mercer 1981: 152).

Hall's New Left milieu was dissenting, middle or lower middle class, largely masculine, with an employment base largely in the public sector and particularly the universities. Of the central figures, only Raymond Williams could be legitimately identified as a son of the unskilled or semi-skilled proletariat. His father was a railwayman. Edward Thompson's father was a Methodist missionary who converted to Buddhism. The family background of Benedict and Perry Anderson was located in the diplomatic corps. Raphael

Samuel's formidable mother, Minna, was a successful musical composer and Communist Party activist, and his uncle, Chimen Abramsky, was a noted historian of the First International. Hall's father was upwardly mobile and became Chief Accountant of the United Fruit Company, the largest corporation in Jamaica. The central figures in the New Left were not people who hailed from a long line of peasants, mill-hands or factory workers. They earned their living as university teachers and writers. Inevitably, for many on the traditional Left located in the shopfloor trade union movement and the Labour Party, the populist socialism of the New Left had latent elitist overtones. To be sure, Hall's readiness to publish non-academic pieces in the *New Left Review* during his tenure as editor, his involvement in the Communist University of London, which convened at the University of London Union and focused on extracurricular topics relating to gender, race, sexual identity and urban youth politics, and his work with a variety of working-class and ethnic grassroots groups were conscious attempts to put the theory of the organic intellectual into practice. But the university was perhaps not the best power base to achieve socialist transformation.

Certainly, there was a preference for theory over empirical investigation that resulted in a curious atmosphere of didacticism and remoteness in much of the New Left work in the 1970s. Although the New Left covered questions of embodiment and emplacement, the social and political consequences of these issues sometimes crept up and took them by surprise. For example, they were slow to respond to feminism and to grasp the far-reaching implications of the feminist critique of patriarchy and the construction of the subject. In the 1980s, other intellectual formations represented in other journals, notably *Theory, Culture & Society* and *Cultural Studies*, were quicker to address questions of the body, globalization, citizenship and postmodernism. The New Left was not quite eclipsed, but its political position hobbled its ability to think anew from first principles if necessary. Thus, for example, to begin with, they treated the challenges of postmodernism rather circumspectly and imperiously. The postmodern dividend was branded as 'New Times'. These 'New Times' were interrogated as an opportunity to rehabilitate left-wing thought rather than to explore what validity the Left retained in a culture and politics that made a virtue of *bricolage* and irony. The didactic overtones of the New Left project prevailed.

Globalization was also handled in a peculiar way. The *New Left Review* had a long and honourable tradition of covering the development gap and the lack of profile in the West of Third World issues. But it was oddly indifferent to the cultural uniformities engineered by multinational corporations, financial deregulation and the rise of net society. For example, a significant part of Hall's aggravation with New Labour derived from his proposition that the Blair government adopted a supine view of globalization. Hall goes out of his way to kick into touch the idea that the operations of globalization are beyond the control of nation-states and regional and international agencies (1998a: 11). But he is less convincing in establishing the consequences of isolationism for generations who consume MTV, Nike, McDonald's and Panasonic, buy stocks and shares through Fidelity or JP Morgan Asset Management and surf the net for pleasure in the evenings or weekends. Hall's attack on New Labour (1998a) accuses the Blair government of treating globalization as a *fait accompli* and calls for the reassertion of national independence in the state management of the economy, culture and civil society. The New Left produced nothing as sophisticated as Castells's analysis of network society and the 'weightless economy' (1996; 1997; 1998). Its approach to globalization tended to fall back on nationalist state solutions. However, one of the main arguments in globalization theory is that global integration leaves little room for national autonomy.

The problem of 'Englishness'

John Hartley argues that a preoccupation with British questions is a central defect of what he calls 'Hallism' (1996: 233). He makes the point to illustrate the limitations of Hall's approach in the analysis of the global media. The question of Hall's relation to Britain is complex. He has gone on record to proclaim that he is not, and never will, be 'English' (1996e: 490). He recalls with a shudder the upper-class English voices 'commanding attention to confidently expressed banalities as a sort of seigneurial right' (1989f: 19) that he encountered at Oxford, with their barely concealed condescension and racism. Hall's sense of not being English possesses added resonance because his colonial education in Jamaica privileged English culture as the zenith of Western achievement. His sense of the gap between the reality of English culture and its representation in the education system and the mass media is therefore perhaps particularly acute.

But one should not exaggerate Hall's singularity among the New Left in this respect. Williams was a Welsh scholarship boy who described the upper- and middle-class students that he encountered at Cambridge as 'loud, competitive and deprived' (1990: 6). The Andersons came from an Anglo-Irish family and Benedict Anderson commented that although he was educated in England from the age of eleven, he found it difficult to imagine himself English (1990: 2). Ioan Davies was right to submit that this ambivalence of the New Left towards English culture was bound up in the politics of displacement (1995: 61–2). Hall was a Jamaican migrant; the Andersons possessed a strong sense of hybridity in their family background and both have lived for much of their adult lives in the United States; Samuel belonged to the Jewish émigré intelligentsia; and Williams, although educated, and for most of his working life employed, by the University of Cambridge, never felt at home in the milieu of English privilege. The New Left displayed the identifying characteristics of racial and class nomads, which perhaps reduced their capacity to establish roots in the labour movement. Certainly, Davies contended that the Andersons' connection with the working class was primarily 'cerebral', and that both belong ultimately to 'the academic set which contemplates from a great political distance, the fate of humankind' (1995: 62–3).

It is unfair to extend the comment to the New Left *in toto*. Samuel actively mixed with trade unionists and working-class students at Ruskin College. He was also a leading figure in the History Workshop, founded in 1967, which was an umbrella organization for community-based publishing projects, local history workshops, oral history groups, and independent writers as well as socialist scholars working in universities and polytechnics. Hall has been involved in many working-class grassroots meetings and discussion groups. He cited the Open University's policy of greater access as a major factor in persuading him to leave Birmingham in 1979. Nonetheless, there is truth in the argument that the New Left's engagement with the working class was pre-eminently academic and that it was mediated through community-based contact rather than in the form of an organized class movement.

At the same time, the significance of the New Left for British culture and political life is undeniable. Its agenda of interests was diverse and contradictory, but it acted as a rallying point for those who were disaffected both with nationalist-centrist hegemony and the 'verities' of traditional Marxism. Thompson, Williams and Hall adopted the role of public intellectuals and their interventions in the mass media were important in popularizing the ideas formed in their academic writings. Hall's analysis of Thatcherism, albeit conducted chiefly through the pages of *Marxism Today*, was politically significant. The same is true of his contributions on new ethnicity and hyphenated identity in Britain.

Yet he came to all of these issues with the gravitas of a New Left grandee. This carried with it preconceptions about political reality and the options for change that other critics in the 1980s and 1990s did not necessarily share. Although Hall was quick to absorb some aspects of postmodernism, he did so on his own terms, never once accepting the nihilistic or hedonistic aspects of the postmodern intellectual formation. The New Times thesis was an attempt to revitalize the Left by rehabilitating socialist theory. It never threw its hat in with Lyotard or Baudrillard, who argued that postmodernism signified a break or collapse in politics that made socialism obsolete. Hall's identification with New Left preconceptions is also evident in his criticism of New Labour which mobilizes traditional socialist demands for more public investment, progressive taxation, more state intervention in the market and an end to the public/private divide in the provision of health and education (1998a). Hall has shown himself to be an adept and versatile theorist, but in respect of the requirement for state intervention, the curtailment of the freedom of capitalist corporations and multinationals, and the establishment of economic, political and civil equalities there is a *plus ça change* quality to much of what is fundamental to his work. The critique of capitalism is obviously still relevant, but there is a depressing tendency to fail to go beyond the level of critique to social, economic and cultural reconstruction.

Problems of embodiment and emplacement

Arguably, the condition of contemporary society in the early twenty-first century requires the reconstruction of civil society around radically revised notions of embodiment and emplacement. Other intellectual traditions have recognized the vulnerability of the body, the frailty of the biosphere and the emergence of transnational dialogic communities as foundations for the reinvention of solidarity (Bauman 1992; 1993; 1998; Beck 1992; Turner and Rojek 2001). In contrast, Hall's post-identity thinking envisages a reflexively constituted, dialogic politics of embodiment and emplacement

in which solidarity is, somewhat oddly, extrapolated from the interruption and erasure of identity.

Other approaches to culture, notably the work of Paul Willis
(1977; 1978; 2001), are much sounder in placing emplacement and
embodiment at the centre of culture. For Willis, the 'laff', swearing,
dress, sport, dancing and other bodily practices create liminal space,
'profane' space, beyond the reach of ideology. In Hall's work ideology is all-encompassing. The result is that the body and place tend
to be 'written over' by ideological 'positioning'. Indeed, during the
1970s, at what might be termed the apogee of Hall's insistence on
the 'positioning' effect of ideology in respect of subjectivity, he
comes perilously close to assigning to ideology the function of the
very sociologism that he elsewhere deplores.

In his later work, after the 1980s, he returns to the theme of unity
through difference that characterized his understanding of the New
Left project (1989f; 1989h). The Parekh Report (2000) on multi-ethnic
Britain, to which Hall was a prominent signatory, advocates equality, difference and cohesion as the central pillars of reform in race
and society. But what does it mean to match equality and difference
as the progenitors of cohesion in conditions in which identity is
chronically interrupted and deconstructed? Equality gives you standardization, uniformity and a central enforcing agency – generally,
in industrial society, the state – which is acknowledged to be the
prior legitimate source of management and arbitration. Difference
gives you diversity, variety and a frequently rather volatile system
of castes, parties and social movements which recognize that the
legitimacy of the state is contingent and, in certain circumstances,
revocable. If, in post-identity thinking, no identity can be regarded
as stable or veridical, it follows that equality and difference must
operate 'under erasure'. It is not apparent that political cohesion is
amenable to being reconstructed around a cultural economy of
ambivalence, contingency, hybridity and deconstruction.

The recommendations that the Parekh Report makes in respect
of police and policing, the criminal justice system, education, arts,
media, sports, employment, health and welfare, immigration, politics and representation, religion and belief are predicated in revitalized roles for the state in the management of civil society. Other
approaches stress the declining role of the nation-state and the
increasing significance of globalization, disembeddedness, life politics and the emergence of cosmopolitan citizenship (Giddens 1998;
2000; Castells 1996; 1997; 1998; Linklater 1998; Beck 1999). But Hall's
work on post-identity thinking (1993d; 1992e) holds that meaning

continues to unfold, so to speak, beyond the 'arbitrary closure' that makes it, at any moment, tenable. The advocacy of equality, difference and cohesion in the Parekh Report does not get around the problem of 'arbitrary closure'. For it necessarily raises the questions of who is articulating social values as socially commendable; what these values are understood to mean; and why they are regarded as culturally superior. The concept of 'dialogical citizenship' starts the debate but it begs the difficult question of what the proper ends of anti-racist policy should be.

Some commentators submit that the development of civil society has culminated in 'reflexive modernism', in which the dichotomy between citizens and 'aliens' is chronically problematized as an ordinary accomplishment of the relations of everyday life (Beck, Giddens and Lash 1994). In as much as this is so, it is reasonable to propose that communities may be more politically autonomous and morally self-regulating than earlier models of governance based around either the market or the state allowed. Hall's advocacy of the political formation achieved under Ken Livingstone in the Greater London Council as 'pre-figurative' of an efficient form of 'counter-hegemonic' politics (1991b: 64–5) seems to say as much. But the precise form of counter-hegemonic democratization envisaged and its relationship to the difficult questions of governance are not clearly enunciated. Hall's bizarre nomination of the old-fashioned Labour politician John Prescott as a 'great hope' for the revitalization of the Left (1997a: 38–9) is not a good omen. Prescott may be a Labour traditionalist who has grappled with the new issues of the 1990s and welcomed the new century as a fresh start for the compact between the public and the private. Further, he may have been, as Hall claims, to some extent radicalized by the process of government in a multicultural, global society. Yet his roots remain ineluctably in the orthodox party divisions between Left and Right, which he addresses with a dirigiste mentality.

Underlying Hall's view of a politics of difference is a revisionist reading of the long-standing relationship between the community and the state. His analysis of cultural diversity and difference points to a crisis in the nation-state and a new confidence among hitherto marginalized communities. Orthodox political science emphasizes the strong correlation between nationalism and culture. Ernest Gellner, in fact, defines nationalism as 'a political principle which maintains that similarity of culture is the basic social bond' (1997: 3). Hall's Cultural Studies can, in part, be read as a rejoinder to this definition. He dismisses the pairing of nationalism with 'similarity of culture' because he regards it to be reductive. His reflections on diaspora and hybridity oppose the notions of national and cultural purity. His critique of nationalism and colonialism treats both as the fruit of Enlightenment positivism. His work on representation, postcolonialism and post-identity thought is really an attempt to replace positivism with hermeneutics. Thus he attacks 'the West' for self-idealization; for omitting to recognize or respect difference; for propounding the Western idiom of perception and representation as universal; and, in general, as the political cliché coined by Sir Robert Armstrong during the Thatcher years has it, for being 'economical with the truth' (Hall 1992b: 308).

Hall regards his intellectual labour as a contribution to the process of cognitive realignment, replacing the abstract European values of 'truth' and 'reason' with context-related conceptions of truth as interpretation. He lists among the benefits of this 'perspectival' shift the following (1999: 17):

1   The radical awareness by the marginalized of the symbolic power involved in the activity of representation.
2   An increasing recognition of the centrality of culture and its connection to meaning.
3   A growing reflexivity about cultural and political hierarchy.
4   The increasing significance of a 'politics of recognition' which supplements the traditional politics of equality.

Strictly speaking, this is not a novel argument. A good case can be made that the shift to which Hall alludes reaches back to the English, French and American revolutions in the seventeenth and eighteenth centuries. In England and France the execution of the king was the symbol of reconstituted representation, reflexivity and the 'politics of recognition' in favour of the Commons, while the American War of Independence broke the colonial tradition of vassalage to the monarch. A deep-rooted historical perspective is therefore required to understand the politics of national belonging and the processes of social inclusion and exclusion. C. L. R. James certainly argued in this vein, in his brilliant account of Toussaint L'Ouverture and the revolution in Haiti, and its relationship to the French and American revolutions (James 1938).

But, of course, the reason why Hall regards the ground to be 'shaking' beneath his feet is that he believes a new conjuncture has emerged that radically undermines the stability of the Enlightenment tradition (Jaggi 2000: 9). Interestingly, *contra* Tudor's (1999) proposition that Cultural Studies has neglected the question of epistemology, Hall regards the new conjuncture as deriving primarily from a crisis in Western cosmology and the Western *episteme*. To use an analogy of which he is inordinately fond, 'the rules of the game' have changed. Postmodernism proposes that current cultural and economic conditions have fatefully unravelled the status of the human subject. Hence the prominence of hybridity, diaspora and multi-accented meaning in his later work. The Enlightenment understanding of identity as fixed, solid and bounded has been replaced by an understanding of position and agency that emphasizes mobility, porosity and fluency.

Prima facie, this emphasis on diversity, plurality and multiplicities of identity and the presentation of the self is reminiscent of the themes raised by symbolic interactionists and postindustrial society theorists in the 1960s. But whereas Goffman's sociology never abandoned the notion of 'paramount reality', which acts as an independent grounded context to particular social encounters, and Daniel Bell (1971) regarded postindustrial society as portending some kind of new social and cultural integration built around technology and pluralism, Hall seems to consign us to cold comfort farm. Once the limitations of identity thinking are recognized there is no going back to the old Cartesian logic of the integrated, stable subject, continuously pursuing the inner dialectic of selfhood. Instead the subject – identity – is literally opened up. What Foucault called 'the technologies of the self' are reflexively narrativized in everyday social encounters, thus making ordinary interchange more permeated with critical and reflexive consciousness than hitherto. Equally, the old, homogenizing collective identities of class, gender, race and ethnicity have had their totalizing function dismantled. We no longer recognize the quick of our being through them. Even if we acknowledge a resonance with them, it is pregnant with the realization of difference and schism. Evidently, feminism, Lacan, Derrida and Laclau and Mouffe have left an indelible mark on Hall's thinking. As he now puts it, identity 'is always constructed through ambivalence. Always constructed through splitting' (1991b: 47–8).

We shall come to consider the foundations and consequences of this standpoint later in the book (see pp. 178–81). Here it is enough to note that Hall's argument carries an important sociological insight having to do with the dynamics of interdependence and co-presence. Others working in the field of Cultural Studies have elected to examine these matters through the prism of embodiment and emplacement, in particular the sensuous relationship between

humans and the world (Turner 1984; Willis 2001). However, Hall
elects to conceptualize them chiefly in linguistic and philosophical
terms. Thus he postulates 'the notion of identity as contradictory,
as composed of more than one discourse, as composed always
across the silences of the other, as written in and through ambivalence and desire' (1991b: 49). One problem with this passage, and
it is a general problem with linguistic-psychoanalytic models of
culture, is that it presents the Other, ambivalence and desire in
abstract terms. The questions are, what 'Other' is being enunciated,
and what is the content of ambivalence and desire?

To some extent Hall's analysis of race, the media and the state
provides concrete answers to these questions. For example, his
discussion of Thatcherism argues that 'authoritarian populism'
momentarily welded the floating signifiers of the market, the nation
and the individual into a unitary network of meaning which centred
on the ideology of subjective freedom. It was a very effective illus-
tration of the Althusserian thesis of interpellation, which proposes
that the human subject is not pregiven or fixed but, on the contrary,
'summoned', 'hailed' or 'called into being' through the operation of
ideology. For Althusser, writes Hall, 'there is no social practice
outside of ideology' (1985a: 103).

In the 1970s and 1980s Hall broadly endorsed this view, albeit via
a more sophisticated, nuanced reading of the multi-accented, contingent character of interpellation. However, from the 1990s his perspective shifts again. Althusser always assumed that ideological
interpellation is not necessarily successful. Moreover, to the extent
that he recognized that we are all interpellated by different ideologies, 'interruptions' are always and already implicit in his approach.
But after the 1970s Hall presents identity as beset with 'interruptions' that create lesions in the appearance of totality and unity.
Ideology no longer successfully 'positions' homology or difference.
Established hierarchy and authority are subject to strong decentring
pressures. Interruptions are now chronic, making traditional ways
of thinking about, and relating to, identity deeply problematic.
However, the causality, in the Weberian sense of the term, is not
clearly explained. Usually in Hall's work, social change is attributed
to transformations in the concatenation of variables that constitute
a conjuncture which articulate positions and tendencies in determinate levels of the social formation which run against the grain of
ideology. But the mechanisms of transformation are often elusive.

In large measure, the problem derives from the nature of the
Gramscian approach to cultural analysis that Hall champions above

all others. As we shall see in more detail later (see chapter 2), Gramsci holds that, at the epistemological level, concepts operate at distinct and discrete levels of abstraction. Societies are presented as complexly structured totalities, involving different levels of articulation (the economic, the political, the ideological, the cultural) intermeshing in distinctive, mobile constellations. Each constellation is theorized as eliciting a distinctive configuration of social forces, which is not repeatable, and which provides the given social situation with its 'conjunctural' character or stamp. The levels that constitute social situations are therefore understood to be multiple, and the elements within each level are polyvalent, both in relation to the other elements within their level of operation and to elements situated at different levels. Polyvalence is theorized as stretching across space and time, so that changes in, say, concrete cultural relations may occur at a faster or slower pace than changes at the political or economic levels.

Moreover, concrete relations are understood to consist of 'many determinations', with 'epochal', 'organic' relations, having to do with the constitution of 'common sense' and the mode of production, being analytically distinct from the historically specific level of 'immediate' relations of state, party, class and community. Hence the significance of the 'moment' in cultural articulation, and the stress on the condensation or 'overdetermination' of elements in the 'power bloc' behind shifts in conjuncture. Nothing is static in Gramsci's paradigm, and the multiple, polyvalent levels of causality and reciprocity place stringent demands on interpretation to recognize the 'periodicity' of change and the various, discrete levels of determination and overdetermination.

This is evidently a complex, multilayered approach to social and cultural analysis. One serious problem hampering its dissemination in the social sciences is that it emerged organically from Gramsci's engagement with the Italian case. To some extent, its wider application in comparative and historical analysis is inhibited by its cultural and historical specificity. Hall's appropriation of Gramsci has been criticized on the same grounds. This returns to Hartley's point that the dissemination and development of what he terms 'Hallism' is obstructed by Hall's excessive preoccupation with British questions (Hartley 1996: 235–40).

Against this one should note that Hall acknowledges that Gramsci's approach does not constitute a general social science in the manner of, say, the formulations of Marx, Durkheim, Weber or Parsons (Hall 1986b: 5–6). To be sure, Hall's sympathy for Gramsci's approach derives in no small part from the latter's insistence that theory must demonstrate ineradicable respect for the concrete, and resist empirically disassociated forms of comparative and historical analysis. For Gramsci and Hall, the concrete level is the *modus operandi* for effecting genuine political change. It is precisely the privileging of abstraction over the concrete, political level that Hall imputes as the central defect in the 'explosion' of Cultural Studies in the US (1992f: 285–6). His disapproval and frustration are unmistakable.

This introduction is not the place to go into any detail on the question of what Hall recommends as valuable in Gramsci for the study of society and culture. What is incontrovertible is that Gramsci's work is of seminal importance in Hall's approach to Cultural Studies. So the question cannot be avoided, and will be merely postponed until chapter 2 of the study. At this stage of the discussion, I simply wish to note that Hall's application of Gramsci's approach in the study of culture is faithful in illustrating the importance of 'hegemony', 'articulation', 'overdetermination', 'conjuncture', 'organic intellectual', and 'unstable balance' in the 'relations of force'. Gramsci undoubtedly provided Hall with a cogent formulation of a non-teleological, dynamic, historical, anti-reductionist way of doing cultural analysis.

Conversely, Hall's application of Gramsci's thought also illustrates the main defects of the Gramscian approach. If I can put it like this, Gramsci constructs a multi-lane highway approach to the analysis of culture and society. It postulates different lanes of force, composed of distinct levels of density and therefore porosity, and requires interpretation to recognize that velocity and articulation in each lane is not uniform or homologous. It is a form of analysis in which indications of lane changes are *de rigueur*, since propositions that apply to, for example, the epochal-organic, do not necessarily apply to the historically specific-concrete. However, Gramsci did not consistently signal his movements from one lane or level to the next, and neither does Hall. The result is a sort of inbuilt infallibility to the Gramscian/Hallian approach. Thus propositions regarding say, working-class activism which appear to be falsified at the level of the historically specific-concrete are conducive to revision in relation to the epochal-organic level, or vice versa. However, revision typically takes the form of retrospective wisdom and not coterminous, integrated interpretation. As with all multilevel paradigms, it is effectively impossible to test propositions since what is being proposed can always be modified in relation to a more (or less) dense/porous lane of analysis at either the synchronic or diachronic dimensions. In so far as this is so, it provides another insight into why Hall is often accused of slippage. Critics who falsify his analysis at one level of interpretation can always be referred back to another level which situates his analysis into a more 'complete' picture. David Harris (1992) has noted the tendency towards circularity in this form of cultural and theoretical reasoning.

Given this stance to analysis, which is integral to Gramsci's thought as opposed to Hall's application of this thought, it is all the more surprising that Hall, since the mid-1980s, has embraced the 'decentred' refutation of identity thinking so enthusiastically. Granted, Hall maintains that Gramscianism regards personal consciousness to be 'multi-faceted' and 'plural' (1986b). But this reflects the indexical relation that is postulated between the subject and the terrain of history and culture. As Gramsci puts it, in a quotation which Hall (1986b) quotes approvingly: 'The personality is strangely composite [it contains] . . . Stone Age elements and principles of a more advanced science, prejudices from all past phases of history . . . and intuitions of a future philosophy' (Gramsci 1971: 324). This is very different from the implosion of the subject documented at length in postmodern and poststructuralist accounts. Most obviously, Gramsci retains the orthodox Marxist conviction as to the 'master' identity of collective subjects like class, gender and race, as pivotal levers of social change. Hall's later work on 'interruption' and 'deconstruction' does more than expose the monolithic/complacent character of our traditional conceptions of identity (1996a; 1997c; 1999). He blows the belief in master narratives and hence foundational identity out of the water. In his own words:

> The question of how to begin to think questions of identity, either social or individual, not in the wake of their disappearance but in the wake of their erosion, of their fading, of their not having the kind of purchase and comprehensive explanatory power they had before, that is what it seems to me has gone. They used to be thought of – and it is a wonderfully gendered definition – as 'master concepts', the 'master concepts' of class. It is not tolerable any longer to have a 'master concept' like that. Once it loses its 'master' status its explanatory reach weakens, becomes more problematic. We can think of some things in relation to questions of class, though always recognizing its real historical complexity. Yet there are certain things it simply will not, or cannot decipher or explain. And this brings us face to face with the increasing social diversity and plurality, the technologies of the self which characterize the modern world in which we live. (1991b: 46–7)

Although Hall focuses on class in this passage, the argument of the defunct utility of the collective subject/master identity in the condition of postmodernity possesses general application in his current perspective. How can we situate this argument in relation to the lineage between Gramsci and Hall?

Somewhere in Gramsci, there is a metaphor, borrowed from Nietzsche, of the old dying and the new being unable to be born. This captures the nucleus of Hall's position on identity in contemporary culture very well. One might express it like this: Western culture has reached a stage in which the proposition that identity is unified and stable is no longer tenable. While this realization is by no means ubiquitous, neither is it confined to the ivory tower. In the areas of nationalism, gender, race and class, the awareness of the internal contradictions and crude simplicities of collective social identities and the fractured and fragmented condition of being has advanced significantly. Postcolonialism and postmodernism enunciate the dyad between presence and absence as a generalized social force, and therefore contribute to a radically decentred view of identity. On this reckoning, the self is always and already positioned in the gaze of the Other so that all points of origination and singularity are 'under erasure'. However, the conceptual categories and social institutions constructed under the Enlightenment *episteme* continue to narrativize identity in fixed, bounded terms. The tension between Hall's refutation of the primary significance of the nation-state at the level of theory, and his application of the nation-state as the primary category in understanding culture, is a case in point. In as much as the politics of difference has an agenda, it consists in forcing the contradictions of the Enlightenment *episteme* to be articulated in everyday practice.

Hall's (1999) advocacy of 'hyphenated-identity' may be cited as an example of how intellectual labour contributes to the 'interruption' of Enlightenment categories (see also the Parekh Report 2000). Through the articulation of the violence latent in central Enlightenment categories of progress and rationality, the potential for a more inclusive, democratic social order may be realized. This is not, however, conceptualized as an order in which the subordinate collective subject is transcendent. Hall is not, in fact, candid about his aspirations for the future social order. However, given his views on social inclusion and the split subject one might safely infer that dialogic communities and reflexive governance are functional prerequisites.

Earlier, I used the term 'cold comfort farm' as a reproachful metaphor of the kind of culture and society that Hall now asserts is becoming normative. However, it is not a metaphor to which Hall would subscribe. For him, the ontology and politics of difference do not give you dissonance, aggravation and disagreement, although in fact, all of these consequences are logically compatible with the scale of epistemic collapse that he describes. Instead he regards the chronic interruption of identity thinking as presaging a profound reorientation in society and culture. From it, new forms of subnational and transnational belonging have the potential to emerge which signal the end of the damaging polarization between citizen and alien, self and other. Alternative means of organizing human beings in communication communities in which insiders and outsiders are regarded as different but equal, and in which the categories of the domestic subaltern and subordinate citizens are erased, are already evident in social movements addressing questions of ecology, biology and the ascendancy of corporate capitalism. These various tendencies coalesce in the somewhat awkward concept of 'multiculturalism'.

Hall is not, of course, turning into a latter-day Rousseau. He does not gloss over the difficulties and dangers involved in creating a society in which citizens are free, as they had been in the state of nature, on the basis of utopian beliefs about the inherent goodness or rationality of mankind.[4] But his work on the politics of difference shares Rousseau's aspiration that dialogic communities can be constructed and reflexive governance can be sustained. Even so, he also cautions against a celebratory drift in the New Times thesis. The expansion of cultural diversity and difference is not universally welcomed. The resurgence of fundamentalism, expressed in the form of nationalism, sexism and racism, is testimony to that. Nor does the recognition of diversity and difference necessarily end in cooperation and harmony. Hall understands only too well that political will is required to prevent the deterioration of the politics of difference into a Hobbesian war of all against all. 'I'm interested in a politics that makes links,' explains Hall, 'without ignoring difference' (Jaggi 2000: 9).

Hall and the public sphere

As befits someone who believes that popular culture was undervalued for much of the last century, Hall has always been interested in reaching a wide public. One of his reasons for leaving the Centre for Contemporary Cultural Studies at Birmingham University and joining the Open University in 1979 was the opportunity to work in an 'unconventional setting' and talk to 'ordinary people' (Hall 1996e: 501). From 1979 until his retirement in 1997, Hall was the public face of Sociology at the Open University, familiar to thousands through his regular television and radio broadcasts. In the 1980s his articles in _Marxism Today_ on Thatcherism, and the political options for the Left, commanded a wide readership. His national television series in the late 1990s on Afro-Caribbean migration to the UK added to his celebrity. Even in retirement, Hall remains a regular figure in left-wing think tanks and radio and television broadcasts. He is perhaps the leading black public intellectual in British life today.

But what does 'Britain' mean to Hall? Without doubt, the relationship between nation, culture and state is a constant in Hall's work. Following Benedict Anderson (1991), he proposes that the nation must be conceptualized as a system of representation that elicits an 'imagined community'. His argument in fact proceeds to deconstruct the category of nation as it has been conventionally understood. Thus he postulates that the nationalist advocacy of racial purity is always founded on a kind of slash and burn technique, in which the history of diasporic migration is defoliated and incinerated. For Hall, the category of nation always contains latent violence since it sets up the spurious division between 'us and them' and rides roughshod over the subject of hybridity. It is his contention that on the dialogic recognition of this violence a tenable politics of difference can be formulated and practised.

Once again, the argument is not in fact novel. Some time ago, the anthropologist Claude Lévi-Strauss proposed that all cultures should be regarded as a 'mish-mash' of borrowings and mixtures, accrued over time, and that nationalist attempts to cleanse hybridity from history simply create myths (Lévi-Strauss 1952). Hall reaches this insight by mining in a very different, more overtly politicized vein that is predicated in a dialectical view of history. From it he extrapolates the thesis that the isolation and marginalization of individuals and social formations arise from the division of power between the established and the subalterns, the dominant class and subordinate classes. This approach privileges the significance of power and struggle in the analysis of culture and society. On this basis Hall argues that the solution to hierarchies of domination and subordination is the construction of a politics of social inclusion.

There is, of course, good reason to read difference, inclusion and exclusion dialectically as the expression of the power relations between the sexes, classes, nations, status groups and other collective agents. But it is not the only way to read them. Interestingly, Lévi-Strauss argues that difference is not primarily a consequence of the isolation or marginalization of individuals and social formations. Instead, he prefers to analyse difference as the affective and cognitive response to interdependence. Through ties of consanguinity, kinship, incest taboos and the division of labour, individuals and groups construct their own space. Emplacement and embodiment are integral to this approach because they posit that difference is not primarily a reflection of material power struggles between individuals and strata but arises from symbolic differentiation within homologous structures. It is not a question of one agent attempting to dominate or annihilate another, but concerns the affectual and cognitive desire to register particularistic correspondence through different cultural materials and embodied, emplaced distinctions.[5]

In this approach the use of cultural materials is pivotal. Significantly, the use values of culture are not theorized in terms of a conjuncture between the variables of social formation which are conducive to organizing 'floating signifiers' in determinate ways. Rather, use values derive from the affectual desire for cultural correspondence based on the recognition of common homologies of embodiment and emplacement, and the cognitive attempt to work on and with the material and cultural world. Crucially, Lévi-Strauss stresses the learning capacity of the human mind. His work looks to science rather than politics to construct dialogic communities and reflexive government.[6]

Of course, Hall is aware of the tradition of structuralist anthropology that Lévi-Strauss represents. It has influenced his own work, albeit primarily through the mediation of Althusser's theory, especially in the analysis of ideology. Structuralism enabled Hall to depart from classical Marxist readings of ideology as false consciousness, and to analyse it instead as the mechanism for social positioning and enunciation in the arrangement of consciousness and agency. Yet he continues to prefer an emancipatory project in the reorganization of society and culture which utilizes politics to achieve its ends.

Hall's work on the collapse of the dichotomy between self and other in the Western *episteme*, and his concomitant reflections on the interruption and deconstruction of identity, suggest the necessity of developing a position on the nation-state. However, while Hall has written prolifically on nationalism, he has remained relatively silent on the nation-state. Within international relations there is a long-standing debate between, broadly speaking, Hegelian and Kantian traditions. The Hegelian tradition argues that harmonizing universal citizenship rights with particular citizenship rights is a notable achievement of the modern nation-state. The Kantian tradition dwells on the failure of the modern state to comply with the obligations of world citizenship. In as much as Hall contributes to this debate, he tends to side with the Kantians (1992b; 1999). Nation-states have not met their obligation to extend rights of social inclusion to citizens or their responsibility for the welfare of the whole community. The tension between 'the West and the rest' is, for Hall, an important example of the fatigue of the Hegelian tradition.

Nationalism is the attribution of common culture within a territorially bounded unit of government. The nation-state, following Weber (1947: 156), is conceived of as an administrative and legal order in which the compulsory association of citizens is organized on a territorial basis, and in which the legitimate use of physical force is monopolized by appointed state officials. Nationalism is the expression of 'pre-contractual' sentiments of embodiment and emplacement that are manifest, *inter alia*, in race, language, heritage and codes of civility. It follows that nationalism can exist without nation-states. Indeed, Gellner observes that stateless, tribal societies have strongly developed ties of common culture without adopting the centralized form of the modern nation-state (1997: 7). Similarly, nation-states may enforce legally binding rights of citizenship that recognize the validity of nationalisms within the territorial boundaries circumscribed by the state apparatus.

These are questions of citizenship. Within international relations they have prompted a significant debate on globalization and the blinkers of nationalism (Linklater 1998: 204–20). From this, the notion of the cosmopolitan citizen has emerged as a strategy for reorienting politics in transnational dialogic communities. Cosmopolitanism acknowledges the limitations of nationalism without proposing that national identity is 'interrupted' or 'under erasure'. Instead it is predicated on what Hannerz calls 'a willingness to engage with the Other' (1990: 239). This debate revives the notion of identity since it posits forms of reflexive agency in which transnational rights and responsibilities are constituted and exercised. Identity is not 'interrupted' or 'erased' but, rather, enriched through the recognition of interdependence and mutual rights and responsibilities.

Interestingly, Hall came late to the debate on citizenship. Arguably, his contribution is tangential and expressed largely through the prism of British experience. The Parekh Report certainly recognizes globalization and citizenship. However, it dwells primarily on the prominence of 'Euroscepticism' in Britain, and the perpetuation of traditional beliefs, ideals and practices that reinforce the notion of an 'island destiny' (2000: 24). Hall, of course, is dismissive of British insularity. The 'New Times' thesis skilfully adumbrates the challenge of globalization to British national identity. However, it concentrates on the delusions of nationalism rather than the reconstruction of the nation-state as part of a wider transnational dialogic community. As we have already noted, Hartley (1996) attacks Hall for focusing narrowly on the British case, implying, *en passant*, that Hall's work is disfigured by latent insularity. The point is overstated, because Hall's critique of colonialism is based on the premise of British universalism. Colonialism is intrinsically brutal, contends Hall, because it cannot appreciate difference and seeks to paint the whole world in its own image.

Historians like David Cannadine (2001) would regard this position as too extreme. Cannadine's analysis of the role of the British in India demonstrates that rule was accomplished by recognizing and institutionalizing analogues between the British and Indian hierarchies of power, rather than merely seeking to replace one with the other. I shall return to take up this point in greater detail in chapter 4.

Despite all of the urging to look outwards in the New Times thesis there is an undeniable flavour of insularity in Hall's outlook. His socialism is of a rather old-fashioned kind, based in the notion of the Keynesian state, as witness the broadside he fired across the bows of 'new Labour' for being 'seduced' by the 'neo-liberal gospel of the global market' (1998a: 11). Hall is dismissive of the perspective that assumes globalization to be a *fait accompli*. Instead he addresses the obligation of the state to manage the effects of globalization to ensure redistributive justice against the tide of 'global' opinion expressed in the boardrooms of Western capitalism. The argument calls for the expansion of the public sphere and the renewal of citizenship as alternatives to the fetishization of neoliberalism and the sovereign consumer.

Hall's focus on the shortcomings of New Labour implies that the state is the central agent in this process. Other critical traditions, notably the Third Way position of Giddens (1998; 2000) and Beck (1999), maintain that the state is too remote from the interests of ordinary citizens. They look beyond the state and party politics for the revival of citizenship. Beck's concept of 'subpolitics' is the collective term for the various associations and fringe groups that politicize questions of citizenship in non-party ways (1992; 1999). The concept is partly designed to highlight the importance of volunteerism and social movements in the political reconstruction of environmental issues, bio-engineering, race relations and gay and lesbian rights issues. Hall's declared sympathies with the old Greater London Council in the 1980s as a model of effective politics (1991b) suggests a predisposition for recognizing the importance of subpolitics as defined by Beck. But nowhere in Hall is there an explanation of how this relates to the renewal of citizenship.

Again the proposition that Hall is a better cultural critic than theorist begs to be repeated. Where can a theorist who insists on the facticity of hybridity and hyphenated identity, but who neglects to adumbrate the detailed rights and responsibilities of agency that follow from this submission, take us? What reason is there to search for new forms of solidarity around hybridity and contingency? Why should we entertain the proposition that these problems, constructed around the pretext of 'New Times', are actually novel?

The criticisms of slippage, absence of methodology, modishness, radicalism, the limitations of Englishness, embodiment and emplacement will be substantiated in the following chapters. The aim is to critically investigate Hall's essential published writings. I will give due credit to Hall's innovative pedagogy, especially during his time in Birmingham. However, I will not comment in detail on Hall's work with course teams in the Open University in seeking to realign the fields of Crime and Society, State and Society, Beliefs and Ideologies, Introduction to Sociology, Social Science Foundation Courses, Understanding Modernities and Representations. Nor do I comment on the many TV, radio and cassette productions by Hall associated with these courses. Plainly, Hall devoted a great deal of energy to these activities. Arguably, they were a major reason in diverting him from producing a single-authored book-length work during this time. Because they made extensive use of electronic media, they reached a much wider audience than the students enrolled at Milton Keynes. But they were also governed by the institutional constraints of course delivery and carried all the compromises and concessions that collaborative work ruled by committee bound by university regulations brings in its wake. For me, Hall's articles on Thatcherism and his writings on hybridity and the politics of difference convey a more accurate bearing of where Hall was at in the 1980s and 1990s.

In researching Hall's published writings, and trying to trace through the many complex threads of the shifts of emphasis in his intellectual position over the years, I have reached the conclusion that Hall's background in Jamaica must be confronted. He has made great play of hailing from a colonial background, but the particularity of his colonial status may not be immediately apparent, especially to white European-American-Australasian readers. The conditions of the Jamaican system of stratification are salient, both in illuminating why Hall felt himself to be so sharply located on the margins during much of his time in England, and in explaining his receptivity to the perspective of hybridity and the politics of difference after the 1980s. This is why the next chapter addresses the theme at some length. As we shall see presently, Hall regards himself to be not merely a cultural hybrid but an 'absolute cultural hybrid'. This awkward mix between singularity and uniformity is a keynote of Hall's writings and is perhaps also redolent of a certain kind of wider tension in the New Left's engagement with the proletariat and the public sphere. It is also reminiscent of 'brown man'/'black man' frictions in the politics in Jamaica in Hall's youth. The question of for whom Hall is talking in his maturity can only be illuminated by considering where he is coming from. The matter of Hall's background is thus germane to understanding his intellectual proclivities and political aspirations.

1

The 'Absolute Cultural Hybrid'

Stuart Hall was born in Kingston, Jamaica in 1932. He was the son of lower middle-class, upwardly mobile parents. His father rose through the ranks of the major corporate employer on the island, the American-owned United Fruit Company, eventually becoming Chief Accountant.[1] Hall describes each of his parents as possessing a strong streak of conservatism. Both were uncomfortable with the movement for Jamaican independence. Each instinctively regarded Britain as the mother country, an outlook that the young Hall repudiated as 'anachronistic' (1995c: 660). He disapproved of their *arriviste* identification with the Jamaican establishment, and the collusion it implied with colonial rule.

In retrospect, Hall declares that he always 'felt as if I were a kind of stranger in my own family' (Jaggi 2000: 8). The sense of estrangement went further than the tension between his parents' dogged colonial loyalism and his incipient attachment to the cause of Jamaican independence. Frictions of class and colour were also at play. Hall's father, Herman, was the product of the coloured lower middle class, only two generations removed from his African ancestors (Hall 1995c: 661). Hall's mother, Jessie, was from a different class and colour formation, only two generations on from an ancestry which included some white forebears. Although she was born into relative poverty, she was adopted by an Anglophile lawyer uncle, and raised in some style.[2] Hall regards his family of origin as overdetermined by class, colonial and racial tensions. He was born, he remarks, 'in a lower-middle-class family that was trying to be a middle-class Jamaican family trying to be an upper-middle-class

Jamaican family trying to be an English Victorian family' (1993d: 135). Hall's father represented the dark-skinned, country faction in Jamaican society, while his mother was lighter skinned and identified with the English-plantation oriented faction. Hall identifies traces of African, East Indian, Portuguese Jewish and 'low, probably convict' Scottish blood in the family, which, he maintains, stamps him as 'a mongrel culturally, the absolute cultural hybrid' (1995c: 661; 1995b: 7). He describes himself as the blackest member of the family, and, on several occasions in interviews, recalls being teased by his sister, for being a 'coolie baby' (1996e: 485; Jaggi 2000: 8).

Hall, class and colour in Jamaica

However, it is questionable whether Hall then, or now, would be properly regarded as 'black' in Jamaican society. As Hall notes, gradations of colour are fundamental in Jamaican society (Jaggi 2000: 8). In an aside, he contends that Jamaica has the most complicated colour stratification system in the world (1991b: 53). In terms of the gradations of Jamaican society, Hall belongs to the 'brown man' category. It is important for non-Jamaican readers to understand that, in Jamaica, this nomenclature has significant racial and political overtones. Far from being a digression from an accurate understanding of Hall's writings, it is essential to go through the details.

The classical statement of the hierarchy of gradations regarding class and colour in Jamaican society was produced by the Jamaican anthropologist M. G. Smith (1965). Although a good deal of controversy now surrounds Smith's methodology and intellectual independence, his study is the classical resource in academic discussions about the subject (for contrasting versions of the controversy, see Robotham 1980; Scott 2000).

Smith portrays Jamaican society as an extraordinary mixture of racial and cultural blending. According to him, four-fifths of the population is 'black', nine-tenths of the rest is coloured, 'of mixed ancestry, and subsidiary minorities are white, Chinese, East Indian, Portuguese, Syrian and Jewish'. His account of the operation of this racial and cultural mélange of peoples and mixtures is grounded in history. He proposes that in the early nineteenth century, Jamaican society consisted of a complex hierarchy of differentiated social categories (1965: 92–101). Broadly speaking, this was conceptualized in triangular fashion. Thus, at the head, the whites constituted the economically and culturally dominant class. Below them, Smith identified the free coloureds and the free blacks. The base of the class system was the slave class. Smith described the slave class as numerically dominant, but culturally and economically subjugated.

Within each of these divisions, Smith noted a series of subdivisions. Hence, the white class was differentiated into creole strata (those born in the West Indies) and immigrants. Overlaying this division was a distinction between 'principal' and 'secondary' whites, the former holding authority over the latter. Creole whites were further subdivided into planters, the professional class and merchants; immigrant whites were subdivided into administrator, militia and planter groups. Migrant planters, in turn, were divided into owners; those who work for them (overseers, book-keepers, master masons); and owners of small estates who hired out slaves as field and domestic labourers. At the cultural level, Smith made the distinction that the principal whites, in general, tended to be 'better educated' than the secondary whites and, further, that creole and white immigrants formed separate social groups (1965: 95).

Turning now to the analysis of the free 'coloured population', Smith maintained that coloured slaves were differentiated by the traditional plantation practice of employing them as estate craftsmen or domestic servants (1965: 99). They constituted a distinctively graded social group, separated from the black field-work slave labourer, and possessing a closer association with principal and secondary whites. Free blacks were recipients of property, gifted by 'affectionate masters', and allowed to pursue their own subsistence. However, because the plantation economy was based on the full employment of slave labour, the opportunities for free blacks to prosper were limited. In cultural terms, Smith suggests, free blacks did not possess the social and cultural affinities with the creole and white dominant class possessed by the free coloured class.

As for the slave class, Smith argued a basic status distinction applied in respect of occupation, as tradesmen, domestic slaves and field slaves (1965: 101). Coloureds tended to be predominant in occupying the roles of tradesmen and domestic slaves, while most field slaves were black. Within the slave class, domestic slaves possessed superior status, since they enjoyed greater opportunities for contact in white households (1965: 102). Next were tradesmen, whose technical knowledge assigned them certain latitudes of conduct, such that they constituted a 'small, select group' (1965: 102). Field slaves were also subdivided into different categories. The senior stratum acquired status through longevity and often regarded manual labour of any type as beneath their standing.

Below them were the creole slaves, and at the bottom of the slave status hierarchy were the newly imported 'African' slaves.

Smith's elaboration of the historical nuances of class and colour distinctions in Jamaican society was partly designed to oppose Parsonian models of society which emphasized binding common values as the cement of social cohesion. For Smith, nation-states founded on the legacy of conquest and violence are necessarily predisposed to hierarchical segmentation, since questions of embodiment and emplacement are irretrievably permeated with colonial racial distinctions. In addition, Smith clearly regarded the segmented hierarchy of Jamaican society as posing substantial obstacles of culture and race in the nation-building process. Crucially, Smith conceptualized culture as a social construction, transmitted and assimilated between the physicality of groups (1965: 15). Thus he regarded race to be a genetic condition of embodiment, impermeable to human control. The latter distinction is, of course, quite contrary to Hall's conception of race as a 'floating signifier', which possesses a history and discourse that can be destabilized and reflexively reconstituted as a politics of difference, through cultural and economic intervention. The inference of Smith's analysis is that while cultural differences between strata can be gradually mitigated, usually through strong central leadership, so that they become less significant, racial differences do not follow the same logic, or succumb to the same remedy.

Viewed synoptically, as Robotham (1980) observes, Smith's discussion of pluralism in Jamaica explains cohesion in terms of acculturation. The discussion of the various gradations of class and colour operates on the presupposition that the values and practices of the various subordinate classes voluntarily emulate those of the principal whites, albeit, of course, with differing chances of convergence. Hall himself has questioned the 'extensive' social cohesion, adaptation and accommodation between different groups in the pluralist model of Jamaican society (1978c; 1985c). Smith, of course, accepted that white rule deliberately set out to marginalize the cultures of the other groups in Jamaican society. Yet, curiously, his view of the characteristic cultural values of the dominant class is reminiscent of the Eliot/Leavis tradition, which regards white elite culture as 'the best that has been thought and done'. Thus Smith holds that the subordinate classes, free brown, free black and black plantation slave, voluntarily gravitate towards white colonial normative precedents of organization, association, practice and belief, because they are regarded to be the most rational known to mankind.

The consequence is a peculiarly rigid reading of hierarchy and segmentation. For critics like Robotham (1980), cultural and racial distinctions are not simply ordained by the status ladder erected by the colonial power, but also entail the reflexive responses of creole and migrant subaltern populations to the fact of conquest. Acculturation is not a satisfactory concept to encapsulate this response, because it conceives of development as a one-way process in which the standards and values of the dominant class are emulated by other social strata.

The contradictions in acculturation theory are thrown into sharper relief when one turns to schisms in the power balance in Jamaica precipitated by free brown and free black aspirations for national independence. Smith supported the nationalist movement in Jamaica that began in the late 1930s. Brown man middle-class activists occupied the vanguard of this movement. They identified strongly with the Eurocentric values of principal white strata. Thus they were in favour of parliamentary democracy, the codified law, a rational education system, sport and the retention of colonial institutions of finance, technology and industry. Their ideals of respectability, personal decorum and manners were drawn from Britain, nowhere more so than in the value attributed to education as a means of upward mobility and a mark of social status. Oxford and Cambridge were fetishized as the pinnacle of academic learning and cultural cachet. In this respect, it is revealing that Hall went through all the arduous hoops to gain an Oxford education. For him at this time, largely one suspects at the prompting of his parents, and particularly his mother, gaining a place at Oxbridge was the summit of academic achievement. But going to Oxford also signified relations of cultural dependence, and perhaps even illustrated in Hall's mind the operation of the Hegelian master–slave relationship. I shall return to the question of Hall's Oxford experience, and its place in his intellectual pedigree, presently. At this stage of the discussion it is necessary to explore some of the tensions in the Jamaican nationalist movement at greater length.

The nationalist movement sought independence from colonial rule, but it divided internally in respect of the tactics designed to accomplish this end, and the extent of political, economic and cultural divergence from Britain. On the one hand stood a landed, pro-colonial enclave that visualized independence as the nationalist management of the institutions and codes of practice introduced by the British, and sought political advantage in rendering them, formally at least, inclusive to the popular constituency. This group regarded the goal of Jamaican society to lie ultimately in the direction of a harmonious, more equal relationship with Britain. Against them was situated an equally prosperous anti-colonial enclave, intent on preserving the foundations of British institutions and practices but fundamentally reforming them, via an egalitarian alliance between middle-class brown men activists and the subaltern black population. This group, of which the Manley family was a prominent example, favoured self-government under the retention of dominion status within the British Commonwealth. Both enclaves were faithful to the institutional and cultural essentials of the colonial programme of acculturation, albeit with the important proviso that brown men would either lead, or join with the British in running, the country. In particular, neither envisaged the abandonment of Eurocentricism, and still less, the positive promotion of Africa and 'African' culture.

Robotham (1980) and Scott (2000) argue that the aspirations of the acculturalist brown middle class were untenable, since they neglected to encompass a sustainable politics of difference. Smith's theory of acculturation identified the transition of power to the brown man class as a progressive feature of social and political development in Jamaica. However, in two respects it was seriously faulty. First, it precluded the possibility of racial hybridity in government because it presupposed revised acculturation as the dividend of brown man ascendancy. Thus brown man government was conceptualized as reforming colonial racism, and thus affirming aspirations for self-determination, but crucially, the ultimate consequence of self determination was conceptualized as the renewal of the culture and institutions introduced by the British. This raises difficult questions about the conditionality of independence. In particular, it implies that brown man nationalism presupposed continuing subsidiarity to Eurocentric cultural and economic hegemony.

Second, it was not sufficiently reflexive about the racism inherent in brown man categories of belonging and recognition that enforced the devaluation of African culture. The pro-colonial brown man enclave, to which Smith's personal sympathies were most closely attached, was left in an invidious, contradictory position. 'Neither able to support colonialism because of its blatantly repressive character, nor able to support the radical anti-colonial movement because of its revolutionary character' (Robotham 1980: 86). Brown man government pursued a policy of reheated acculturation, which is negatively associated with the elaboration of racial patronage and clientism, and which failed to address the aspirations of the subordinate blacks. The eclipse of brown man power after the 1970s is partly the result of the ascendancy of a new black middle class, which draws its power from the market, and maintains reflexive, critical distance from the colonial acculturation process and the renewal of this process under brown man hegemony.

Although there are necessarily many lacunae in this account of race and colour in Jamaica, some of the issues raised help to clarify several of Hall's lifelong intellectual preoccupations. Thus, through-out his writing, Hall has continuously returned to problems of position and difference. In his public accounts of the frictions in his own family, these questions have precedence. Hall's family was upwardly mobile, brown middle class and, through his father's job, dependent on the interests of the dominant business corporation on the island. In class and income terms it is probably correct to clas-sify Hall's family as middle class rather than 'lower middle class'. After all, his father rose to be Chief Accountant in the main source of corporate employment in the country, and his mother, although technically *déclassé*, was clearly raised in a social milieu with strong links with the Jamaican brown and white middle class. By Hall's own account, throughout her life she was more or less consumed with the need to maintain the appearance of superior colour and class status (Jaggi 2000: 8). Smith's account of colour and class in Jamaica demonstrates that the nuances of position and difference permeate Jamaican culture. Jesse Hall's consciousness of these issues may have been importunate; her son certainly found them to be so. Yet on Smith's account the entire social structure during Hall's boyhood was riddled with conflict and friction over these issues.

This placed Hall in a contradictory position. To use a phrase that he has somewhat popularized in his later writings, he was 'doubly inscribed'. As the brown man son of the man who rose to be the Chief Accountant of the premier business corporation on the island, he was symbolically identified as part of the hegemonic bloc that succeeded white rule in Jamaica. The United Fruit Company was at the centre of Jamaican landowning issues. The company operated a neo-feudal system in which land was rented to farmers on a bonded basis. Resources for planting and cash were advanced to the farm labourers. In return the produce was sold to United Fruit at a price set by the company. Hall's family was positioned in direct collision with the peasantry and the nationalist uprising in 1938, in which land ownership and low plantation wages were key issues.

His privileged education at Jamaica College and Oxford, and his successful career in the Western academy and media reinforced the populist view that Hall was a brown man of the middle or upper middle class. Yet his intellectual and political outlook predisposed him to identify with black nationalism. This identification carried over into Hall's migrant experience. Certainly, as we shall see later, *Policing the Crisis* (Hall et al. 1978) tends to romanticize black street crime, or at least, refuses to accept police and populist accounts on a priori grounds. For the 'doubly inscribed body', hybridity, hyphenated identity and the third space might seem attractive solutions to the contradictions of embodiment and emplacement. But they also encourage critics to see slippage and modishness as attendants of this intellectual stance.

Being black in the UK

Hall (1991b) tells of returning to the Caribbean in the 1960s, after his Oxford years, and finding his parents worrying that he might be regarded as a black immigrant in the UK. This was a moment of epiphany for Hall. He reminisces that his parents wholly misunderstood the nature of racism in Britain (1991b: 55). In the UK he was interpellated as a black man (1991b: 53). The nuances of colour that his mother and father recognized in Jamaica were negated in Britain. Later, in the 1960s and 1970s, and perhaps not unexpectedly, he identified with the black Rastafarian movement. In a telling memory, Hall recalls:

> At that very moment, my son, who was two and a half, was learning the colours. I said to him, transmitting the message at last, 'You're Black.' And he said, 'No. I'm brown.' And I said, 'Wrong referent. Mistaken concreteness, philosophical mistake. I'm not talking about your paintbox. I'm talking about your head.' That is something different. The question of learning, learning to be Black. (1991b: 55)

It is an unequivocal identification with the most oppressed elements in Jamaican society.

Within the England of the 1960s and 1970s with its crude division between black and white one can see the point. But in the context of Jamaican society at the same time, it is a muddled message. Brown man hegemony was more rooted, entrenched and privileged than Hall's testimony allows. In Jamaica, through his father's job and his Oxford education, he was implicitly associated with brown man domination and capitalist exploitation. It would be overstating the case to maintain that Hall's course was 'determined' by this situation. On the other hand, Cultural Studies is a very long way from the neo-feudal system run by the United Fruit Company and the intellectual milieu of Merton College, Oxford. In taking the journey, Hall was not merely making a voyage of discovery, he was also making a personal and political point.

At the same time, presenting oneself as black in the body of a brown man raises difficult questions of position, emplacement and embodiment in Jamaica, which Hall perhaps sweeps aside too easily. Brown man hegemony can also be related to Hall's powerful elucidation of the concept of authoritarian populism, in respect of Thatcherism. Unquestionably, the thread of authoritarianism is prefigured, but not of course determined, in Hall's own family. Both parents were quite strict. Hall is particularly critical of their part in destroying a relationship involving his sister, because they attributed inferior status on grounds of colour to her suitor, a black student doctor from Barbados (1995c: 660; 1996e: 488). The incident occurred when Hall was seventeen. It left his sister 'seriously ill' (1996e: 488; Jaggi 2000: 8). Hall clearly took her side in the family conflict. His deliberate, and heartfelt, reference to the incident, in two interviews when he was over sixty, suggests that it was a profound turning point for him.

The episode reveals his acute early sensitivity to issues of power and positionality. He clearly judged the actions of his parents to be reprehensible. He was especially critical of his mother, a strong personality, whose influence he describes, variously, as 'overwhelmingly dominant' and 'devouring' (Hall 1996e: 489; Jaggi 2000: 8). He confesses that the desire to escape her was the main reason behind his decision to migrate to England (1993d: 135). His academic work returned repeatedly to the issues of the misuses of power and the importance of resistance.

Yet overarching these family tensions was the friction in the Jamaican nationalist movement. The struggle between the pro- and anti-colonial enclaves formed the political backcloth to Hall's childhood and adolescence. The landed pro-colonial group formed their own political party and won the first general election held on universal adult suffrage in 1944. Their slogan was 'Socialism is slavery! Socialism is brown man rule!' Hall must have regarded this campaign as deeply cynical, and he would have been struck by the populist approval of policies that directly contributed to the marginalization of the black population in the market and the public sphere. Perhaps there is an inkling here of Hall's later antipathy to the monetarist and nationalist rhetoric deployed by Thatcher in the 1980s. Certainly, the attempt by the landed-colonial interests to define nationalism in this period in terms of their own interests would have taught Hall early important lessons about the political appeal of essentialism and its various delusions.

The acculturation programme validated by both wings of the brown man nationalist movement privileged education as a route of upward mobility. In many respects, Hall's schooling conformed to the archetype of the brown man model of respectability. Hall was educated at Jamaica College, Kingston. To some extent, he undersells his secondary education by describing it as 'one of the big Colleges in Jamaica, strongly modelled after the English public school system' (1996e: 486). In fact, Jamaica College was the country's premier boarding school, faithfully enshrining all of the familiar 'old country' public school rituals, of chapel every morning, houses and prefects, school tie, cap and crest, cricket, shooting and swimming. The headmasters were either 'Jamaica white' or imported from Britain. The total number of pupils was no more than 350. A handful of scholarships were available, but most pupils were fee-paying.

Hall's schooling was designed to equip him with the habitus and skills to become a professional son of the colonies. As Hall himself testifies, 'I was formed, brought up, reared, taught, educated, nursed and nurtured to be, a kind of black Englishman' (1995b: 8). Of course, by no stretch of the imagination can Hall be regarded as a scion of the old Jamaican upper crust, unlike Roddy Edwards who set up the now famous Walkerswood Jerk Sauce company, or Chris Blackwell who made his fortune promoting Bob Marley and Island Records. However, he went to school with some of them. It was a schooling and adolescence liberally sprinkled with the saccharine of Empire duty and loyalty. Hall is gracious about the role that individual schoolteachers played in his education, but rather dismissive about the general system. Yet it was incontestably a more privileged education than that experienced by most of the British students he went on to teach in Britain.

In 1951 Hall left Jamaica, as a Rhodes scholar, to study at Merton College, Oxford. At Oxford, he felt divorced from the white British establishment university culture, a fish out of water. He was a victim of racism and ineffable Oxford snobbery. He remembers the 'willed triviality' of Oxford in the 1950s. His description of the dominant stratum of 'Hooray Henries' attempting to 'relive *Brideshead Revisited*' rings true (1989f: 19). His middle-class, brown man status in Jamaica was lost on most of the white British students of the day. To them, as his parents feared, Hall would have been an undifferentiated 'black' student.

He found refuge with fellow students from America and the Caribbean and developed a deeper interest in Caribbean politics. Intellectually, he describes himself at the time as a 'left Leavisite' (1995c: 663), drawn to Leavis because Leavis undertook to define literature as a serious issue, but critical of the intrinsic elitism in Leavis's position. For a while, he contemplated returning to Jamaica to pursue a political career, but instead, surprisingly, given his emotional antipathy to Oxbridge, decided to embark on a Ph.D. in Oxford. Hall's topic was the relationship between Europe and America in the novels of Henry James. With hindsight, it seems an odd choice for someone who ended his academic career as Professor of Sociology at the Open University. Yet one should remember that while James is the novelist *par excellence* of manner, style and high society, his work also deals continuously with questions of power, difference, representation and emplacement. All these are lifelong interests in Hall's sociology and cultural studies.

During this period Hall increased his acquaintance with people on the Left, mainly from the Communist Party and the Labour Club. For example, Hall met Raymond Williams, who worked as an extra-mural lecturer in Oxford, and developed friendships with student members of the Communist Party, including Raphael Samuel and Peter Sedgwick. Hall characterizes his political stance at this time as 'independent left' and 'anti-Stalinist', sympathetic to Marxism, but eschewing Marxist dogmatism (1996e: 492). He was in dialogue with the Communist Party, but on intellectual and moral grounds could not defend the Soviet system. In an attempt to create intellectual space for the 'independent Left', Hall and his circle 'occupied and revived' the Socialist Club and tried to bring together British Marxists, dissidents from the British Communist Party, anti-colonial intellectuals, fellow travellers in the Labour Party and other left-wing intellectuals (Hall 1997b: 120).

If Hall was repulsed by the Hooray Henries of Oxford in the 1950s, he also encountered another England there, composed of demobbed young veterans and national servicemen, Ruskin College trade unionists and scholarship boys and girls, from home and abroad. Hall clearly discovered something of the independent Left with which to empathize here. For example, he remembers

G. D. H. Cole, rooted in the co-operativist and workers' council traditions of Guild Socialism, convening seminars that brought together a stimulating discussion group of left-leaning students (1989f: 15). Cole's seminars were formative in the New Left circle, of which Hall became a prominent member, that eventually went on to establish the *Universities and Left Review* (*ULR*), one of two precursors to the *New Left Review* (*NLR*).

The 'double conjuncture'

Appropriately, the catalyst for Hall's political and intellectual activism was what he calls the 'double conjuncture' (1995c: 663) of external events, that is, the twin crises in Hungary and Suez in 1956. The Soviet suppression of the Hungarian Revolution, and the British and French invasion of the Suez Canal occurred within days of each other, and crystallized Hall's anti-Stalinism and anti-imperialism.

Hall quit Oxford in 1957 and worked as a supply teacher in South London. In the same year he co-founded and co-edited the *Universities and Left Review* with colleagues from the Socialist Society, Charles Taylor, a Canadian, and Raphael Samuel and Gabriel Pearson, two British Jews. The internationalism of the editorial board was important, even though copy was mainly directed at a British readership. The mixture of a Jamaican, a Canadian and two Britons, albeit from ethnic minorities, on the editorial board signified sympathies with globalization and multiculturalism which contrasted sharply with the insularity of the traditional Left in Britain. For Communist Party members of Hall's generation, the Soviet suppression of Imre Nagy's government in Hungary was traumatic. Hall recollects that Raphael Samuel's 'whole political world' was 'blown apart' by the invasion, which was regarded to signify 'the apotheosis of the degeneration of Stalinism and Soviet communism' (Hall 1997b: 120). After 1956 the romantic attachment to Moscow and the anti-capitalist revolution in Eastern Europe exhibited by the vanguard of the British Communist Party became a point of odium for the New Left. The youth of the editors was also significant. Hall and his colleagues self-consciously regarded themselves to be members of a new generation, addressing a new agenda for socialist change. The new broom had arrived and it was left to Hall and his new socialist colleagues to seize the opportunity and wield it.

It was perhaps at this time that Hall recognized the impossibility of ever returning to Jamaica or ever 'becoming truly British'. The intellectual preference for concepts of diaspora, hybridity and emergent identity in his later writings is perhaps related to his experience of displacement, in terms of class and colour, in Jamaica, and the trauma of his migration to the UK. Arguably, the recurring 'problems' of slippage and modishness in his work spring from the same fountain.

In a paper written later in his career, Hall observes that the processes of racial, economic and cultural assimilation, translation, adaptation, resistance and reselection combine to make the search for origins a fruitless quest in Jamaican society (1995b). In this deeply hybrid, nuanced formation, cultural community is always and already, imagined community. As such, it is subject to the same dilemmas of representation, invention, selective memory and repression that, for Hall, always accompany the attribution of identity.

Hall regards his own position to be 'twice diasporized' (1995b: 6). In Jamaica he lived in a place in which the cultural and economic centre was acknowledged to be Britain; and on migrating to Britain he was conscious from the start of being racially positioned as a representative of 'the Other'. As he elaborates in respect of his migration:

> Having been prepared by the colonial education, I knew England from the inside. But I'm not and never will be 'English'. I know both places intimately, but I am not wholly of either place. And that's exactly the diasporic experience, far away enough to experience the sense of exile and loss, close enough to understand the enigma of an always-postponed 'arrival'. (1996e: 490)

Although exile is generally beclouded with metaphors of loss, displacement and pain, there are, unquestionably, positive analytical resources in occupying outsider status. Living on the borders often has profound advantages for intellectual labour, since it allows one to treat the habitual practices of the surrounding natives as an anthropologist would. Raymond Williams, a scion of the border country between England and Wales, never lost sight of the strategic advantages it conferred on him. By never 'quite arriving', one can immediately see the limitations of those natives who confidently believe they know the lie of the land. The metaphysical strangeness of habitual practice has been a rich seam mined by Hall, in his writings on race, class and hegemony. One definition of his concept of articulation might be the process of making the absence of the exoticism that underlies native renderings of 'common sense' transparent. For him, the migrant experience was also racially loaded, conveying indelible lessons about emplacement, empowerment and ideology. In respect of his relationship to his family, and his connections with Britain and Jamaica, Hall has a strong sense of subjective displacement. 'I was always aware', he writes, 'of the self as only constituted in that kind of absent–present contestation with something else, with some other "real me", which is and isn't there' (1993d: 135).

The New Left

In 1960, *ULR* was merged with the *New Reasoner* (*NR*) to become the *New Left Review*. The *New Reasoner* was initially edited by Edward and Dorothy Thompson and John Saville from the North of England. As I noted in the first chapter, it represented a socialist humanist, critical flank in the communist movement. There was therefore a measure of tension between it and the *ULR*. The *New Reasoner* was edited by a generation older than Hall's, formed in the 1930s and 1940s through the Popular Front, the humiliation of the politics of appeasement and the war against fascism. After Khrushchev's 'secret speech' at the Twentieth Annual Congress of the Soviet Communist Party and the Soviet invasion of Hungary, the *NR* became an important front for communist dissidence.

In contrast, the *ULR* emerged from the postwar student generation of the 1950s and operated around an Oxford–London axis. The journal was less embroiled in the doctrinal disputes of the Communist Party. It regarded itself to be a rallying point for the independent Left and deliberately eschewed party political involvement. It pursued an editorial line that argued that the institutions and language of normative coercion in Britain were failing. The national crisis in Britain was paralleled in the hegemonic decomposition of the socialist alternative in Eastern Europe. The *ULR* proposed that socialist renewal had to commence with a new conception of socialism and an analysis of the dramatic realignment of the economic relations, social formations and cultural dynamics of postwar capitalism. This translated into the publication of topical articles along with more theoretical papers. The *ULR* deliberately sought to convey that the Left had moved into, if one may borrow a term that Hall popularized over thirty years later, 'New Times'.

The NR and ULR merged to create the *New Left Review* in 1960.[3] Hall edited the journal between 1960 and 1961. Raymond Williams recalls that Hall 'produced a style of journal closer to the original *ULR*, in contact with new cultural styles, new modes of visual presentation, in a language that differed from the typical left magazine' (1979: 365). Williams sympathized with this approach, but he noted that it did not impress all members of the editorial board, particularly those with roots in the *NR*.

The journal fostered the umbrella organization of New Left Clubs, in which discussion groups on education, literature, new theatre and race were regularly held. The clubs were catalysts for the Campaign for Nuclear Disarmament and, as Ioan Davies (1993) observes, were frequently formed from local groups of the Workers' Educational Association and National Council of Labour Colleges. The origins of the New Left were therefore outside the established university sector and, importantly, were not concentrated in the London metropolis.[4]

The schisms in the editorial board of the *NLR* placed Hall under enormous pressure. As Williams recollects, Hall's role was encumbered

> with constant circulation of internal memoranda about the policy of the magazine. I think the editor never got either the proper backing for what in the event he was more or less left to do on his own, or clear directives for which the editorial board took collective responsibility. Working under great difficulties, he was often just blamed for whatever came out – a fairly typical situation on the Left. There were endless arguments within the board over whether it was running a political movement or a magazine. There were also the mundane problems of the usual sort about the temporary debts of the journal. (1979: 365)

In 1962 Hall resigned his editorship to teach media, film and popular culture at Chelsea College, University of London.[5] He combined this with research for the British Film Institute into the pedagogy of popular culture, conducted with Paddy Whannel. This was eventually published as *The Popular Arts* in 1964. At Chelsea, Hall began to read anthropology and sociology more systematically. The new insights he acquired, together with the idea of culture as 'ordinary' and 'a whole way of life' which Raymond Williams championed at the *NLR*, further exposed the limitations of the

Eliot/Leavisite tradition on culture, which Hall encountered and substantially rejected, at Oxford. In addition, the bankruptcy of traditional Conservativism, the evident decline of British pre-eminence in the world as the loss of Empire exposed foundational weaknesses in the domestic economy, and the superficiality of Western consumer culture made this a particularly rich moment for left-wing criticism. Before the emergence of public social movements concentrating on, for example, gay and lesbian rights, environmental erosion, health issues and particular instances of social injustice, the New Left constituted a popular front of solidarity through which the rule of capital could be meaningfully challenged.

The Birmingham Centre for Contemporary Cultural Studies

In 1964 Hall was appointed as Research Fellow at the newly established Birmingham Centre for Contemporary Cultural Studies (CCCS). Richard Hoggart, a professor in English at Birmingham University, founded the Centre. As he observed, Cultural Studies did not exist in British universities at this time (Gibson and Hartley 1998: 17). The Centre was therefore a unique venture. It was financed from outside public funding by a tax deductible covenant from the publisher, Sir Allen Lane of Penguin books.[6] Additional funding from the publishing firm Chatto and the *Observer* produced £2,500 per year over a seven-year period. Further funding was provided through grant applications, notably an award from the Rowntree Trust for a study of the press.

Hoggart's original vision envisaged the Centre as a tripartite project: one part historical-philosophical, another sociological, and the third literary-critical. For Hoggart the literary-critical element was the 'most important' element (1970: 254). Hoggart's book *The Uses of Literacy* (1958), a nostalgic account of traditional working-class culture in the North of England, was clearly a template for the programme of study in the Centre, but not an exclusive or intimidating one. His main influence on the development of Cultural Studies at Birmingham was as a moral leader and manager, especially with the university hierarchy in the departments of English and Sociology. Rather like Ilya Neustadt, who assembled an outstanding Sociology department at the nearby University of Leicester, Hoggart played a crucial role in keeping the Centre afloat, and gaining respect for it from critical elements in the University of Birmingham.

Hoggart did not seek to take teaching and research in the Centre down a political road. His own intellectual background was working class and aspirational, in the widest sense of recognizing the value of 'ordinary' culture and supporting the means of expression for marginalized cultures. This predisposed him to oppose the pomposity and self-regard of elite culture, and to demonstrate that marginal and subordinate forms of cultural expression have their own validity, and are worthy of scholarly regard. But it was no part of a neo-Marxist project. This inflection came later in the Centre's history, under Hall's directorship.

It is worth noting *en passant* that Raymond Williams argued that it is significant that the origins of Cultural Studies lay in non-metropolitan, 'non-traditional' pedagogic traditions (Laing 1991: 145). The three key figures in the incipient growth of Cultural Studies in Britain – Richard Hoggart, Raymond Williams and E. P. Thompson – all taught in extra-mural departments and Workers' Educational Associations. To some extent then, it is tenable to maintain that Cultural Studies was founded by intellectual misfits in the traditional British university system. This sense of being outsiders and operating on the edges of knowledge and power is still central to the self-image of Cultural Studies. Thus Richard Johnson, who succeeded Hall as Director of the Birmingham Centre, submitted that Cultural Studies must constantly resist academicism, and strive to relate cultural questions to the analysis of power, and 'social possibilities' (1983: 9).

Under Hoggart the research agenda of the Birmingham School was dominated by broad questions of class inequality, cultural representation and the mechanics of cultural gatekeeping. Predictably, the role of the media emerged as a pivotal research focus. To begin with this work was heavily influenced by American communication research. Theory was an underdeveloped resource. Perhaps Hall's first significant intellectual contribution to the Centre was to lever media research away from the quantitative, empirical American tradition and steer it towards the subject of ideology.

Hall has acknowledged the crucial significance of Raymond Williams's contribution of the study of culture as 'the relationships in a whole way of life' in the intellectual development of the Centre (Hall 1980a; Williams 1958; 1961). Equally significant were Williams's concepts of 'the selective tradition' and 'structure of feeling'. By the term 'selective tradition' Williams meant the institutional and textual funnelling of cultural data to produce the notion of a dominant tradition and agenda of cultural debate and practice. For Williams, selection always involves a degree of fabrication, since to valorize the 'core' necessarily peripheralizes 'the margins'. The 'great tradition' of English novelists constructed in Leavisite pedagogy is a case in point. Leavis's roll-call of the great and the good was both prejudiced and partial. Williams held that the central defect of the selective tradition as a methodological device in organizing culture is that it mistakes contemporary preoccupations for eternal verities. The composition of Leavis's great tradition is certainly vulnerable to this charge.

'Structure of feeling' is a complex concept, referring *inter alia* to the *episteme*, concerns and sensibility of a generation that is reflexively rendered in cultural forms. The New Left group was certainly bound up with a common structure of feeling that shaped their outlook, their writings and their political interventions. Moreover, the Centre, in its heroic period, certainly conveyed an organic 'structure of feeling', a connotation with a theoretical and political project which was absolutely distinct.

The more combative influence of Edward Thompson, evident in his approach to culture as 'a way of struggle', was also pivotal in the development of the Centre. Interestingly, aside from the work of Richard Johnson and Bill Schwarz, the tradition of long-range, detailed historical research never flourished in the Centre. On the other hand, Thompson's methodological proposition that the historical study of culture is always a matter of a dialogue between concepts and empirical evidence was a considerable general influence on Birmingham thinking and debate. Thompson's history of the English working class (1963) held a totemic significance in the Centre, even if it failed to engender a trend of emulative historical research. Johnson recollects that the intellectual labour at the Centre engaged more strongly with Literary Studies than History (2001: 261). Even so, he goes on to note that history was a significant theme in collective work at the Centre between 1974 and 1979. Group work and doctoral theses explored the subjects of history and theory, historical transitions (from feudalism to capitalism and laissez-faire to monopoly capitalism), radical movements, the crisis in state hegemony, the peculiarities of the English and the popular politics of the Second World War. Historical approaches to culture survived until the mid 1980s through the work of subgroups and the increasing importance given to memory in the partly collectively organized M.A. But while history can certainly be said to be part of the context of intellectual labour in Birmingham, and in particular, Hall returns repeatedly to the importance of the period between the 1880s and

1920s as *formative* for understanding contemporary British culture (1981b), it did not occupy the foreground.

In part, perhaps, this was a reaction to Thompson. His contribution to the history of the English working class was recognized to be immense. Yet as a cultural theorist, he was also an obvious loose cannon. Nowhere more so than in his superbly marshalled, but cruel and one-sided denunciation of Althusserian Marxism (1978). An attack, moreover, that was delivered at the very apogee of Althusser's influence over Hall and his associates, as they published what is, arguably, the single most important work to emerge from the Centre, *Policing the Crisis.*

'Culturalism' and 'structuralism'

When asked to comment on the direction the Centre took under Hall's leadership, Richard Hoggart replied, somewhat laconically, that it became 'a) more political and b) more theoretic' (Gibson and Hartley 1998: 19). Hall's famous paper on the aetiology of Cultural Studies (1980a) recognizes 'two paradigms'. *Culturalism* is the British tradition, associated with the work of Hoggart, Williams and, to a lesser extent, Thompson. It rejects the anthropological emphasis on culture as 'practice' or 'mores and folkways' of society. Instead it focuses on the organization of cultural relations with material conditions, institutions and traditions. Culturalism addresses the ensemble of relations that constitute 'the whole way of life' of a determinate social formation. In contrast with elitist approaches, it emphasizes the 'ordinary' nature of culture. Politically, culturalism tends to favour the values of the Left or Centre-Left, without however, identifying with Marxism. Indeed, Williams was always very critical of the base–superstructure model in which the economy is understood as determining cultural relations. It is a criticism fully shared by Hall, who objected to the essentialism of 'vulgar materialism'.

Nonetheless, Hall clearly regards the culturalist tradition to be inadequate (1980a: 63–4; 1981b: 228, 233–5). Firstly, its emphasis on agency and experience is held to perpetuate a tendency towards humanism in culturalist analysis, which Hall plainly regards as naive. Secondly, culturalism is criticized for condensing levels of analysis through means which are not sufficiently reflexive. Thirdly, culturalism fails to delineate clearly and consistently the levels in the ensemble of relations that constitute the whole historical process, the 'cultural totality', as Hall terms it.

Structuralism was incorporated into the Birmingham project as a way of remedying the perceived defects of culturalism and to produce a more adequate approach to the study of culture. For Hall, the key structuralists are Louis Althusser, Claude Lévi-Strauss and, of course, Marx. What is the central contribution of structuralism to cultural analysis? Hall lists four points (1980a: 67–8):

1 *Theoretical determinacy* Structuralism locates cultural experience in relation to the network of the relations under capitalism which position men and women as social agents. Against the 'heroic affirmation' of agency offered by classical culturalism, structuralism contextualizes agency in relation to structures of power.

2 *Recognition of the necessity of abstraction* Structuralism deploys abstraction to elucidate social reality. It distinguishes different levels of abstraction and analyses relations between these levels and the correspondence that these levels have with concrete agency.

3 *Emphasis on totality* Structuralism examines agency and history as part of a complex unity composed of differences as well as homologies of practice. The emphasis on 'unity in difference' and 'complex unity' clarifies the contextual relations behind agency and reveals the process of 'overdetermination' in relation to cultural and historic specificity.

4 *Emphasis on ideology* Structuralism 'decentres' experience by locating structures of power and agency in relation to the terrain of ideology. Culturalism is unable to command this terrain because its emphasis on the authenticating power of 'experience' imposes a barrier between culturalism and 'a proper conception of ideology'.

Hall recognizes the tendencies towards pure abstraction, functionalism and theoretical closure in structuralist thought, and deplores them. To some extent, culturalism supplies answers to these weaknesses. In particular, it refuses to treat agents as 'cultural dopes' (Garfinkel) or to treat agency as the mere reflection of ideology. Hall advocates Gramsci's approach as a fruitful way of combating these unfortunate tendencies in structuralist thought and retaining the meaning of the agent as an informed, reflexive actor.

Hall's valuable discussion of the two paradigms is clearly intended to accomplish syncretic narrative fusion between what he regards as the best elements in each one. He does not intend to replace culturalism with structuralism. Nevertheless, as Hoggart recognized (Gibson and Hartley 1998), the inflection of culturalism through the lens of structuralism makes Cultural Studies more theoretical and political. Interestingly, at the height of the New Times thesis in the early 1990s, Hall lamented the socialist 'problem' of 'translating everything into the language of "structures"' (1991d: 59). Yet within the context of British Marxism, Hall's advocacy of structuralism in the Birmingham years was a major catalyst in popularizing structuralist analysis.

Hall's espousal of structuralism was not, of course, an isolated event. After the climacteric of 1968 in which the hopes of 'Socialist Man' were dashed by the collapse of the student and worker revolt in Paris, the British Left became more critical of the lacuna in Marxism. Hall identifies two journals, *Screen* and *Screen Education* (sponsored by the Society for Film and Television) as being particularly significant in this regard (Hall 1980c: 157). *Screen* theory drew on the contribution to semiotics made by Christian Metz, and the debates between the journals *Cahiers du Cinéma* and *Cinétique*, Althusser's theory of ideology, theories of language and discourse associated with Julia Kristeva and Michel Foucault, the Brechtian critique of 'realism' and, perhaps above all, the psychoanalytic theory of Jacques Lacan. Hall is critical of *Screen* theory (1980c), and his criticism helps to clarify the distinctive features of the Birmingham approach to culture at this time. Although he is broadly sympathetic to semiotics, seeing in it a useful mechanism of decoding common-sense meaning and thus exposing the hand of ideology, he refutes the textual turn taken by the *Screen* group.

The crux of the matter is *Screen's* appropriation of Lacan's psychoanalytic theory. Hall proposes that Lacan follows Lévi-Strauss in regarding the subjective 'entry into culture' as decisive in signification and symbolic representation (1980c: 158–9). However, whereas in Lévi-Strauss this transition is located outside the subject in the cultural and social structure, in Lacan it is internalized in the constitution of the subject in the 'symbolic', in language, the system of signifiers. For Lacan this occurs at an unconscious level, a caveat that violates the Freudian concept of the integrated subject by retheorizing the subject as a set of 'positions' formed in relation to knowledge and language. Hall notes that Lacanianism gives primary significance to language and relies on a series of visual analogues to explain agency and meaning – the 'mirror phase', the 'gaze', the 'look', the 'scenario of vision'. The Birmingham position, asserts Hall, is different. The crucial distinction is that the Birmingham approach emphasizes the operation of signification and ideology in specific social formations and historical formations. In this perspective the positioning of the subject is concrete and historically specific, while in the *Screen* approach it is transcultural and ahistorical.

Coward (1977) launched a famous poststructuralist attack on the Birmingham approach, accusing it of determinism and theoretical naivety for taking class and gender as unproblematically 'given' and cultural practice as expressions of class and other structures. Hall may have been influenced by this critique, but his turn towards representation, signification and the nature of identity predates it by at least five years.

The crux of the distinction is that the Birmingham approach rejects textual determinacy and embraces relative textual polysemy, while the *Screen* approach inverts these polarities. Tudor fastens on an interesting contradiction in the Birmingham perspective in this regard (1999: 112–14). He comments that David Morley advances the Birmingham perspective as being more sensitive to the polysemic nature of signs and sign-based discourses and is supportive of interrogative/expansive readings of culture (Morley 1980: 167). This is the corollary of the Birmingham accent on 'struggle in ideology' and the crucial significance of resistance to domination. From the Birmingham standpoint this accent is absent in *Screen* theory because it presents the entry into culture, and hence ideology, as a universal, text-driven unconscious process. However, as Tudor correctly notes (1999: 113), the notion of infinite polysemy is anathema to the Birmingham approach, since it rules out a basis for concrete political intervention. The solution was to devise the concept of the 'preferred reading'. The concept retained the Gramscian stress on ideological dominance and hegemony, and equipped the Birmingham School with the political role of penetrating the mist-enveloped regions of habit, convention and 'common sense' that gathered around the ascent of ideology.

The concept of 'preferred reading' was to prove problematic for the Birmingham School, because the criteria for claiming preference appeared to treat ideology and hegemony as a text within which the subject is positioned, thus raising difficult questions about the real nature of agency and struggle in capitalist society. I will take up this matter at greater length in the next chapter in relation to Hall's encoding/decoding model (1973a; 1993e).

Being at the Centre: pedagogy and research in Birmingham

To concentrate only on the theoretical and political turn taken by the Centre produces an unbalanced view of its extraordinary achievements under Hall's stewardship. In respect of pedagogy, training and publications, Hall's term of office was associated with some major innovations. As will quickly become apparent, boundaries between pedagogy, research and writing were not recognized by members of the Centre. To be sure, the method of graduate teaching was deliberately organized to raise research issues and to explore them through subgroups. Similarly, research was expected to feed back into teaching and colloquia work. However, as a way of organizing the material relating to the Birmingham tradition, the division between pedagogic, research and publishing innovative interventions is helpful.

Firstly, on the level of pedagogy, Hall pioneered a collaborative spirit of teaching that was unprecedented in the British university system. Tutorials, seminars and lectures in Birmingham were non-hierarchical and aimed to maximize student participation. Hall and his associates were among the first academics to adopt workshops and colloquia as pedagogic devices. Socializing with students was treated as a formative part of the education process. Weekly Centre general meetings were held which covered everything from curriculum content to current affairs issues such as the firemen's strike, or the rise of Thatcher. A general theory seminar open to all sub-groups also allowed wide-ranging debate about theoretical matters, such as the value of Althusser or the significance of Gramsci.

The sense of being engaged in a collective pursuit with political as well as intellectual dimensions perhaps best defines the atmosphere of the Centre in its heyday. Above all, there was the intoxicating 'structure of feeling', the exciting sense of exploring a new terrain and inventing new methods and theories to encompass it. 'We made the curriculum up,' Hall recalls. 'It was the inauguration of, not a discipline, but a field of inquiry that . . . is interested in how culture organizes everyday life. It was a very creative moment' (Jaggi 2000: 8).

Two M.A. postgraduate degrees were offered at the Centre: M.A. by course work and dissertation, and M.A. by thesis. It is particularly interesting to reflect on the course content of the M.A. by course work and dissertation, since this may be regarded as evidence of the technical training in Cultural Studies that was regarded as fundamental under Hall's leadership.[7]

The M.A. was a twelve-month 'taught' degree, comprising three courses and a dissertation. Faculty regulations required two of the three courses to be assessed by examination; the third was assessed by a seminar paper of not less than 5,000 words. The dissertation, approximately a 12,000-word study, was normally written over the summer and submitted in October.

Course 1: Theory and Method in Cultural Studies

The course in theory and method addressed the main ways in which 'culture' has been deployed in contrasting intellectual traditions: the culture-society tradition, the Weberian tradition, Durkheim and the 'sociological' tradition, the anthropological tradition, the Marxist critique, mass society and mass culture theory. The second part of the course moved on to five substantive concerns. These were:

(i)   *Culture, meaning and meaning construction*   The role of language and communication in the 'objectification' of culture.
(ii) *Culture and ideology*   The relation of culture to belief systems, cognitive frameworks, ideologies and consciousness.
(iii) *Culture and structure*   The relation of culture to social structure, the determination of culture and cultural institutions.
(iv) *Cultures, subcultures and classes*   The formation and transmission of culture through groups and their historical practice.
(v)   *Dominant, subordinate, alternative and countercultures*   The 'elementary forms' of the cultural process as a whole.

Course 2: British Society and Culture, 1880–1970

The course in British society and culture related changes in selected cultural institutions, with reference to the 'specific' conjuncture for 1978–9, to historical changes between the 1880s and 1926. The course concentrated on:

1 *General problems in cultural history and cultural analysis*   The sites of culture; culture and ideology; the location of the conjuncture within a larger historical framework; problems of transitions; the notion of hegemony.
2 *Political parties, political ideologies and political philosophies* Including schooling, mass media and literature; the cultures of 'popular classes' in relation especially to family and work.

3   *Interrelations between cultural shifts illustrating theoretical issues*
    Questions of 'levels', for example, from philosophies to informal
    practices and 'common sense'; implications for the study of
    recent conjunctures, continuities and breaks.

Course 3: A Subject Area in Cultural Studies

Course 3 was designed to intensify familiarity with the basic literature, problems and methods involved in the cultural study of
a particular subject area. In practice this involved becoming a
member of one of the existing subgroups. Subgroups were partly
constructed as efficient mechanisms for sharing information and
participating in theoretical refinement. However, attached to these
technical pedagogic functions was also the aim of creating a sense
of collective solidarity and common purpose. We shall not understand Hall's work in Birmingham correctly unless we constantly
bear in mind that it was a political as well as an intellectual project.

In addition to taught courses and examined research, the Centre
also regarded itself to be a sort of open think-tank in the study of
culture. Links with scholars from other universities, through attachments, seminar presentations, symposia and public lectures, were
actively encouraged and pursued.

Turning now to the question of interventions in research, Hoggart
pays tribute to Hall's high intellectual standards (Gibson and
Hartley 1998). This is certainly reflected in the quality of graduates
who engaged in research projects during his tenure. Under Hall's
leadership, research in Birmingham involved some of the most tal-
ented students of culture of their generation. Consider: Paul Willis,
Dick Hebdige, Janice Winship, Larry Grossberg, Angela McRobbie,
Paul Gilroy, Hazel Corby, Bill Schwarz, Chas Critcher, Charlotte
Brundson, David Morley, Dorothy Hobson, Iain Chambers, Colin
Sparks, Phil Cohen, Greg McLennan, Stuart Laing, Lucy Bland,
Gary Whannel and Frank Mort were all part of the 'Birmingham
mafia'.

The label is intended to be affectionate, but it does contain the
grit of critical insight. To understand the nature of this insight fully
it is necessary to give an account of the style of intellectual labour
advocated and practised by Hall in Birmingham. To begin with, it
was an omnivorous approach to the study of culture. Hall's Director's Report of 1979 listed ongoing M.Litt. and Ph.D. research in,
inter alia, political/feminist theatre, women and the welfare state,

secretarial work and technological change, press representations of race, European avant-garde movements, cultural and social movements in postwar Italy, the transition from school to work for girls, problems in historiography, sexual ideologies, postwar feminist writers, ideology, technology and practice in photography, lower middle-class culture between 1800 and 1918, science and the Cold War, aspects of nationalism and the Northern Ireland problem, classroom cultures, discourses in TV comedy, the culture of popular conservatism, the emergence of rock music since the 1950s, race and the construction of 'race relations', women and the welfare state, representations of sport in the media, languages of resistance and nationalism, and postwar education.

It is an extraordinarily potent mixture of research activity, supported in sometimes trying circumstances of financial and political conflict with the university. One should particularly note that staff–student ratios were very high. Until 1974, when Hoggart formally resigned, he and Hall were the only full-time faculty. After 1974, Richard Johnson joined from the Department of Economic and Social History and Michael Green arrived as a half-time appointment shared with English (Davies 1995: 36). The range and quality of intellectual work accomplished consistently in Birmingham throughout the 1960s and 1970s are astonishing, and are a great tribute to the dedication and energy of Hall and his colleagues.

The Director's 1979 report locates the main intellectual themes of research in the Centre as cultural history; education; English studies; family/school; language; media, race and politics; state; women's studies; women and fascism; and work. Each of these themes involved orthodox methods of individual study and seminars. However, they also entailed the formation of subgroups, which were explicitly devised as an advance on more traditional and hierarchical modes of research. At the levels of both pedagogy and research, subgroups were intended to be the main creative cell of the Centre's collective work. They allowed for collective discussions of common problems and particular texts in major areas. At the end of each academic year, the subgroups were required to present their year's work to the Centre. Subgroups were also intended to be seed-beds for the production of articles or books. The Centre's research ethic paralleled the ethic of teaching, which was that as many tasks as possible should be undertaken by groups and not by individuals. This was, of course, diametrically opposed to the conventions in postgraduate activity in social science and humanities at the time, which tended to privilege the importance of individual self-discipline and 'originality' through examination performance, the presentation of dissertation work and the defence of research theses. Wherever possible, teaching and research work at the Centre minimized status distinctions between members.

The third area of innovative intervention was in respect of the Centre's publishing programme. The main media outlet for work in the Centre was the serial publication *Working Papers in Cultural Studies*. Until 1978 this was self-published, but under the pressure of slender resources and with the demands of rising circulation, a publishing agreement was struck with Hutchinson Press. In part the journal constituted a forum for the publication of completed work and work in progress from Centre members. However, it was also intended to stimulate dialogue and critical debate. To this end, external papers were published from prestigious national and international contributors such as Stanley Cohen, Umberto Eco, Fred Jameson, Geoff Pearson, Paul Corrigan, Graham Murdock and Simon Frith. The Centre also published stencilled papers and special numbers of the journal, such as *Women Take Issue*, *On Ideology*, *Resistance through Rituals*, and *Policy and Practice* (*Schooling England since 1944*). The publishing programme also produced a valuable income stream to support the Centre's activities.

The publishing milieu was very novel. Lecturers and research students often wrote together, and commented on each other's drafts. Hall remembers that research issues and responses were frequently circulated by means of internal bulletins and papers (1997a: 39). Anyone could put a position into circulation.

This method of collaboration maximizes collective involvement, but it can dilute the focus of arguments on the principle that 'too many cooks spoil the broth'. Much of the published work that emerged from the Centre during Hall's term of office has the quality of an open seminar. 'If you look at the books we produced,' Hall elaborates, 'they are in a sense unfinished. They lack the tightness of argument that you can get out of a singly authored book. They don't have the coherence of conception. But we were making up the field as we went along' (1997a: 39). As with an open seminar, the topic of publication tended to follow fashion or respond to public issues of the day. Hall's thoughtful and rigorous reading of Marx's method (1973b), and his charismatic and compelling elucidation of the relevance of Gramsci and Althusser to Cultural Studies attempted to bolster the intellectual spine of the research and publishing programme at Birmingham. But the difficulties of accommodating cultural development with theoretical coherence were always very great, and they became particularly severe after feminism began to make a contribution.

Hutchinson provided an international platform from which to disseminate the Centre's ideas and projects. The publishing programme was intended to offer direct interventions in culture. Hall dismisses the allegation that the Centre was a political agent intent on precipitating class revolution (1995c: 666–7). Not unreasonably, he claims that had it acted thus, it would have been disowned by the university, and financial support would have been withdrawn.

Hall's conception of intellectual work at the Centre recognized several different tasks, relating, most obviously, to cultural analysis, cultural critique and theory. Each of these tasks was regarded as having an active relation to politics. But, in his view, the Centre never aspired to establish a Marxist monoculture. As he points out (1995c: 667), he and his associates were hostile to the base–superstructure reductionism in Marxism, which they regarded as mechanistic and crudely overdeterministic.[8] Marxism was certainly a major influence in the intellectual development of the Centre, especially during the 1970s, when the work of Gramsci and Althusser suggested new neo-Marxist ways of working around the base–superstructure problem. The attack on *Screen* and Coward and Ellis's book *Language and Materialism* (1978) reasserted the value of materialist approaches to culture. However, in Hall's judgement, Marxism was always only one element in a rich theoretical mix of influences, including sociology, anthropology, symbolic interactionism, feminism, criminology, linguistics, French structuralism, semiotics, Lacanian psychoanalysis and poststructuralism. To some extent, he saw his responsibility as Director partly to defend dialogic relationships between different analytical, critical and theoretical positions. Using these relationships to articulate contradictions in the economy and body politic was, however, regarded as a legitimate part of Birmingham practice. This is certainly reflected in the publishing programme pursued by the Centre.

With one or two exceptions, notably the collections of working papers *On Ideology* (Hall, Lumley and McLennan 1978) and *Culture, Media, Language* (Hall et al. 1980), titles were not prepared or published with narrow pedagogic or academic intent. Rather the aim was to contribute books and papers which would contribute to the articulation of contradictions in contemporary culture, most obviously so in the case of *Resistance through Rituals* (Hall and Jefferson 1976) and *Policing the Crisis* (Hall et al. 1978).

Several students in Birmingham during the 1960s and 1970s described the institution as a 'laboratory' of pedagogy and research. Although the Centre was not immune from the usual academic frictions caused by careerism, individual jealousies and struggles with the administration over funding, it was remarkable for the spirit of genuine collectivism that it cultivated, and achieved, in the late 1960s and up to 1978. In part, this derived from the conviction of its members that they were embarked on an important new project of study that required constant innovation in respect of methodology, theory and pedagogy.

Also, after Hall became de facto Director, the political complexion of the Centre became more obviously harnessed to a public critique of capitalism, and to the advance of socialist transformation. One of the principal intellectual achievements, regularly mooted by Hall in his reminiscences of his time at the Centre, was the prediction of the rebirth of right-wing authoritarianism in Britain. It is a prominent theme in *Policing the Crisis* (Hall et al. 1978), and Hall returned to it in his lecture to the Cobden Trust (1979), which concentrated on the drift into a law and order society. Yet political activism, in the revolutionary sense, was never really on the table.

Why then do many people remember the Birmingham Centre as an axis of political opposition? Hall submits that one reason is that the Centre was explicitly organized to produce the democratization of knowledge (1997a: 39). It sought to engender a genuinely collective way of creating knowledge, based on a critique of the established disciplines, a critique of the university as a structure of power, and a critique of the institutionalization of knowledge as an ideological operation. According to Hall, the student movement of 1968 was the decisive factor in radicalizing and politicizing the Centre (1995c: 666–7; 1997a: 39). Many students who enrolled after that date were activists in the '68 student protests and occupations. Against the backdrop of escalating American involvement in the Vietnam war, the central institutions of capitalist society, notably patriarchy, the family, the education system, the law and the police, came under ferocious critical scrutiny from the students. They undoubtedly contributed to the ethical milieu that emerged in Centre after 1968.

Organic and traditional intellectuals

However, a more profound political and ethical influence was the ideal of intellectual labour fostered by Hall. Pivotal to this was

Gramsci's (1971) concept of the 'organic intellectual'. As Hall put it in 1992:

> The 'organic intellectual' must work on two fronts at one and the same time. On the one hand, we had to be at the very forefront of intellectual theoretical work because, as Gramsci says, it is the job of the organic intellectual to know more than the traditional intellectuals do: really know, not just pretend to know, not just have the facility of knowledge, but to know deeply and profoundly . . . If you are in the game of hegemony you have to be smarter than 'them'. Hence, there are no theoretical limits from which cultural studies can turn back. But the second aspect is just as crucial: that the organic intellectual cannot absolve himself or herself from the responsibility of transmitting those ideas, that knowledge, through the intellectual function, to those who do not belong, professionally, in the intellectual class. And unless those two fronts are operating at the same time, or at least unless these two ambitions are part of the project of cultural studies, you can get enormous theoretical advance without any engagement at the level of the political project. (Hall in Morley and Chen 1996: 268)

This amounts to Hall's fullest expression of the ideal of intellectual work required by the Centre, and is, I submit, his best testament of the substance of intellectual craftsmanship. Several issues in the passage repay our attention.

To begin with, Hall, following Gramsci, pointedly contrasts the labour of the organic intellectual with that of the traditional intellectual. The organic intellectual is an agent charged with conserving and disseminating the distinctive knowledge, ideas and values of a particular social class or group. The organic intellectual is *not* necessarily a revolutionary agent, since the ruling power bloc also relies on intellectual labourers to conserve and disseminate the mental relations of force which distinguish it from other strata. However, it is clear that Gramsci regards the organic intellectual as pivotal in socialist construction through, *inter alia*, breaking down the barriers between mental and manual labour and raising consciousness of hegemony as an organized network of force. Gramsci also identifies the 'traditional intellectual', who looks for authority in 'detachment' and 'objectivity'. According to Hall, the decisive difference is that organic intellectuals recognize a determinate class affiliation, while traditional intellectuals see themselves as 'free floaters', lacking this affiliation (Hall, Lumley and McLennan 1978). The inference is that the labour of the traditional intellectual is often hidebound by mere academicism.[9] In contrast, the organic intellectual is not constrained by the boundaries of academic disciplines, but instead makes a virtue of interdisciplinary study and research. At its best, this results in better questions being formulated, and better solutions being proposed.

For Hall, the crucial issue is the *relevance* of knowledge produced through intellectual labour. He proceeds on the basis that the labour of the organic intellectual recognizes no limits, and addresses knowledge as a resource to answer the power relations that characterize capitalist society. This is why he deliberately rejects the traditional boundary between the university and society, in favour of a more dialogic model of cultural intervention. In this respect, his observation that he, and the students in the Birmingham years, 'made up the field as they went along' pointed to a big strategic advantage since, at one leap, it freed them from the seigneurial introspection and self-satisfaction that is often found in traditional intellectual labour.

This may have been one reason why ethnographic work featured so prominently in the research activities of the Centre. Hall was always more at home with writing, debating and theory than interviewing or survey work. Nonetheless, he presided over a research programme in which Paul Willis, Christine Griffin, Dorothy Hobson, Phil Cohen, Tricia McCabe and David Morley all used innovative ethnographic methods to exploit and develop cultural research. It would be quite wrong to think of the Centre as a talking shop. Qualitative research was privileged over quantitative methods as the best means to explore empirical data in culture. The quality and range of ethnography conducted in Birmingham during Hall's term as Director illustrates the diversity of work conducted at the Centre. As with the discursive labour produced at the Centre, an important aim behind ethnographic work was to elucidate hegemony and to precipitate cultural intervention.

However, one of the prices of entering 'the game of hegemony' is to engage in a struggle with established academic disciplines. Hoggart gives an interesting concrete instance of this struggle in Birmingham (Gibson and Hartley 1998: 17–18). He recounts that the Vice-Chancellor in 1968 decided that the Centre was instrumental in fomenting student activism and precipitating riots and unrest. He attempted to close it down, or at least significantly reduce the scale of its operation, by establishing an independent commission to report on its activities. The commission found against some aspects of intellectual work at the Centre. For example, it criticized the tendency for 'abstract, polysyllabic complicated' language to dominate research theses, and the collectivist 'ownership' of some theses which, the Commission held, was counter to good academic practice. However, to the chagrin of critical factions within the university, it praised the quality of intellectual work conducted at the Centre as being of the highest calibre, and vindicated it from the charge of acting as a political *agent provocateur* in student unrest.

It should now be clear that Hall's understanding and application of the concept of the 'organic intellectual' carried with it deep ethical responsibilities. It is not enough for the intellectual to 'know', he or she must 'really know', and use knowledge to answer power. The labour of the organic intellectual is therefore predicated on a dialogic relationship between research and cultural and political intervention.

The ethical responsibilities demanded of intellectual work at the Centre were enormously attractive to students and researchers. But they were also associated with intellectual overconfidence and a predilection to regard Birmingham work as morally superior on a priori grounds. Hall's pointed contrast between the labour of the organic intellectual and the traditional intellectual was a predisposing factor in this. Theoretically, at least, it conferred the advantage of political relevance to the organic intellectual, while simultaneously ascribing a lack of political relevance, and therefore a degree of ethical bad faith, to the labour of the traditional intellectual. The practice of democratizing knowledge and challenging the structure of institutionalized pedagogy in the university was also significant. The students and researchers working in the Centre were conscious of working on the frontline of what was institutionally acceptable, and this doubtless carried considerable cultural *cachet*.

This relates back to the soubriquet of the 'Birmingham mafia', which is sometimes negatively applied to describe researchers and graduates of the Centre. Birmingham 'organic intellectuals' frequently occupy the moral high ground, as if it is their natural habitat, and their research work and writing possess a proselytizing quality, as if they have a duty to correct the obfuscation and woolly thinking that dominate the field. No doubt this also relates to the tenor of intellectual work at the Centre which pursued the discipline of social criticism more avidly, and with greater distinction, than the practice of social construction. Given the Centre's self-image of an institution actively challenging the traditional disciplinary organization of knowledge, the established pedagogic and administrative apparatus of the university, and the orthodox detachment of the Academy from cultural intervention, there was good reason to foreground social criticism. Moreover, at the level of pedagogy, the creation of subgroups was unquestionably a creative innovation which constructed solidarity through collective work in ways that were very imaginative and novel, at least in the context of the British system of tertiary education. Nonetheless, at the levels of research labour and writing, the comparative neglect of questions concerning detailed policy, strategy and a vision for the future left the Centre open to the charge of making a fetish of abstract criticism.

Remarkably, the core unit of capitalist culture, namely the business/industrial corporation, was not seriously investigated. All the Birmingham work presented capitalism as the context in which culture and agency develop. But the differences between capitalist corporations, and the shifting balance of power between national and multinational organizations remained a closed book in the Centre. Instead, especially after the infusion of Althusserian ideas in the 1970s, the Centre concentrated on the capitalist state. The latter was regarded as the major player in determining the rules of capitalist operations, and it was also identified as the lever for meaningful socialist change.

It is perhaps also worth observing that the existence of the Centre was heavily dependent on public funding. Many of the students who enrolled in the 1970s relied on state grants, often supplemented by part-time college teaching. Under Thatcherism a squeeze on grants for study in 'liberal' subjects like Sociology and Cultural Studies was introduced and part-time teaching opportunities diminished. The loss of Social Science Research Council and Arts 'quotas' imperilled graduate work at the Centre and contributed significantly to the decline of Birmingham as an intellectual powerhouse in the 1980s.

The Birmingham 'project'

For many traditional academics, and not a few university administrators and Department of Education personnel, the Birmingham 'project' was frequently associated with semi-subversion. This was unjust. The Centre was always stronger on analysis than feasible plans for action. The work on the interventionist state, schooling, racism and policing purported to strip capitalist ideology naked.

But despite Hall's emphasis on the need to make ideas politically relevant, there was a clear predisposition in the Centre towards discourse, debate and intellectual exchange over direct political action. In reality the sheer range of subgroups and intellectual activities meant that the Centre was never firmly focused around a coherent political strategy. Needless to say, everyone who worked at Birmingham to a lesser or greater degree was in favour of emancipatory politics. Yet this covered a good deal of ground, including support for class resistance, feminism and the contradictions of heteronormativity. These trajectories did not always converge. Indeed, as we shall see in more detail below (pp. 127–9), the Women's Studies subgroup was highly critical of 'male-stream' dominance in the Centre's intellectual and social activity. If there was a Birmingham 'project' it boiled down to encouraging maximum, diverse, mobile investigation into questions of culture in a milieu that was shaped by a number of theoretical influences among which Marxism was, for much of the time, pre-eminent.

While there was a good deal of gesturing and uncoordinated activity in favour of radical social transformation, the immediate role of the Centre as an instrument of political change was modest. Birmingham's real legacy was in raising the consciousness of both students and the public about the role of ideology in everyday life and the various cultures of inequality in Britain. But, to date, this work has never really engendered either a coherent view of political agency or a tenable political strategy. To be sure, the work on school youth cultures, race, patriarchy, the distortions of the mass media and the transition from school to work for working-class kids in the 1970s articulated profound questions of injustice and inequality centred around class. Yet arguably with the exception of Paul Willis's brilliant work on cultural homology and difference (1977; 1978), the Centre in the 1970s and 1980s tended to reproduce an overconsensual and holistic view of resistant agency. Edward Thompson observed that

> We should not forget that 'culture' is a clumpish term, which by gathering up so many activities and attributes into one common bundle may actually confuse or disguise discriminations that should be made between them. We need to take this bundle apart, and examine the components with more care: rites, symbolic modes, the cultural attributes of hegemony, the inter-generational transmission of custom and custom's evolution within historically specific forms of working and social relations. (1991: 13)

The cleavages, and necessary discriminations, within the concept of resistant agency are undertheorized in Birmingham work. Although divisions of class and race are acknowledged, the levels and components of cultural friction, fusion and fission, and their various implications for cultural intervention, are inadequately elucidated.

This produces serious difficulties in the application of the concept of resistant agency, not least in respect of the analysis of class, gender, subcultural and racial mobilization. These difficulties are compounded when one considers the Birmingham elucidation of the hegemonic structures within which resistant agency is located. Following Gramsci (1971), there is a lucid treatment of the contingent, negotiated character of hegemony. This connects up with a positive aspirational role for cultural intervention which the Centre always optimistically subscribed to, since it suggests that under capitalist hegemony there is everything still to play for. At the level of theory, the hydraulics of hegemony, particularly in respect of the operation of the state in capitalist society, were impressively dismantled, and the circuits of power revealed. As already noted, the role of the corporation in capitalist society was handled less satisfactorily. Research at the Centre in the 1970s was influenced by Althusser's theory of the state apparatus and ideology (1971; 1977), and the debate between Miliband and Poulantzas in respect of class power and the state (Poulantzas 1973; Miliband 1983). This work privileged the state in the orchestration of hegemonic rule. In so far as the corporation figured at all in research conducted at the Centre, it was presented in 'clumpish' terms, as the exemplar of Fordism.[10] But as the work on globalization and postmodernism in the 1980s and 1990s made clear, there was considerably more diversity and flexibility in the form and actions of corporations than Fordist models allowed. In particular, corporate branding and theming in consumer culture energized and divided people in ways that the Centre failed to fully recognize. The failure to take consumer culture seriously was a general fault of the Birmingham Centre in the 1970s and 1980s. It limited debates around embodiment and emplacement to neo-Marxist assumptions of commodity fetishism. These limitations were exposed in the 1980s by other groups, notably the *Theory, Culture & Society* formation, who were not so obviously bound by a political agenda.

I propose that 1978 was the Centre's climacteric. With the publication of perhaps the most triumphant example of the Birmingham approach, *Policing the Crisis*, in that year, latent tensions became manifest. In particular, the conflict between the 'scientific' struc-

turalism of the Althusserian tradition and the more open and interpretive Gramscian tradition became pronounced, and feminist criticisms of the 'male-stream' Birmingham tradition became sharper.[11]

In 1979 Hall left Birmingham to become Professor of Sociology
at the Open University. Richard Johnson succeeded him. Under
Johnson, the emphasis on the historical construction of everyday
life was revived, a move that some commentators interpreted as a
veiled criticism of the prominence of textual analysis and ethnography under Hall's stewardship. Turner records Johnson's view that
ethnography in Birmingham was relatively 'undertheorized' and
carried a tendency towards 'elitist paternalism' (G. Turner 1990: 73;
Johnson 1983).

After Hall's departure, it is perhaps fair to say that the Centre
never achieved the same level of dynamism or public profile. Some
of the most promising Birmingham graduates were establishing careers outside the region and indeed, outside the UK. The
Birmingham project was gradually disseminated through the
national and international expansion of Cultural Studies and Media
and Communication courses. In the 1980s, as part of the general
retrenchment in higher education under Margaret Thatcher, the
existence of the Centre was imperilled. Both Johnson and his suc-
cessor, Jorge Larrain, devoted much of their energies to securing
the intellectual and financial security of the Centre and blocking
pressure from the university to reallocate it to the Department of
English. The Centre became a Department of Cultural Studies and,
for the first time, offered an undergraduate programme to supple-
ment postgraduate Masters and doctoral work.

From coercion to consent and hyphenated identity

Hall left the Birmingham Centre and became Professor of Sociology
at the Open University in 1979. At Milton Keynes he co-produced
the U203 'Popular Culture' interdisciplinary undergraduate course
convened by Tony Bennett, which ran from 1982 to 1987. In its first
year the course attracted over 1,000 students. Anthony Easthope
placed U203 as second only to the Birmingham Centre as the most
significant institutional intervention in Cultural Studies in the UK
(1991: 74).

Interestingly, Williams had misgivings about the Open University project (1989a: 157–8). He argued that the technocratic style of
course committee widened access but separated faculty from the

local conditions of students. As one might expect of Williams, he was critical of forms of delivery in education that decoupled the connection between pedagogy and the 'whole way of life' in culture.[12] In a criticism directed more pointedly at U203 and perhaps Hall himself, Williams lamented the turn towards structuralism in Cultural Studies. He regarded this as 'a new form of idealist theory' which produced an unsatisfactory view of agency (1989a: 157). In his view structuralism reinforced the tendency towards 'decoupling' in the Open University by encouraging course planners 'not to look' at 'the practical encounters of people in society' but instead to position these encounters in 'deeper' structuralist frameworks. Williams also takes a pot-shot at the eclecticism and partiality of the structuralist tradition in Cultural Studies. He complains that the tradition 'subsumes' the 'quite different' work of 'Gramsci and Benjamin' and provides a limited reading of culture by, for example, neglecting the critique of idealism associated with the writings of Bakhtin and Medvedev (1989a: 158).

The year of Hall's move in 1979 was also the year that Margaret Thatcher was elected to power. Throughout the 1980s, most obviously via a torrent of trenchant and influential articles in *Marxism Today*, Hall established himself as one of the foremost public critics of Thatcherism. If, before the late 1970s, he dreamed of a personal nemesis that would embody the relations of force, hegemony and overdetermination that he analysed in abstract terms at the level of society and culture, he located it thereafter in Margaret Hilda Thatcher. Thatcherism embodied all of the key themes, concerning ideological manipulation and the organization of popular consent to an authoritarian programme, that Hall had been working on for two decades. But Margaret Thatcher constituted a peculiarly virulent point of articulation, an individual that personally aggravated Hall and stimulated his critical imagination. Some of Hall's best, most enduring writing was produced in these years.

Initially, the central problem that he confronted was why the working class 'voluntarily' voted for a government openly committed to dismantling the postwar welfare settlement. The tight control over public finances and the narrow moral agenda promised by Thatcher in 1979, as the antidote to 'the winter of discontent' under James Callaghan's Labour administration, directly threatened hard-won civil rights in respect of health, education, unemployment and welfare provision. Why, asked Hall, should the working class voluntarily vote to cut its own throat? Gradually, as Thatcher proceeded to achieve two more election victories, only to be finally extirpated by a putsch from within the Tory Party, Hall's interests broadened to embrace the repertoires of English (as opposed to Scottish, Welsh or Irish) nationalism and the cultural, economic and political consequences of globalization. Hall coined and developed the concept of authoritarian populism to describe the democratically constituted civil, moral and economic closure accomplished by Thatcherism.

The analysis of authoritarian populism followed *Policing the Crisis* (Hall et al. 1978) in insisting on the virtue of historical specificity in theoretical labour. From the outset it portrayed much of the traditional Left as becalmed in the problematics of the past. The success of Thatcherism, Hall maintained, lay in addressing the real historical moment, albeit in terms which distorted reality by framing it overwhelmingly through the interests of capital. Hall's analysis demonstrated how Thatcherism was able to utilize and weld together outwardly incompatible elements to achieve popular control. It did not spare the Left. Labour in government under James Callaghan was upbraided by Hall for introducing the 'monetarist realism' which he regarded as paving the way for full-blown authoritarian populism. Labour in opposition he excoriated for either indulging in a complacent and profitless yearning for the revival of class struggle or colluding with the central tenets of Thatcherist 'reform', and so diluting the socialist promise. In these years, the organization of subjectivity comes to occupy the forefront of Hall's intellectual concerns, but always in the political context of the revision of socialism as a counter-hegemonic force to capital.

Much of Hall's ire against the Left at this time derives from his conviction that traditional socialists failed to recognize the seismic nature of the social and economic change which Thatcherism both exploited and expressed. The New Times thesis proposed that the last quarter of the twentieth century underwent an epochal transition from organized to flexible accumulation. Further, it argued that this change is equivalent in significance to the transition in the closing decades of the nineteenth century from the 'laissez-faire' to the advanced or organized stage in capitalist development which eventually culminated in Fordism. Because Hall was understood to claim that New Times revolutionized both the objective conditions of life and the subjective formation of interpersonal relations, thus eventuating in a break or rupture with organized capitalism and its accessories, he was widely criticized by left-wing associates for converting to postmodernism.

In fact Hall distanced himself from prominent aspects of post-modernism, notably its apocalyptic model of change and its propo-sition of the death of the social. However, as ever, when fashionable new theories challenged his understanding of emancipatory poli-tics, Hall's response to postmodernism is vulnerable to the charge that he wants to have his cake and eat it.[13] The New Times thesis refers to the 'ambiguous and treacherous reaches of postmod-ernism' (Hall and Jacques 1989: 15). Nevertheless, from the late 1980s, Lyotard's hypothesis of the collapse of grand narratives is appropriated as the central premise of Hall's writings on culture and politics. Difference, dissemination and *différance* now occupy the fulcrum of his thought on identity, although always with a con-tinuing commitment to socialist intervention. Then, after the mid 1980s his thought becomes increasingly receptive to poststructural-ism and postmodernism. So much so that Sparks argues that Hall's work gradually moves away from an identification with Marxism (Sparks 1996: 88–90). The decisive intellectual inheritance behind this shift is the work of Laclau (1977) and Laclau and Mouffe (1985). This work weakened the Althusserian legacy by rejecting the thesis that ideological elements have any necessary class connotation. Laclau's position advances a more culturalist reading of ideology by shifting the notion of the interpellation of the subject from social class to multiple identities. The effect was to produce a concretized, differentiated approach to ideology capable of exploring how ideo-logical discourse operates to interpellate, for example, racial, gay and lesbian identity, without positing class struggle as the floor or foundation of the social formation.

Laclau further shifted the discussion of representation and ideology away from class by redefining the central contradiction in politics as that between 'the people' and the power bloc. This was an important resource for Hall's discussion of authoritarian populism. It promoted a reading of culture, in all of its concrete variable forms, as an axial site of political struggle in the process of consent and resistance. It also opened up the question of nationalism, which Hall used to illustrate the ideological subtlety of Thatcherism's appropriation of decline, heritage and freedom around what it is to be 'British'. The emphasis that Laclau placed on contingency and discourse clearly liberated Hall from what might be called the ideological fundamentalism of Althusserianism. Ideology remained central to his work, but he now took its refraction through concrete, contingent formations more seriously.

After the mid 1980s the subject of identity emerges as a pre-eminent theme in Hall's writing. Doubtless this reflects the New Times thesis which, as Hall noted elsewhere (1991d), involved 'the return of subjectivity' as a focal topic of social theory. But it also mirrors Halls growing interest in poststructuralism, feminism and postcolonialism. Hall has never adequately explained how 'interrupted identities' and 'sliding', 'fragmented' subjectivities, emerging in his work during the 1990s, can achieve the collective solidarity necessary to effect socialist change. This has led some critics to complain that Hall's espousal of New Times is a *trompe-l'oeil* (Mulgan 1998; Giddens 2000).[14] Perhaps with half an eye to the dilemma of wanting to have socialist change but propagating a range of theoretical observations that appear to pre-empt solidarity and collective agency, Hall has taken to describing his position as 'pessimism of the intellect, optimism of the will'.[15]

Hall always recognized that socialism, and any radical move-ment, must be rooted in the recognition of difference. Arguably, the issue of race made this more acute for him during the rise of the New Left. Different by virtue of colour, Hall was doubtless sensi-tive to the immature New Left conceptions of belonging and recog-nition. His later work tries to envisage forms of collective agency and solidarity that are 'always conditional, never complete, always operating through difference' (Hall 1989h: 154). The paternalist, patriarchal connotations with the old New Left notion of 'Socialist Man' has been revised to incorporate feminist insights and issues of race. Although Hall claims that feminism led him to recast his whole way of thinking about identity, agency and politics, he has not written much directly on the subject. Instead, his writings about the revision and transcendence of 'Socialist Man' have tended to concentrate on issues of race. He maintains that Britain has become a more multicultural society since 1951 when he migrated to the country, but crucially he insists that multiculturalism co-exists with racism (2000b: 8–9).

The Parekh Report (2000) propounds a number of policies that government and local communities can implement to lower the racial barriers and inhibitions that prevent social inclusion. It parallels the Macpherson Report (1999) on the racially motivated murder of the black teenager Stephen Lawrence, which identified the presence of 'institutional racism' in British society. Institutional racism refers to 'unwitting', 'unconscious' racial stereotypes and prejudice which inhere in the organizational structure and routine practices of public and private bodies. Hall rightly notes that the term is problematic in at least two respects (2000b: 8). Firstly, the emphasis on the unwitting, unconscious nature of prejudice underplays the real levels of conscious racism in British society. Secondly, by applying the term indiscriminately to private and public bodies, it is in danger of attributing racism as a universal fault of society, a fault that is so widespread that some people will think that we must live with it rather than take active steps to uproot it. True to the Gramscian maxim, Hall is a 'pessimist of the intellect and optimist of the will' in this matter. He evaluates Macpherson's recognition of institutional racism in the Metropolitan Police as 'a real advance', but regards it as one episode in 'a long campaign which is unlikely to have many short term or any total victories' (2000b: 8). In general, Hall eschews the celebratory sentiments that are found in some versions of multiculturalism (McLaren 1997). Radical by inclination, but stoical by temperament, Hall prefers instead, as with his work on socialism, to emphasize 'the long hard road to renewal'.

A crucial element in this campaign, reviewed at length in the Parekh Report (2000), is the need to revise the concept of British heritage from the perspective of multi-ethnic Britain. Part of this involves engineering a new cultural habitus in Britain which recognizes social inclusion regardless of race, and revises the concept of national heritage to fully reveal the contribution of people of colour. The challenge for the Left, Hall wrote elsewhere, is 'to *constitute* classes and individuals as a popular force – that is the nature of political and cultural struggle: to *make* the divided classes and the separated peoples – divided and separated by culture as much as by other factors – *into* a popular-democratic cultural force' (1981b: 239; emphasis in original).

The Parekh Report calls for a re-examination of British heritage, a great national debate, in order to explore the roots of multi-ethnicity and hybridity in Britain. The object is to produce a new and more inclusive conception of what it might mean to be British, a conception which recognizes hyphenated identity around colour (Afro-British, Asian-British, Caribbean-British, Chinese-British) on a par with white hyphenated identity (Anglo-Irish, Anglo-Welsh and Anglo-Scots).

In this respect Hall's thought has come full circle. The New Left, he recalls, was not a socialism of political dogma, but a socialism of 'the social imaginary' (1989h: 153). It was, he continues, a quest to construct a radical perspective that refused to be locked into the language of the present, and sought to engage with the, frequently conflicting and hectic, political, social and cultural realities in which people are moving. It allowed different experiences and different senses of oppression to puncture the terms of the traditional British debate between Left and Right. Hall argues cogently that the problem for the Left is to engage and respect difference without replacing a politics of articulation with a politics of infinite dispersal (1993d: 137). However, his solution of constructing 'unities through difference' is obscure. His growing interest in visual culture (1991b; 2000c), especially black photography, suggests that he may regard aesthetics as one avenue through which that unity-through-difference might be solidified. If so, it parallels the later work of Herbert Marcuse (1978) on the radical potential of art to operate as a catalyst for constituting classes and individuals into a 'popular-democratic cultural force'. Hall would doubtless object to the 'bourgeois' solution of aesthetics as an instrument of unity, on the grounds that it fails to engage adequately with the material realities of inequality and exclusion. Be that as it may, the mantra of 'unity through difference' leaves many difficult questions unanswered.

In some ways, the emphasis on hybridity and the politics of difference that is accentuated in Hall's later work should be regarded as the culmination of the inherent anti-essentialism that distinguishes his approach to culture. In the 1980s his engagement with Thatcherism and analysis of the failures of the Left played a part in creating the intellectual and political climate that allowed New Labour to flourish. But as we shall see presently (pp. 153–5), Hall was later very critical of many aspects of New Labour policy, thus providing further ammunition for critics who regard his work to be prone to modishness and slippage. A coherent view of the kind of society and culture that Hall wants to see is still absent from his work. Arguably his role as a public intellectual has dissipated his energies.

The next three chapters explore Hall's contribution to understanding representation and ideology, state and society and culture and civilization. I submit that his attempt to relate representation and ideology to material questions of inequality and exclusion constitutes the most distinctive feature of his contribution to cultural studies. Similarly, while his approach allows for a variety of extra-state networks to exert political influence, he never departed from the traditional Marxist premise that the state is the key tool of socialist transformation. His accounts of the rise of the interventionist state, and his analysis of the capitalist state under Thatcherism and

New Labour, provide important insights into the uses of the state apparatus to both promote and hinder socialist change. Although questions of civilization pervade his work, especially in relation to his critique of the West, Hall assigns to the concept of culture the lion's share in his analysis. This has led to some misguided and misleading turns of thought in relation to 'the West' and the potential of the politics of difference to fully erase the conventional politics of emplacement and embodiment.

Although all three chapters consist of an effort to critically engage with Hall, they are also structured as an exposition of his ideas. In my own undergraduate and postgraduate teaching I have found that today's students often find it hard to understand the sequence of Hall's analysis. In part, this reflects the fecundity of Hall's writings. Over the years he has contributed to so many areas of academic and popular debate, from the role of the media in shaping public opinion to the challenges of hybridity to identity thinking, that it is often difficult to see how the various strands are connected. By working through the sequence of Hall's writings, from his early contribution to encoding/decoding processes in the media, through the contributions of Gramsci and Althusser, to the work on the interventionist state, authoritarian populism, the West and the politics of difference, both the range of his intellectual activities and the interconnections between them will hopefully be made more apparent.

2

Representation and Ideology

The concepts of representation and ideology are pivotal in Hall's approach to the analysis of society and culture. Hall proposes first, that points of enunciation are always implicated by the practices of representation, and second, that representation bears a subsidiary relationship to ideology. By the term 'enunciation' Hall means not merely speaking and writing, but all modalities through which agency is expressed in what Marx and Engels (1965) called 'man's double relation' to nature and other wo/men. For Marx, wo/man intervenes upon nature and, with the help of certain instruments and tools, adapts nature to reproduce the material conditions of human existence. As Hall observes in one of his first important essays on ideology (1977a: 315), Marx understood that from an early point in the history of the human intervention into nature, labour is socially organized. The generation of surplus wealth extends the forms through which wo/man's mediation with nature is conducted, and eventually supports a complex, multilayered set of distinctions between and within manual and mental specialization in the division of labour.

At this juncture, there is no need to go into the complexities that Hall, following Marx, locates in manual and mental specialization and the various ensembles, sub-ensembles and sedimentations in the process of ideology in social reproduction. It is enough to note two things. Firstly, Hall submits that there is no space of representation, including theoretical space, which exists outside ideology (1984a: 11). As we shall see later, this proposition exists in some tension with other approaches to culture which prefigure embodiment, emplacement and sensuality in man's 'double relation' with nature and other wo/men (Willis 1977; 2001; Turner 1984). In addition, it drives a coach and horses through the argument of academics situated outside the 'organic intellectual' tradition, who submit that principled academic labour proffers a 'detour via detachment' (Elias 1956).

Secondly, Hall reiterates his antipathy to essentialism by rejecting models of ideology that posit false consciousness in favour of an approach that presents and analyses representation and ideology as a mobile *field* of relations. This is consistent with Gramsci's understanding of culture as striated, constituted through relations of reciprocity and conflict, and always 'in process'. Hall's construction of the concepts of representation and ideology is elaborated through close readings of certain key texts in Marx, notably *The German Ideology* and the 1857 Introduction to the *Grundrisse*, and the writings of Gramsci, Althusser and, to a lesser extent, Volosinov. But his initial written confrontation with the problem was through his early work in Birmingham on the media.

In particular, the faults he perceived in the American behaviourist model of mass communications led him to postulate ideology as central in analysing the media and mass communications. Hall has convincingly argued that media and communication studies constitute a 'regional' rather than a 'self-sustaining' discipline (1989d: 43). That is, they are ineradicably bound up with the theoretical efficacy or lacunae of the general social sciences that take as their subject matter the social and economic formation as a whole. Hence, the problematic of 'the ideological effect' that Hall first ventured in relation to media and communication studies inevitably reflects the whole social formation, and requires an encounter with the general social sciences entrained upon questions of communication and power. However, to begin with, the problematic is addressed in short-range terms. Hall's much cited paper on encoding and decoding targets television discourse (1973a), although it is apparent throughout that the issues raised in relation to the representation of facticity in the media are connected with wider questions of privilege and power. However, in this paper the questions are substantially undertheorized, a condition rectified by Hall in his published work on representation and ideology between the mid 1970s and mid 1980s.

Encoding and decoding

As Hall notes elsewhere (1989d; 1993e), the origins of the encoding/decoding paper are partly polemical. His immediate target is the

Centre for Mass Communications Research at the University of Leicester. Hall regards the Leicester School as representing the dominant paradigm of the day in media and communication studies in the UK, namely behaviourism.[1] The crux of Hall's dissatisfaction with it is his contention that 'reception isn't the open-ended, perfectly transparent thing at the other end of the communication chain' (1993e: 254). On this reading, behaviourism assigns too much freedom to the individual and exaggerates the transparency of the communication process. It is insufficiently reflexive about the context of identity formation and communication exchange, postulating transcendental naturalism where historical specificity should go, and hypothesizing communication processes as technical, apolitical effects of modernization rather than regarding them as the phenomenal forms of capitalist power.

Hall's contention is that media messages are embedded with presuppositions about beliefs and practices that shape everyday perceptions of reality. Further, these presuppositions operate finally to reproduce hegemony. The effect of his argument is to topple the behaviourist claim of transparency in communication and objectivity in media research and to replace it with a thoroughly politicized approach to the media. Thus the behaviourist proposition that the media message is a transcription of social reality is challenged with a redefinition that attributes ideological transformation to the media process. Hall's concern is not merely to focus on the relationship between ideology and communication. He also seeks to establish the principle that decoding is an ordinary accomplishment of audiences through the practices of reflexive assimilation and critical exchange.

The emphasis on the active audience is consistent with the intellectual mood of the early 1970s. Terry Eagleton (1996) observes that Hall's most persistent political strength is a deep-seated belief in popular democracy. With hindsight, the early 1970s, building on the counterculture movement of the 1960s, constituted a 'democratizing moment' in a variety of areas in academic life. For example, ethnomethodology succeeded in challenging the positivist assumptions of structural functionalism by focusing on the tacit knowledge and members' methods in constructing social reality. For its part, semiology demonstrated the importance of sign economies in agency and culture, and argued that meaning is subject to infinite semiosis that is beyond the control of any social agent.[2] Similarly, feminism revealed the disturbing extent of patriarchy in the Academy, and generated a serious debate about the politics of identity. All three offered the Left the prospect of revival after the battering taken by Marxism following the fiasco of the May 1968 'revolution' in Paris.

Hall's appropriation of these influences was connected with a recasting of his relationship with Marxism. Of fundamental importance here was his close reading of Marx's 1857 Introduction to the *Grundrisse* (Hall 1973b). As we shall see presently, Hall used this work to overcome the productivist bent that he castigated in classical Marxism. In the 1857 Introduction he found a classical pretext in Marxism for emancipating consumption and culture from their subaltern status to production. The encoding/decoding paper and the remarks on the 1857 Introduction were published in the same year: 1973. Much of the theoretical élan exhibited in the encoding/decoding piece can be put down to Hall's exploits in Marxist revisionism.

Hall understands encoding and decoding to operate in complex ways. As usual with his analysis of representation, multiple layers of meaning and circuits of communication are posited as integral to the encoding and decoding process, and the Gramscian notion of 'unstable equilibria' is implicit. In large measure, Hall's criticism has become the conventional wisdom in the field. As such it perhaps obscures nuances in the position of the Leicester School that Hall omitted to recognize in his scene-changing piece. James Halloran (1970) and his colleagues at Leicester were certainly aware of the effect of distortion in media communication and they recognized that the manipulation of meaning was logically compatible with the assembly and transmission of media messages. However, they conceptualized these matters in terms of negotiated transaction between the audience and the producer, a liberal-pluralist interpretation that fails to hold water for Hall. He rejects the Leicester School approach because it neglects to base the question of media distortion in the Marxist theory of power and agency, opting instead, as was the field convention of the day, to pursue media and communication studies as a self-sustaining discipline. For Hall, Leicester was therefore insufficiently political in its representation of culture and power and inadequately theoretical. The encoding/decoding paper was his response to this impasse.

The paper is organized into three broad sections. First, Hall refutes the proposition that the media merely reflect facts. Instead he redefines the media as producers of messages or transmitters of 'sign vehicles'. The media 'effect' is to place a particular gloss on social reality. Hall acknowledges that meaning is polysemic in its nature. However, the effect of ideology is to seek to negate polysemy. As he explains:

> I use ideology as that which cuts into the infinite semiosis of language. Language is pure textuality, but ideology wants to make a particular meaning . . . it's the point where power cuts into discourse, where power overcuts knowledge and discourse; at that point you get a cut, you get a stoppage, you get a suture, you get an overdetermination. The meaning constructed by that cut into language is never permanent, because the next sentence will take it back, will open the semiosis again. And it can't fix it, but ideology is an attempt to fix it. (1993e: 263–4)

Hall's wording here is slightly misleading, since it implies that ideology exists outside of discourse and knowledge. As his wider writings on ideology and representation affirm, it is more accurate to regard discourse and knowledge as always and already inscribed with ideology. However, leaving that aside, the passage reveals both Hall's understanding of the force of ideology in constructing meaning as 'obvious' or 'natural', and his conviction that the role of intellectual labour is to expose and unpack this force. Hall's interest in the media is partly based on his recognition that it is axial in the construction of meaning in advanced capitalist society. He regards its professional codes and technological practices as making a decisive 'cut' or 'overcut' into the semiosis of language in the culture at large. This brings me to the second section of the paper.

Much of the impetus in the encoding/decoding paper is directed towards confirming the notion of 'the active audience' as an antidote to the blank social subject constructed by behaviourism. However, Hall is also concerned to demonstrate that the media play a constructionist role in advancing some narratives and meanings at the expense of others. The process of encoding and decoding is clearly very complex. It functions as a mixture of conscious and unconscious levels, and involves perpetual struggle over the specific type of representational practices. Gramsci's notion of dominance as a structured field of relations in which relations of force constitute 'unstable equilibria' informs Hall's analysis throughout. Hegemony is therefore never irreversible or univocal. Rather, it always involves a balance of power that is contested, redressed and opposed through ordinary agency. These are significant caveats, but they should not be allowed to obscure the fact that Hall regards media representation as finally operating through determinate codes which anchor semiosis and ultimately enhance 'the dominant cultural order' (1973a: 13).

Hall's position on this matter is nuanced and sophisticated. Elsewhere, he has criticized the 'conspiracy theory' of vulgar Marxism that portrays the media as the simple ideological instrument of capital (Hall, Connell and Curti 1976: 51). Hall is an implacable opponent of the notion of 'false consciousness' since the term implies that the goal of analysis should be to elucidate the so-called reality underlying ideological distortion. Instead he submits that the notion of social reality is always discursively constituted, and further, that representation inevitably bears the inflections of class, gender, race and status. For these reasons Hall refuses to countenance a version of the dominant ideology thesis which hypothesizes class control over the popular. On the contrary, for Hall, the popular is always contested terrain, cultural space in which resistance and opposition foment and evolve as ordinary accessories of agency. As he advises in another place:

> In the study of popular culture, we should always start here: with the double-stake in popular culture, the double movement of containment and resistance, which is always inevitably inside it . . . I think there is a continuous and necessarily uneven and unequal struggle, by the dominant culture; to enclose and confine its definitions and forms. There are points of resistance; there are also moments of supersession. This is the dialectic of cultural struggle. In our times, it goes on continuously, in the complex lines of resistance and acceptance, refusal and capitulation, which make in the field of culture a sort of constant battlefield. A battlefield where no once-and-for-all victories are obtained but where there are always strategic positions to be won and lost. (1981b: 227, 233)

At the same time Hall is at pains to pre-empt the inference that society is a completely open discursive field in which all readings or 'battle reports' are of equivalent analytic value. His remedy is to introduce the vexatious notion of 'preferred readings'. The notion is vexatious because both the criteria for determining preferred readings, and the consequences that follow from it have proved to be mercurial. I will take up this point in more detail later.

The third section of Hall's paper examines the concrete mechanisms through which media representations are constructed by producers and assimilated by audiences. To this end he constructs a typology of four codes by which, he contends, audiences read media messages.

(1) The dominant or hegemonic code   When audiences assimilate media messages as 'straight' reflections of reality they are operating in the code of the dominant or hegemonic order. This is a state of 'transparent communication' in which the critical reflexivity of the audience is suspended or at least decisively checked. Given Hall's emphasis on the 'active audience', he stresses that transparent communication is an ideal-type case. Nonetheless, because he is concerned to demonstrate that the media operate within the field of dominant ideology, he is required to nominate closure in the dominant code as a logical possibility in the communication process.

(2) The professional code   The professional code refers to the techniques and practices deployed by media personnel to construct and transmit messages. A good deal of the encoding/decoding paper is devoted to nullifying the self-image of impartiality and objectivity cultivated by media professionals. Hall does not wish to impute bad faith to them. On the other hand, he attributes 'over-defensiveness' to them on the question of bias (1974: 24). For Hall, media professionals are not autonomous agents. This is a proposition that ruffles media feathers. Hall understands that impartiality and neutral reporting of the 'facts' have totemic significance in the self-image of media professionals. Against this, he argues that the concepts of impartiality and neutrality already presuppose a 'natural' order in which notions of justice, difference and inclusion reflect dominant values. It is not a matter of positing media conspiracy, although rather contrarily Hall claims that media professionals are organically linked with dominant elites through the structural position of the media as an 'ideological apparatus', and their privileged access to elite constructions of reality (1973a: 17).[3] Rather it is at the level of connotative 'metacodes' that Hall identifies complicity between elites and the media. This is not necessarily a conscious complicity. Rather Hall maintains that it typically operates through unspoken shared understandings of the 'common ground' of debate and agency, so that 'ideological reproduction therefore takes place here inadvertently, unconsciously, "behind men's backs"' (1973a: 17). Hall therefore theorizes the professional code as compliant with the hegemony of the dominant code. It transmits a staged version of reality to the consumer that is inscribed with the 'cut' of dominant ideology.

(3) The negotiated code   This is the most common code in assimilating media messages. It recognizes that media messages are

dominantly defined and professionally signified. As such, it might
be said to constitute a reflexive engagement with the media. Reflexivity is understood to comprise a mixture of adaptive and oppositional elements. For example, it acknowledges the legitimacy of
hegemonic definitions of the national interest, while simultaneously
reading these definitions in relation to habitus and experience. Hall
uses the term 'situated logics' to describe the operation of this code
(1973a: 18). By this term he means that media messages are assimilated according to the particular life circumstances of the audience.
The negotiated code reflects high levels of ambivalence and inconsistency about political, economic and cultural matters. For
example, Hall mentions that agreement with the hegemonic mantra
that it is in the national interest to practise pay restraint as a hedge
against inflation does not necessarily carry over into a readiness to
accept a low pay offer on the shopfloor (1973a: 18). The ambivalence
intrinsic to the negotiated code makes it a fruitful space in political
agency. For the mismatches between the hegemonic code and the
situated logic of lived experience potentially expose the hiatus
between fact and bias which ideology labours to disguise.

(4) *The oppositional code*   When audiences respond to media messages as mere ideology they operate in the oppositional code. Here
the literal and connotative inflection given to a particular event is
understood by the audience, but read in a converse way. The audience decodes the preferred code of referencing and presenting an
event and 'retotalizes' it in an alternative framework. The oppositional code may be a continuous way of reading media messages
for some strata. These strata may have developed lifestyles with
values that are inimical to hegemonic order and therefore automatically discount and oppose the media messages through which this
order is represented. Willis's study of 'profane culture' in the
habitus and practice of bikers and hippies (1978) may be referred to
as an example of the inimical values at issue here. The people he
studied maintain a highly conditional relation with hegemonic
culture. They transgress it through their means of material and symbolic subsistence, inhabiting, so to speak, a self-validating ring of
culture within the universe of hegemony. Moreover, their discourse
about the latter is often automatically dismissive and carnivalesque
in form, hence Willis's choice of the label 'profane' to describe it.

However, Hall's interest in oppositional readings is primarily
directed towards conjunctures of instability in hegemony which are
conducive to the articulation of transformative intervention. As he

concludes, 'one of the most significant political moments (they also coincide with crisis points within the broadcasting organizations themselves for obvious reasons) is the point when events that are normally signified and decoded in a negotiated way begin to be given an oppositional reading' (1973a: 18).

The encoding/decoding paper was not based on empirical research. It was left to David Morley, an associate of Hall's in Birmingham, to test the propositions. He showed episodes of the BBC current affairs programme *Nationwide* to social groups representing the middle and working classes and asked them to comment on the output (Morley 1980). Broadly speaking, his findings confirm Hall's fourfold typology. However, he also discovered significant anomalies in the audience response which cross-cut class, status, race and gender lines. Following the discourse theorist Michel Pêcheux, Morley argues that the operation of codes must be understood in relation to *interdiscourse*, a term designed to render the interpellation of social subjects as involving a multiplicity of discourses. The inference is that the closure denoted in Hall's fourfold typology is untenable. To some extent, Hall's readiness to acknowledge ambivalence and slippage in the coding process anticipates this manoeuvre. All the same, Morley's intervention suggests that Hall did not go far enough in clarifying the dialectics of ambivalence and slippage.

Morley's critics responded by submitting that he himself did not go far enough in practising what he preached. In particular, Lewis (1983) complains that Morley underestimated the autonomy of media professionals and caricatured them as agents of 'primary definitions'. This again raises difficult empirical questions relating to the class backgrounds, education history and lifestyle practices of media professionals and elite members in business, the state and the celebrity sector that remain substantially underresearched in the field. On this basis Lewis queries the validity of the concept of 'preferred reading' in Morley's research, observing that the verification of the concept is always a matter of empirical research and never theoretical fiat. The import of this remark is that Morley, and implicitly Hall, are overdependent on theoretical categories to support their claims in respect of the ideological effectivity of the media.

Jordin and Brunt (1988) offer a countervailing view, criticizing Morley's methodology for replicating positivist assumptions in its application of quantitative analysis. *Contra* Lewis they hold that preferred readings can be established textually prior to empirical research. The empirical task that derives from this is to establish the range of decodings attached to encoded preferred readings. As empirical tasks go it is a daunting prospect, since the range of encoded and decoded readings is potentially infinite. Nor is the ideological pretext governing preferred readings adequately explained.

Morley himself became dissatisfied with the ethnographic limitations of his original research, forsaking the controlled ambience of his research groups for investigation into audience responses in 'natural settings' (Morley 1986; 1980). This involved a loosening of the ideological problematic formulated in the original encoding/decoding model in favour of a more diversified reading which embraced factors of age, race, gender and generation as well as class in the 'viewing context'. Morley argued that the subject is split both psychologically and sociologically, so that it is a mistake to impute identity to audience responses. The result is a more multilayered model of coding than envisaged in the original encoding/decoding paper.

Underlying these various reformulations is dissatisfaction with the criteria of encoding and decoding elaborated by Hall (1973a). Jim McGuigan gets to the nub of the matter with his observation that Hall's insistence on ideological effectivity and audience activity is 'flexible almost to the point of incoherence' (1992: 131). Hall's criteria of audience activity in decoding and ideological effectivity in encoding are undersubstantiated. The encoding/decoding model strives to defend relative autonomy in the negotiated and oppositional codes, but is nebulous on the question of the route or passport that audiences use to achieve this end. Simultaneously, he wants to retain two arguments that point in contrary directions.

In an important interview (1993e), Hall recognizes that the original encoding/decoding paper is faulty in at least four respects. Firstly, the distinction between signification at the level of society, culture and politics, and encoding at the level of the media message, is not adequately adumbrated. The dialogue between hegemonic reproduction and the encoding practices of media professionals is poorly enunciated. Other traditions regard reflexivity to be a general characteristic of communication (Beck, Giddens and Lash 1994). In contrast Hall's fourfold typology posits a polarized view of reflexivity in which reflexive consciousness is concentrated at the end of the negotiated and oppositional pairing, and is virtually absent in the dominant and professional codes.

Secondly, the formulation of the encoding/decoding paradigm suggests that signification works in the real world. The analytic task becomes to determine how a preferred reading is attempted through the encoding process, and how a preferred meaning is achieved by the audience.[4] However, the distinction between signification and the real world overturns Hall's thesis on ideology, which is that ideology 'pre-signifies' or 'overdetermines' the 'natural' world, thus making 'the real' a dubious category. As Hall attests:

> I really create problems for myself by looking as if there is a sort of moment there. So you read the circuit as if there is a real world, then somebody speaks about it and encodes it, and then somebody reads it, then there's a real world again. But of course, the real world is not outside of discourse; it's not outside of signification. It's practice and discourse like everything else is. (1993e: 260–1)

Thirdly, the dynamics of preferred meaning and preferred reading are obscure. Hall wants to use the terms in order to get away from any connotation of determinism. Both the active agent and the active audience are consistent with his view of ideology as positioning actors in situations. The criteria of preferred meaning and preferred reading cannot be simply inferred from hegemony. As Morley's work demonstrated (1980; 1986), preference in the polysemy of the TV broadcasting process can only be established by assigning diligence to the particular context in which communication messages are assembled and assimilated. Preference cannot be pre-designated or inferred since its efficacy is a matter of the specific exchange of reflexivity between the producer of the communication message and the audience. Because this is the case, Hall's conflation of preferred reading and meaning with ideology needs to be much more carefully expressed. No one would seriously quibble with the argument that communication operates within the force of normative coercion and that the media constitute a central institution of normative coercion. The question is the nature of coercion. For Hall, coercion tends to operate to reproduce the rule of capital. But this requires more explication than is achieved in the encoding/decoding paper.

Fourthly, the paper continuously begs the question of the relationship between the real and the discursive in the capitalist mode of production. The encoding/decoding paper ends up framing everything as discourse. But as Hall recognizes (1993e: 267–8), this is unsatisfactory because it dissolves the question of the relationship between discourse and history. Hall's approach aims to avoid assigning determinacy to discourse. However, the analytical edge of his work is the proposition that discourse operates to reinforce the rule of capital. Understandably, Hall does not want to produce a reading that turns the media message into pure polysemy. But in avoiding doing so he is forced to connote the media message with material levels of power and history. The problem is that these levels are precluded by his insistence that power and history are discursively constituted. Hall's effort to wrestle with this difficulty raises more dilemmas than it solves. He writes:

> I simply can't think 'practice' without touching ground, with each practice always touching ground as the necessary but not sufficient element – its materiality, its material registration. Somewhere. What that, however, pushes me to is what I would call the historically real, which is not philosophically real but which has a good deal of determinacy in it. So the historical structures may not be long lasting, they may not be forever, cannot be transcendental, but while they are going, they do structure a particular field. (1993e: 268)

Elsewhere, Hall has complained of his frustration at lacking a language to express his argument adequately (1995a: 68). The remark is made in relation to his attempted exegesis of the politics of difference and interrupted identity. However, it is also relevant to the passage cited above. Thus, in one sentence Hall proposes that history is not 'philosophically real' but confusingly invokes the 'historically real', which, he adds, 'has a good deal of determinacy in it'. What Hall hopes to gain from the concept of the 'historically real' in preference to 'history' is puzzling. Perhaps the overweening confidence of some left-wing writers, *après* Marx, that history is on their side troubled him, and he sought to put distance between himself and them by adopting the concept. Be that as it may, it is not clear that the rejection of 'history' is required to refute historicism. In another sentence, the 'historically real', which he submits exists 'somewhere', is adduced as exerting 'structure' over a particular 'field', albeit structure that may not be 'long lasting' and 'cannot be transcendental'. Nor is the calibre of determinacy specified, which somewhat weakens its analytic purchase. Most historians would regard the proposition that historical forces are variable as unexceptional. However, it reprises the question of why Hall discards 'history' in favour of the 'historically real'.

To be fair, Hall is cognizant of the problem. 'I suppose,' he writes, 'in moving away from the real or the extradiscursive as a kind of transcendental signifier outside of the system, I try to reintroduce it back as an element of tendential structuralism' (1993e: 268). This is perhaps another example of the slippage that critics argue is a general problem with Hall's work. But it is also evidence of the structural opacity between discourse and the extradiscursive that runs right through his writings.

The encoding/decoding paper represents one of Hall's first significant contributions to the investigation of ideology in capitalist society. It has been rightly appreciated as a notable intervention in politicizing the study of the media and communication. Hall's method of syncretic narrative fusion of elements from Marxist theory, structuralism and semiology is imaginative. It generated both critical discourse and a programme of research, conditions that Jeffrey Alexander (2001) proposed as requirements of knowledge in the human sciences to possess canonical status. In as much as this is the case, Hall's paper should be regarded as an addition to the canon. However, the paper was constrained by a focus on the media. Hall's real interest is in how the phenomenal form of ideology functions to organize subjects and to mask the real foundations of capitalist society. Throughout, it is evident that he is straining to stop himself losing his audience in media and communication studies by delving deeper into the societal mechanics of this process. His work between the mid 1970s and 1980s returns repeatedly to the question of the form and functions of ideology in capitalist society. The analysis of authoritarian populism may be regarded as the climax of these efforts.

I shall now turn to this work, leaving aside the subject of authoritarian populism, as it is more apposite to consider it in relation to Hall's position on the state and society, which is the topic of the next chapter. Hall's thought on ideology is best approached via an examination of his use of Marx, especially the 1857 Introduction to the *Grundrisse*, Gramsci, Althusser, Laclau and Mouffe. Other influences are formative in Hall's thought on ideology, notably Lévi-Strauss, Barthes and Eco. However, I think that Marx, Gramsci, Althusser, Laclau and Mouffe can properly be attributed as seminal influences.

Hall's writing has a tendency towards didacticism. In his publications on ideology he is at his most didactic, frequently pulling up others for misreading key texts and conjunctures, and setting readers right, often in somewhat lapidary terms, about what constitutes 'good sense' in the analysis of culture and society.[5] Hall is not a sanctimonious writer, although he possesses a strong moral conscience that occasionally comes over as priggishness. For example, his accounts of the Birmingham tradition in Cultural Studies and the wrong turn taken by Cultural Studies in America

(1989b; 1992f; 1996e) have a certain holier-than-thou quality which grates with some readers. His writings on ideology abound with a sense of delineating the terrain of cultural studies as distinct from sociology, politics and economics. They have an embattled quality as Hall struggled to open up new space, often in opposition to critics who doubted the very legitimacy of his enterprise. This problem loomed large in Hall's revision of culture in the Marxist tradition. The significance that he attached to this revision is evidence of his desire to remain identified with the Left. Later, as the linguistic turn in Hall's thought became pronounced, he grew more comfortable in professing Marxism 'without guarantees'. But in the work on ideology between the mid 1970s and mid 1980s, he is plainly struggling to achieve a new modus operandi within the Marxist legacy.

Marx and the 1857 Introduction

Nowhere is this more apparent than in the close reading of Marx's 1857 Introduction to the *Grundrisse*. Hall is drawn to this work as a means of rebutting the economic reductionism of the base–superstructure reading of Marxism. This reading, which is sometimes called 'vulgar Marxism', holds that Marx proposed that the economic base always and fully determines the psychological, cultural and political superstructure of society. Raymond Williams (1973) famously repudiated the base–superstructure couplet, arguing that to present culture as the reflection of the economic base is untenable. Williams held that culture is material. It is inscribed in the process of production through language and social interaction. Thus nothing can be made without culturally envisioning the object and collaborating in the transformation of nature and the existing products of human labour. Similarly, culture is integral to the process of circulation, distribution and exchange. In short, economy is presupposed by culture and vice versa. So culture cannot be the 'reflection' of the economic base, since it is already enmeshed with economy. The effect of Williams's fusillade against the base–superstructure couplet was to make production more cultural and cultural analysis more conscious of its material roots.

The reason why vulgar Marxists latched on to the economic base as the 'secret' of the laws of capitalist development is that they wanted to conscript scientific status to Marxism. The intention was to pre-empt the taint of cultural and moral relativism from being aimed at Marxist analysis. In the Birmingham School, via Althusser and Poulantzas, this led to an important debate on the nature of the putative 'relative autonomy' of science from ideology (Women's Studies Group 1978), and I shall consider this in the next two sections of this chapter. The point at issue at this stage of the discussion is why the New Left sought to discredit the historicism and reductionism of vulgar Marxism without, however, culminating in a chorus of approval for the inevitability of cultural relativism.

To some extent the reason lies in Hall's disquiet with English culturalism (1980a). As we have seen, Hall believed that culturalism falls into the trap of privileging 'experience' as the focal point of cultural analysis. In as much as this is so, culturalism is held to end in a bog which represents 'undifferentiated human praxis' as the human condition, and so fails to convey the proximate and determinate character of cultural agency. For Hall, and other members of the New Left, continental structuralism offered a way out of this morass by demonstrating the limitations of culturalist humanism and empiricism. In fact, Williams, like Edward Thompson, understood only too well that cultural agency must be analysed as proximate and determinate. But both fled from the conclusive closure of the base–superstructure couplet. This is why neither fully embraced Hall's advocacy of structuralism, opting instead to associate themselves with the more expansive Marxist thesis that 'social being determines consciousness'.

To this end Williams's (1973) paper makes imaginative recourse to Gramsci's concept of hegemony. For Williams the concept is preferable to the dominant ideology model of the base–superstructure dichotomy, because it supports a more nuanced analysis of the complex interplay of social forces within the social totality. In particular it recognizes the contradictory instances of bourgeois rule, the precarious nature of hegemonic ascendancy and the practical necessity of political resistance. Indeed, Williams's endorsement of hegemony as a vital tool of cultural analysis is partly designed to reinforce Gramsci's proposition that the rule of capital is inherently contradictory. Because hegemony is never universal, its contradictions cannot be entirely assuaged or masked by bourgeois organic intellectuals or spin doctors. In as much as this is so, hegemony has to be understood as a matter of perpetual struggle between contending forces. This argument was part of Williams's celebrated 'resources of hope' (1983) for left-wing renewal.

Williams modified Gramsci's concept of hegemony by distinguishing *dominant*, *residual* and *emergent* formations, and differenti-

ating between *alternative* and *oppositional* wings in respect of the
residual and emergent categories (1973). He argued that the dominant formation aims to present the historically specific order as
natural and everlasting. However, because it cannot engineer universal hegemony it is obliged to engage in continuous struggle with
residual and emergent formations. Residual formations have their
roots in history, representing 'whole ways of life' that resist and
challenge the dominant formation. Williams was especially interested in emergent formations, which, he argued, carry the potential
to yield generalized forms of life that transcend dominant and residual categories. In the nature of things, emergent formations typically originate as ascending marginal or peripheral cultures of
transgression which conflict at some level with dominant and residual formations. The introduction of the distinction between alternative and oppositional wings in residual and emergent formations
is critical. Williams held that alternative cultures may be contrary
to many aspects of dominant formations, but they are content to co-
exist within its circle of hegemony. In contrast, oppositional cultures
are counter-hegemonic forces, oriented towards replacing the
dominant order.

Hall's reading of the 1857 Introduction (1973b) was prepared in
the context of increasing frustration among the New Left with the
durability of economic reductionism in the Marxist camp. It aimed
to demonstrate that vulgar Marxism was never part of Marx's
method and, by this resort, to claim a bridgehead in classical
Marxism against the proposition that the economy determines
culture. Hall maintained that to posit the economy as the foundation of the superstructure is contrary to Marx's method. Marx
understood the capitalist mode of production to comprise a multilayered ensemble of mobile relations. He never entertained the
notion that production is independent of culture. On the contrary,
he held that production is predicated in culture in at least two
respects. First, culture and energy are consumed in the process of
labouring on nature or relations with other men to produce value.
This anticipates Williams's point that production is always already
culturally encoded. Second, production is never an end in itself. As
Marx observed elsewhere, the spider labours to weave its web
without knowing why it is engaged in the exercise, while wo/men
always labour with a sense of purpose. Even when this purpose is
imposed on labourers, as is the case under capitalism by virtue of
the logic of bourgeois accumulation, it is conducted on the basis of
answering to conscious human wants. Hall concludes that the 1857

Introduction demonstrates that Marx understood capitalism to rest on a circuit between production and consumption that is mediated through culture.

Hall makes the case that production and consumption are joined together in a circuit because he wants to get away from the vulgar Marxist position that culture bears a subsidiary relation to production. But Hall is also drawn to the 1857 Introduction because it offers a succinct account of how the phenomenal forms of capitalist society tend to disguise the 'real relations' that operate to reproduce bourgeois rule. Hall particularly approves of Marx's dissection of bourgeois political economy, which, pejoratively, he described as the highest form of bourgeois 'common sense'. Locke, Burke, Smith, Ricardo, Bentham and the other lions of classical political economy take the isolated individual to be the nucleus of production and society. Marx, however, commences with the 'socially determinate' individual engaged in 'socially determined individual production'. For Hall, it is Marx's emphasis on the 'all-sided interdependence' of individuals and the categories of life (private right, morality, the family, civil society, the state, etc.), and his post-Hegelian insistence on the material level of social life that decisively lift his analysis as an enduring intellectual resource.[6] Hall celebrates Marx's achievement as revealing how the laws of political economy really work:

> They worked by representing themselves, in theory and conscious-ness, in a mystified and inverted form, as something other than they really were. Thus, in everyday consciousness, wages appear as a proper and equivalent return to labour for its part in production. Only if labour is seen as a commodity which is also *not* a commodity, a power, a source not only of 'value' but of surplus value, can it be shown that wages are indeed a mystified though necessary 'form' with another, deeper contradictory relations hidden within it. (Hall 1973b: 69)

Marx's Introduction answered Hall's requirement for an anti-essentialist reading of culture. From it Hall developed an approach to cultural analysis that is distinguished by three basic principles. First, culture is understood to consist of an ensemble of interdependent relations. Hall eschews a privileged reading of the economic base, and he does not succumb either to a 'prime mover' theory of development. Cultural analysis is a matter of elucidating the interdependent relations between the ensemble of institutions and agents that function to elicit normative coercion.

Second, Hall's approach insists on reading culture as mobile and unfinished. Culture is understood to consist of multiple layers of interdependent relations which range from the abstract to the historically specific. Change in these layers is not uniform. Some relations operate in the *longue durée* so that their consequences emerge gradually, creeping up on the cultural analyst, as it were, 'behind men's backs'. Change in other layers is more transparent. Hall's analysis of authoritarian populism in the 1980s constitutes the fullest realization of this take on cultural analysis.

The third principle of Hall's reading is that the phenomenal form of culture disguises the real relations of cultural reproduction. This is crucial because it equips Hall with a rationale for insisting on the political responsibilities of cultural analysis. The task of the labour of the organic intellectual in the area of cultural analysis is to reveal the place of ideology in phenomenal forms of communication and representation and to elucidate the real relations of cultural reproduction and change.

Hall's (1973b) paper does not quite constitute an encomium of Marxism. But it comes close to doing so, and is the most 'Marxist' of all Hall's writings. The rhythm of his prose and the confident parade of propositions about the tendencies of capitalist accumulation are reminiscent of the master himself. Hall's evident excitement in delving into the quick of the newly published English-language version of the *Grundrisse* (Marx 1971) was shared by many on the Left. The *Grundrisse* fleshed out Marx's method and checked vulgar Marxism. It provided Hall with the pretext to maintain that culture belongs to the classical Marxist tradition, and is not a scarcely developed footnote of *Capital*. However, the execution of Hall's rediscovery of Marxism did not occur in isolation. Hall's route to the 1857 Introduction was via the questions raised by Gramsci and Althusser in respect of normative coercion. In particular, the question of how these theorists regarded the subject to be constituted through ideology was a focus for Hall.

Gramsci, complex unity and hegemony

Antonio Gramsci is the principal intellectual influence on Stuart Hall's thought and approach to cultural analysis. In part, this reflects the historic resonance that Hall recognizes between Gramsci's historical position and his own (Hall 1988a: 161–73).[7] Like Hall, Gramsci hailed from the non-metropolitan periphery. He reached political maturity in the 'conjuncture' of the 'proletarian moment' that followed the First World War. Gramsci became a leading socialist journalist and theorist of the Turin factory councils movement of 1919–20. He regarded direct democracy, based on the factory councils, to be a long-term alternative to parliamentary democracy. He was elected secretary of the Italian Communist Party in 1924. Perceived by the authorities to be a threat to the state, he was arrested and imprisoned in 1926, dying in 1937 in the very month that he regained his freedom. The main themes of his *Prison Notebooks* (1971) are how and why this moment of progressive change faltered, and the elaboration of a 'philosophy of praxis' necessary to secure proletarian party hegemony over the masses.

Hall's socialism, in part a product of the 'double conjuncture' of 1956, blossomed through his involvement with the New Left. During the last quarter of a century his work returns regularly to the question of the opportunities and obstacles to socialist advance in Britain. Thatcherism is, of course, the focal point of his deliberations in the 1980s. However, he traces the relations of force that enabled Thatcherism to seize hegemony back, initally, to the mid 1970s, with the Callaghan government's capitulation to the demands of the International Monetary Fund and recognition of the need for welfare state revisionism, and then to failures of national-centrist consensus politics in the postwar period.[8] Indeed Hall's work on the state suggests that the roots of hegemonic crisis derive from the concessions made in the political power alliances between the 1880s and 1920s to overcome class tensions (1984c; Hall and Schwarz 1985). According to Hall, the power blocs organized around consensus politics and social democracy in the postwar period failed to deliver redistributive justice. This created a crisis of legitimacy in the ideology of centrist national unity which the New Right exploited after the mid 1970s in the turn towards Thatcherism.

Leaving that aside for the moment, Hall's self-image is of an embattled intellectual who, like Gramsci, seeks to trace the contours of the historical conjunctures that simultaneously enable and obstruct left-wing advance. Both participated in popular journalism as a means of communicating with the people. Hall's approach to cultural analysis is generally indebted to Gramsci in three particulars. Firstly, he approves of Gramsci's insistence that the structure/superstructure complex constitutes a 'complex unity'. Gramsci's purpose here is to rebut the economic reductionism of vulgar Marxism and pre-empt the notion that the 'proletarian moment' will arise spontaneously. Instead Gramsci conceptualizes the structure/superstructure complex in terms of a formation of interrelated multiple levels. These levels range from abstract, formal categories that Gramsci calls 'organic-epochal', in the sense that they apply to decades or centuries in capitalist development, down to the historically specific concrete level. Examples of epochal categories include the labour process and the capitalist mode of production, while the historically specific and concrete refers, *inter alia*, to questions of primitive accumulation, factory legislation and the class struggle.

The argument parallels Marx's proposition in the 1857 Introduction that the concrete consists of 'many determinations'. But of course, Gramsci reaches this insight by a different route. Namely by attempting to explain the practical reasons why Italian communism faltered after the heady purpose and direction following the First World War, and how an understanding of the dynamics of the prevailing historical conjuncture can be enlisted to revive socialist advance. This emphasis on the responsibility of analysis to pay due attention to historical specificity and the characteristics of the 'national-popular' have sometimes led to the criticism that Gramsci's approach is constrained by over-reliance on the experience of the Italian nation-state. Hall prefers to see strengths in Gramsci's method of grounding theory in historical specificity and the concrete characteristics of the national-popular. Hall regards this as an essential counterweight to the tendency towards abstraction in cultural theory. At the same time Gramsci's understanding of organic-epochal categories facilitates theoretical work that is genuinely cross-cultural.

Gramsci's proposition that concepts operate at different levels of abstraction has been extremely valuable for Hall. In his analysis of authoritarian populism and racism he returns repeatedly to the position that agency, in the sense of conscious willed action, is mediated through complexly constituted 'relations of force'. He holds that it is a serious error to translate concepts which are designed to operate at a high level of abstraction to more concrete levels of operation (1986b). As noted already, this creates problems in testing theory since falsification at the concrete level does not necessarily confirm or falsify concepts and categories constructed to apply at the abstract level. Perhaps, instead of regarding Gramsci's approach as akin to a multilane highway, it is better to say that it resembles a cat's cradle in which concepts and propositions are interconnected by a plethora of visible and semi-invisible threads. Be that as it may, Hall evidently responds enthusiastically to the complex unity that

Gramsci's approach posits and seeks to adumbrate. This brings me to the second point.

Gramsci's notion of complex unity prohibits the vulgar Marxist notion of the privileged class subject. By situating agency in relations of force and insisting that these relations are continuously *in process*, Gramsci paves the way towards a view of agency as contradictory and fragmentary. He seldom refers to class domination, preferring instead to conceptualize power in terms of a 'ruling bloc' or 'historic bloc' of interests that consist of contradictory and discordant ensembles that hegemonic leadership must 'cement'. Hall has utilized this perspective and elaborated it in his later work on New Times, interrupted identity and hybridity. More broadly, his conception of conjunctural analysis honours Gramsci's position that the historical conjunctures consist of unstable equilibria. That is, the relations between politics, ideology, the state, different political parties, the pre-eminence of national-popular questions and civil society consist of a shifting balance of power in which *nothing* can be taken for granted. Gramsci's sociology holds that power is precarious. Engineering hegemony is a contested process involving a continuous war of movement and war of position. Classical Marxism promoted a dialectical view of history. But vulgar Marxism tended to obscure this by perpetuating a triumphalist view of proletarian progress. By enjoining the dual propositions that power is precarious, and that situated subjective agency mirrors the contradiction and fragmentation of relations of force, Gramsci revives the accent in classical Marxism of a dialectical view of history.

Thirdly, Gramsci champions the importance of the cultural level in Marxist analysis. He constructs an extremely subtle reading of culture that recognizes it as the terrain of practices, representations, languages, customs and 'common sense' of historically specific society. He identifies culture as a primary site in the construction of national hegemony. Gramsci's analysis of popular Catholicism and popular Fascism in Italy provided concrete instances of how culture operates to facilitate and obstruct change. He understood that significant sections in the Italian proletariat rejected the Marxist thesis that religion is 'the opiate of the people' and instead adhered to Catholicism as a progressive alternative to the development of a secular, revolutionary national-popular culture. Likewise, in contrast with many on the Left in his generation, he appreciated the 'modernizing' influence of the Fascist Party in harnessing the backward character of the national-popular in Italy and stamping it with a reactionary face, capable of arousing genuine voluntary support from the masses.

What Hall admires here is Gramsci's unflinching realism, his constant readiness to focus on things as they are and to apprehend them 'violently', rather than on how he would wish them to be. Hall has no need for self-exculpation. In the 1980s and 1990s he saw himself as telling unpopular truths in the presentation of both his New Times thesis and his account of the politics of difference. Each conflicted with the traditional Marxist emphasis on the privileged class subject. Gramsci's penetrating analysis of the antinomies in proletarian common sense and the sophistry of some forms of left-wing thought provided Hall with a crucial historical role model. Like Gramsci, he embraced the role of the embattled intellectual seeking to render the truths of his times against the corrosive forces of sentiment and self-interest.

Hall brings to bear many of what he takes to be the decisive assets of Gramscianism in his analysis of how ideology operates in contemporary culture. Disarmingly, his utilization of Gramsci begins with the admission that Gramsci bequeathed no 'systematic' theory of ideology (Hall, Lumley and McLennan 1978: 45). Many critics would say the same of Hall's theory of culture. Both Hall and Gramsci are preoccupied by the question of normative coercion and the institutions that organize popular consent in a normative order. An example of normative coercion is the identification of the masses with the national-popular, an adhesion that Hall investigated concretely later in his work on the racist legacies of Empire and the integrative function of heritage in contemporary British culture (1998b; 1999; 2000b). Gramsci identifies civil society, the state, the party and the intellectuals as central institutions of normative coercion (Hall, Lumley and McLennan 1978: 45). In Gramsci's sociology, these institutions are not pre-eminently concerned with producing false consciousness. The concept of false consciousness is problematic for Gramsci since it presupposes notions of true consciousness and reality. These notions are anathema to Gramsci's view of the mechanics of normative coercion. The institutions of normative coercion do not generate a set of representations that are inherently false. According to Hall they produce

a *false inflection* of the 'real relations' on which, in fact, they depend ... not only does socially interdependent labour *appear*, in the sphere of the market, as a set of mutually independent and indifferent relations: but this second level of ideological relations gives rise to a whole set of theories, images, representations and discourses which *fill it out*. (1977a: 324; emphasis in the original)

Hall then identifies two functions of ideology in Gramsci's writing on the institutions of normative coercion. Firstly, these institutions systematically construct a false inflection of the 'real relations' on which the system is based. This inflection of course, is ultimately designed to reinforce the rule of capital. Secondly, they generate a supporting network of discourses and theories which naturalize this inflection. It becomes 'common sense'. In Gramsci's sociology, common sense refers to the sedimented layers of consensual knowledge that sustain a shared construct of social reality in a particular class or social group. Because these layers correspond to false inflections, orchestrated by the central institutions of normative coercion, they are not equivalent to collective wisdom. The labour of the organic intellectual is therefore frequently concerned with the task of appropriating and deconstructing common sense. As Hall elaborates:

> It is precisely its 'spontaneous' quality, its transparency, its 'naturalness', its refusal to . . . examine the premises on which it is founded, its resistance to change or correction, its effect of instant recognition, and the closed circle in which it moves which makes common sense, at one and the same time, 'spontaneous', ideological and *unconscious*. You cannot learn, through common sense, *how things are*: you can only discover *where they fit* into the existing scheme of things. In this way, its very taken for grantedness is what establishes it as a medium in which its own premises and presuppositions are being rendered *invisible* by its own transparency. (1977a: 325–6; emphasis in original)

Several features of this passage repay attention. Firstly, Hall reinforces Gramsci's proposition that the central institutions of normative coercion function to naturalize the false inflections of representation so as to achieve adhesion or cementing. Common sense is one of the most potent expressions of this, because it organizes adhesion to the dominant order 'invisibly' and 'transparently'.

Secondly, at the subjective level, Hall locates adhesion in the seat of the unconscious. This assigns, so to speak, a 'pre-critical' dependency between the subject and the objective normative order, since it assumes that identification occurs before it becomes a question of conscious reflection.

Thirdly, against the classical Marxist position, which was also held by Lenin, Hall and Gramsci refuse to regard the state as the organized violence of the ruling class. Instead, they emphasize the 'positive', 'educative' functions of the central institutions of normative coercion. Schooling, the welfare system, political parties and even the police and judiciary cease to maintain popular consent when they stand 'above' society. This was the basis of Hall's attack on the rise of 'the disciplinary state' in his important public lecture to the Cobden Trust (1979), which identified reactionary elements in the police dedicated to the task of organizing 'disciplinary common sense' in the general public. By the same token, Hall and Gramsci regard ideology as operating normatively to 'position' subjects in the social formation. The educative influence of the institutions of normative coercion is concerned with placement. That is, with naturalizing the differences between classes and social groups so that, as Mrs Thatcher was so fond of saying, 'there is no alternative'.

Gramsci uses the term 'hegemony' to refer to the general governance of normalization. However, there are several nuances in his application of the concept that, *pace* Hall, arguably hinder its analytic value. Thus one can distinguish six meanings of the concept in Gramsci's work:

1 Hegemony refers to the engineering of voluntary, popular 'consent'. It operates at multiple levels in the social formation, the most significant of which are the economic, political and cultural.
2 Hegemony establishes the horizon for agency and practice within which conflicts are fought out, appropriated, obscured or contained (Hall and Jefferson 1976: 39).
3 Hegemony frames the terrain that ideas and conflicts occupy. It does not prescribe the content of debate but it *predisposes* debate to occur in particular directions. In social democracy, hegemony ultimately rests on the forces of coercion but it typically operates by persuasion and consent.
4 Hegemony positions difference. A common mistake in commentaries on hegemony is that the concept is held to refer to overcoming or erasing difference. In fact, hegemony operates through positioning difference so that some points of view are pronounced or accentuated and others are situated in a subaltern place (Hall 1995a: 69).
5 Hegemony refers to the form and content of political, intellectual and moral *leadership*. A power bloc acquires hegemonic control politically when it articulates the interests of other groups and harnesses them to its own interests. It cements

control morally and intellectually when it gains consent for the ideological conditions that must be fulfilled for the collective will of leadership to become possible.

6   Hegemony is the representation of mastering a determinate field of force. Gramsci believed that hegemony is never a historical-social moment of unity. On the contrary, it is inherently contradictory and therefore publicly contested. In addition, he held that hegemony is a moment in which many complex determinations are at work that cannot be reduced to the confrontation between capital and labour, or homogeneous cultural modes. A power bloc is assembled around multiple levels of contradiction, different inflections of struggle, different 'regions' of history. The articulation of hegemony depends on an ability to dissolve peripheral, discordant or contrary elements in the central ensemble of relations of leadership.

This fecundity of meaning makes the concept hard to read or apply. It is problematically conceptualized. It is difficult to judge what is actually being said on behalf of hegemony in any particular case. Is it about the exercise of leadership, or the institutional machinery that engineers consent? If it predisposes behaviour, how is predisposition mediated between strata? Doubtless Hall would say that Gramsci regarded these questions as requiring concrete analysis before answers can be given. However, the problem in their writings is that hegemony is often used in a general, descriptive way as well as in a concrete, particular way. The result is that the reader frequently finds it difficult to determine what is being claimed and the import of the implications that follow. This imprecision invites charges of slippage and modishness because it fails to generate testable propositions.

Hall would of course have no truck with the charge of imprecision. An important claim that Gramsci made on behalf of hegemony, and one which is warmly endorsed by Hall in his application of the Gramscian approach, is that the concept enables analysis to keep the levels of social formation distinct, and to identify how fusion elicits fundamental transformations in the system. As we shall see in the next section of the chapter, this connects up with Althusser's concept of 'overdetermination', just as his related concept of 'interpellation' builds on Gramsci's notion of the 'educative' effect of ideology. Morally and intellectually, hegemonic control is fulfilled when popular consent to the collective will of the leadership is achieved. However, there is a good deal of slippage between the various meanings of hegemony, both in Gramsci's work and Hall's application of Gramsci.

Gramsci's approach is typical of its time in attributing the central role to the state in reproducing normative order, and again Hall faithfully adheres to this premise.[9] Through its influence over schooling, the police, the judiciary, health care, employment legislation and the media, the state imprints its values on the public sphere. The struggle for hegemony is therefore a struggle over the political, moral and intellectual leadership of the state. Because Gramsci refuses to cast this leadership as either unified or universal, he assigns special significance to civil society as a site in which agents and networks resist and oppose hegemony. Hall's work on the encoding/decoding process establishes the idea that the correspondence between inscription/encoding and reception is never total. Central to his understanding of representation is that communication always involves a degree of latitude. As he puts it:

> Meaning is polysemic in its intrinsic nature: it remains inextricably context bound. It is caught in and constituted by the struggle to 'prefer' one among many meanings as the dominant. The dominance is not already inscribed in structures and events but it is constructed through the continuous struggle over a specific type of practice-representational practices. (1989d: 47)

Volosinov's 'multi-accentual' approach

Hall consolidates the argument that communication involves a 'struggle over meaning' (1986c), by incorporating Volosinov's (1973) 'multi-accentual' approach to language. Volosinov argues that the field of ideology consists of intersecting social interests. Language is the common denominator in ideological work. However, because different social interests intersect in the production, circulation and exchange of ideological signs, they accent meaning differently, that is, according to their contrasting positions in the social formation. For Volosinov, the sign is an arena of ideological struggle.

This is a significant distinction for Hall, because it frees ideology from a narrow identification with class. For Volosinov, ideology is not the reflection of the economic base because its production, circulation and exchange bend its meaning in different ways as an ordinary part of the communication process. On this reading, accretions and sediments adhere to the ideological sign as an ordinary part of the communication process, transforming its meaning through exchange. Volosinov's contribution historicizes the ideological sign and pre-empts a structuralist interpretation being cast on Hall's analysis of ideology.[10] The classical Marxist tradition located the foundations of ideology in determinate relations of class struggle. Volosinov's contribution retains the notion of struggle, but extends agency and intervention beyond the class base. The effect is twofold: first, it assigns a degree of autonomy to ideology and ideological struggle, so that economic reductionism is precluded; and second, it identifies civil society as a forum for undermining the political, moral and ideological fundamentals of hegemonic leadership.

The recognition of slippage in the production, circulation and exchange of ideology reinforces the Gramscian premise that the relation between the dominant ideology and common sense is not hierarchically fixed. In Gramsci's sociology, hegemonic leadership is designed to reproduce determinate relations of force which reinforce the rule of capital. However, at the same time, Gramsci maintains that hegemonic leadership is bound up with wider relations of force, wider 'multi-accented' agents that prevent hegemony from becoming 'universal'. A crucial responsibility of the organic intellectual, in the revolutionary sense of the term, is to engage consciously in hegemonic struggle so as to expose the limitations of 'false inflections' that contribute to the domination of the ruling bloc. It is because hegemony always elicits a contradictory, episodic and discordant system of domination that it gives the organic intellectual everything to play for.

For Gramsci, hegemony is always a question of contestation, always a matter of winning, securing and defending popular consent. The terrain is in constant process and at any given moment its character depends on the existing relations of force at the ideological level, between the classes, cabals and power factions involved in the struggle for dominance. He holds that classes can rule without gaining hegemony. Moments of 'coercion' can replace moments of 'consent', and the resulting crisis in hegemony need not necessarily culminate in the collapse of the system. This perspective invests particular significance in the concrete analysis of the hegemonic and non-hegemonic forms of domination and the elucidation of conjunctures of hegemony and the relations of class force which precipitate a schism or rupture in hegemony. Like Niccolò Machiavelli, Gramsci understood that power involves calculation, strategy, cooperation and compromise. In order to remain in dominance, the ruling bloc may offer concessions to the subaltern classes. But the logic of hegemonic leadership always seeks to reproduce national-popular consent (Hall, Lumley and McLennan 1978: 68–9).

The 'complex unity' is achieved through a mixture of force and persuasion. In Gramsci's sociology a crucial interface in this process refers to the relations between the state and civil society. The state directly coordinates and manages the forces of coercion. Civil society is a more amorphous space. It consists of a plethora of institutions, including the media, universities, schools, the church, parties, professions and trade unions, which address many foci, including science, politics, aesthetics and religion. The ruling bloc seeks to orchestrate these institutions to achieve hegemony over civil society. Practically speaking, this means engineering a combination of agreements, undertakings and cooperative arrangements between institutions in order to achieve correspondence between the foci of concerns in civil society and the ultimate goal of reproduction at the levels of economy, politics and culture. However, civil society is not subject to the direct authority of the state. It possesses relative autonomy and, as such, is the basis for significant contradictions between different institutions within the complex of civil society, the state and the ruling bloc. This accent is general to Gramscianism but it was of particular moment to Hall's British readers in the 1980s when for long periods Thatcherite hegemony seemed unassailable. Hall's essays in *Marxism Today* were one example of how, even at the apparent zenith of hegemonic control, agents in civil society operated to perforate hegemony.

Hall's appropriation of Gramsci enabled him to break with the vulgar Marxist principle of the pregiven, unified ideological subject. History was no longer theorized pre-eminently in terms of class struggle. Classes remain important for Hall, but following Gramsci, he revises his conception of them. Classes are now theorized as fragmented, fissiparous contradictory agents. The notion of the fragmentation of the subject was of course very much in the air in the late 1960s and 1970s. The symbolic significance of the events in Paris in 1968 cannot be underestimated in this regard. For many in the New Left, the old Marxist principle of the unfolding triumph of the proletariat was decisively exposed as a teleological ruse. The *Screen* group adapted psychoanalytic ideas from Lacan in their bid to elaborate the notion of the split subject. They privileged language and textuality in the organization of the subject and the operation of ideology. Hall and the CCCS circle held on to a more positive view of agency in which ideology is always perceived in terms of struggle, and hegemony is analysed as a perpetual process of winning and holding on to popular consent. It is a more concrete approach that pays attention to history and determinate levels of contestation and negotiation. Hegemony demonstrated the complex unity of the social formation and revealed the interrelations between the levels of economy, politics and ideology. It might be objected that this is also accomplished by the traditional sociological, multifactoral approach to agency and structure. What separated Gramsci's approach from this was, of course, his insistence that hegemony imposes determining priorities on agency. It is a structure in *dominance*, a structure that can be undone through concrete struggle.

For Hall, the next decisive stage in developing this perspective was supplied by conscripting ideas from Louis Althusser. The marriage between the Gramscian and Althusserian traditions would reach its fullest expression in *Policing the Crisis* (Hall et al. 1978), which is the most impressive achievement of the Birmingham Centre under Hall's leadership. An account of this work will be postponed until the next chapter, since to understand it correctly we need to delve into the nature of Althusser's influence on Hall, and also to consider Laclau and Mouffe's (1985) revisionist engagement with the concept of hegemony.

Althusser, difference and the 'imaginary' relation of ideology

In the late 1960s and 1970s, Hall identified Saussure, Lévi-Strauss and Althusser as the principal intellectual resources in the structuralist tradition from which a structuralist approach to culture might be developed.[11] Recall that he was pulled towards structuralism by what he took to be the deficiencies of culturalism, namely parochialism, overdependence on class analysis and humanism. Today, structuralism is routinely criticized for producing abstraction and closure in social and cultural analysis. But it is important to remember that for Hall, and other members of the New Left, it originally promised liberation from what they regarded as the naive essentialism of culturalism.

Of the three intellectual resources identified by Hall, the work of Althusser quickly became ascendant. In part, this reflected fashion. The New Left credited Althusser's rereading of Marx, with its emphasis on the 'break' in classical Marxism, its principled antihistoricism and defence of the scientific basis of Marxist enquiry, as the most significant revision of Marxism in the 1960s and early 1970s. In his most sustained reflection on Althusser, Hall (1985a) identifies three significant contributions in the Althusserian approach.

In the first place, Althusser directly criticized historicism, humanism and empiricism in Marxism. He insisted that social formations constitute a 'complex structured whole', thus reinforcing the principle of 'complex unity' adumbrated in Gramsci's perspective. Althusser rejected the Hegelian notion that history is a process of a self-unfolding essence. Like Gramsci, he imputed reductionism and historicism to vulgar Marxism, and sought to recast causality in agency as a matrix of distinct chains interlinked by contingency rather than laws of historical necessity.

Secondly, Althusser departed from a 'monistic' conception of Marxism by arguing that social contradictions are various, with distinct origins; and that the contradictions behind history are not universal, and do not have the same consequences. Marx's emphasis in the 1857 Introduction on 'many determinations' is therefore redoubled. Remember, after 1968 it became fashionable to maintain that the subject is always and already split, that language and symbol attached to determinate regimes of power shape general conceptions of embodiment and emplacement, and that theory must live with and in difference. Hall cites the work of Derrida and Foucault as advancing these analytical distinctions (Hall 1985a: 92–3). However, he regards Althusser's work to be superior because it resists fetishizing either specificity or difference as 'micro-politics', or positing a perpetual slippage of the signifier. Instead, it embraces the necessary unevenness of a complex structure in which both difference and unity are always present. In a word, it acknowledges the importance of analysing the levels of politics, culture, economy and ideology in the social formation in terms of *unity in difference*. For Hall, the great advantage of this perspective is that it alerts the intellectual labourer to the necessity of regarding history and agency as integrally composed of several different levels and kinds of determination. Again, the overlap with Gramsci is evident. The fact that Hall comments on it at some length suggests that he regarded the fusion of Gramscianism with Althusserianism to offer a potentially decisive departure in the Marxist tradition (1985a: 101, 111; Hall, Lumley and McLennan 1978: 56–65).

Conversely, Hall was not oblivious to the tensions between the two traditions. In particular, Althusser's attempt to replace Gramsci's civil society/state distinction with the more formal concept of the 'ideological apparatuses' is identified as a source of friction (Hall, Lumley, McLennan 1978: 62–4). In time, Hall came to regard the functionalism of Althusser's position on ideological state apparatuses as a serious defect. Althusser's enlarged conception of the state insisted on the importance of class struggle at the level of ideology. But this insistence reads like a non sequitur given that he already maintains that ideology is always inscribed in the ideological state apparatuses, and further, that these structure the condition of dominance in society.

Hall became increasingly dissatisfied with the circularity and closure in this account of ideology. In particular, he realized that it involves the recrudescence of class reductionism, since Althusser assumes that the ideological state apparatuses structure dominance to reproduce the interests of the ruling class. Nonetheless, for most of the 1970s, at the theoretical level, the attempt to merge aspects of the Althusserian and Gramscian traditions stamps Hall's own work, and the collaborative labour in Birmingham, with its distinctive imprimatur.[12]

Thirdly, Althusser offered a reading that presents ideology as the imaginary relation of individuals to the real conditions in which they live. He argues that ideology is the process of fixing an imaginary unity through which we are able to recognize ourselves as subjects. The argument is clearly indebted to the psychoanalytic tradition, particularly the work of Jacques Lacan (1977). According to Lacan the unified self is always and already constituted in a state of *misrecognition*. The decisive influence here is the mirror stage. Between the ages of six months and eighteen months the infant first confronts its image in the mirror. Lacan argued that the image of unity and solidity is a chimera. The infant identifies with the image, but this is misrecognition because it represses the inchoate and unstable state of the subject's body and psyche. Misrecognition carries over into language and therefore culture.

Lacan's perspective is quite controversial and has been widely criticized.[13] However, it is difficult to overemphasize the impact of the theory in philosophical, literary and sociological circles during the 1960s and 1970s. The work of the *Screen* group drew heavily on it, prompting Hall to fire a broadside against them (1980c), complaining that their position universalizes ideology and thus precludes the notion of struggle. For Hall (1985a), Althusser's appropriation of Lacan avoids this trap. Althusser, to repeat, maintains that ideology is the imaginary relation of individuals to the real conditions in which they live. The function of ideology is to reproduce the social relations of production. The state is one of the principal sites in which political and moral practices of different kinds are condensed. Althusser introduced the concept of ideological state apparatuses (ISAs) to refer to state-controlled institutions that articulate and disseminate into a complexly structured instance a range of political, moral and cultural discourses and practices. Examples include schools, universities, social work agencies, training boards and state research centres. These institutions engage directly in the task of reproducing the social relations of production.

However, Althusser argues that increasingly under capitalism, reproduction is elicited through non-government organizations that entwine with the government in civil society, notably the media, trade unions, charities and political parties. A distinctive feature of his argument is that he insists that ideology operates through the 'practices and rituals' of everyday life, and is realized in the mental events communicated, principally, through language. This allows Althusser to claim, famously, that 'ideology is material' because it is 'inscribed in practices'.

Another distinctive feature of Althusser's argument is that it breaks with the vulgar Marxist premise that ideologies produce false consciousness. For Althusser, ideologies represent systems of ideas, concepts, myths, common sense and images through which men and women live in an imaginary relation to the real conditions of existence. The purpose of these systems is to *interpellate* or 'fix' humans into forms of subjectivity and agency that perpetuate social reproduction. Althusser borrows the term interpellation from Lacan, and he shares Lacan's view that the process works primarily at an unconscious level. Thus we are 'summoned' or 'hailed' into being as subjects by discourses and practices that 'recruit' us as 'agents' of our own destinies. In as much as this is so, ideology performs a positive function in supporting and reinforcing agency. True, the inflections that it places on subjectivity and action tend towards the reproduction of the existing hierarchy of power. But ideologies do not operate through single ideas; they operate in clusters, interrelations and semantic fields with discursive configurations. This emphasis on variety and difference within unity is crucial for Hall (1985a: 104) because it shows how ideological consensus or common sense may be ruptured, interrupted or contravened through resistance. But it does not follow from this that resistance necessarily produces 'truth' or 'reality'. Ideology cannot be contrasted with experience or illusion, as occurs in culturalism, because for Althusser there is no way of experiencing the 'real relations' of a particular formation outside of its cultural and ideological categories.

Again, the parallels with Gramsci are evident. Gramsci's sociology is concerned with winning popular consent through hegemony. Althusser wants to demonstrate how subjects are positioned through interpellation, and more broadly how social reproduction is articulated. The neo-Althusserian concepts of articulation and overdetermination were used extensively by Hall in the 1970s and it is worth commenting on their technical meaning. Articulation refers to a combination of distinct determinations, requiring particular preconditions and sustained by specific processes, that contribute to the reproduction of social and economic relations. The combination is not fixed or eternal but instead is best conceptualized as a *process* geared to establishing 'differences within unity'.

There are some difficulties with Hall's application of the concept. Wood alleges considerable slippage in Hall's use of the concept. He counts at least five different meanings of articulation in Hall's work:

1   The 'ensemble of relations' which constitute society.
2   The 'discursive procedures' that transform ideology into culture or combine determinate ideologies together.
3   The 'social force' that 'makes' conceptions of the world.
4   The 'many autonomous' parts of civil society that elicit hegemony.
5   The 'different social practices' and 'range' of political discourses transformed into the operation of 'rule and domination' (Wood 1998: 407).

Hall's interest in the concept derives from his dissatisfaction with the essentialism and humanism of culturalism in which agency is attributed indiscriminately to the subject. Following Althusser, Hall wants to replace this with the notion of 'effective agency', which locates action in the 'complex structured whole' of 'many determinations', each with distinct levels of operation combined to express a unity in difference.

The concept of overdetermination is introduced to explain this unity. Althusser borrowed it from psychoanalysis, where it refers to the merger and fusion of causal processes which result in a condition of symbolic wholeness. The 'reality' of any given condition of fusion is not a matter of ultimate literality for two reasons. First, the multicausal processes that have brought about fusion are laden with the fantasies and illusions that psychoanalysis identifies in all psychological forms. Second, fusion is always subject to contingency. Its appearance, and disappearance, are matters of interrelated processes and not laws of historical necessity. For Althusser, overdetermination operates at an unconscious level to reproduce symbolic unity and difference in the social whole. This is crucial for both Althusser and Hall since both wish to refute the Hegelian view of history as a process of 'self-unfolding'. The concept of overdetermination negates the dichotomy between essence and appearance by denying an ultimate literal 'base' for the symbolic, because the latter itself derives from signification. Identity and patterns of collective life therefore lack 'essence', because they are inseparable from the cultural and ideological categories that constitute the social whole.

Hall's application of Althusser in the 1970s was at times rather gruelling. Colin Sparks comments on the 'increasingly baroque structure' of the Althusserian approach (1996: 88), and argues that by the 1980s Hall's work on representation and ideology was visibly shifting away from Althusser's 'scientific' approach and following the turn towards discourse taken by Laclau and Mouffe (2001).[14] Hall himself attests to a sense of fatigue in 'battling on' with ideology and acknowledges 'loosening the moorings' during the 1980s (1997a: 31). Why did this loosening occur? And what results did it have for Hall's approach to representation and ideology?

Laclau and Mouffe and the discursive turn

Overdetermination gives an approach to representation and ideology that rejects the notion of essence, base or underlying reality. This combats both the essentialism of Hegelian historicism and the reductionism of vulgar Marxism. Both advances were significant for Hall, as he laboured to steer a path away from the pitfalls of culturalism and economic reductionism, to a theoretically more productive union, comprising the engagement of culturalism with concrete experience and the sang-froid of structuralism. Althusser reinforced Gramsci's emphasis on analysing social formations and complex, layered configurations of power, process, difference and contingency, and legitimated the political significance of struggle as the interruption of hegemony. Indeed, he went further than Gramsci in breaking with orthodox essentialism by affirming the incomplete, open and politically negotiable character of identity *per se*.

However, there was also an impediment in the Althusserian position. This concerns Althusser's proposition that, *in the last instance*, the economy is the determining agent. If the laws of development in society are determined by the economy, then the relations between overdetermined instances and the last instance must be causally privileged in favour of the latter. Therefore the gain made in insisting on the overdetermined nature of representation and ideology is weakened by privileging the economy as the determining agent.

The challenge then is to recast the notion of overdetermination so as to preclude the inference that materialism exists outside of meaning. The main contribution in this respect came from Laclau and Mouffe (2001) via their appropriation of Foucault's concept of discourse. They reject both the classic notion of pregiven identity, and Althusser's privileging of the economy. Instead, they hold that identity must be conceptualized as discursively constituted from the different, contingently interrelated resources of the symbolic order. They make four crucial distinctions in revising the relationship between identity and the symbolic order (2001: 105). *Articulation* refers to any practice establishing a relation among resources that modifies identity. *Discourse* is the structured totality reproduced and constituted through articulatory practice. *Moments* refer to the different positions articulated within discourse. An *element* is any difference not discursively articulated.

This is the discursive turn in the Left's approach to representation and ideology and influenced Hall greatly after the mid 1980s. It refutes the principle of autonomous agency that underpins classical liberal political economy, and it breaks with Althusser's unfortunate privileging of the economy. Following Gramsci, it retains the principle that identity is positioned through difference, and that positioning is contingent and subject to reconfiguration. Neither agency nor structure are assigned priority in explaining meaning and development. Instead meaning and development are reconceptualized as partially fixed by the practice of articulation. This practice proceeds from the field of discourse, which is conceived as an uneven, interwoven social terrain of infinite representation. The latter caveat is important, since it retains the Althusserian emphasis on the overdetermination of any given moment. Representation does not follow laws of necessity. Instead, Laclau and Mouffe stress the 'radically contingent' constitution of all discursive formations and practices of articulation. Society is therefore deprived of any realist explanatory power as a pregiven, external or constraining force on agency, because it is redefined as the effect of articulation. Indeed, through the conscription of Lacan's distinction between the real and the imaginary, Laclau and Mouffe submit that the symbolic force of society as a metaphor of human existence reflects the recognition of the absence or lack of a real foundation of agency and experience. The work of ideology and politics is to deflect consciousness from this absence by 'suturing' or filling in the lack of the subject.

Laclau and Mouffe therefore promote a view of identity as multiple, discontinuous, fragmented and dispersed. At the same time, they point to the networks of power through which identity and meaning are partially fixed. These networks are never fully transparent and their obscurity in everyday experience is partly a function of ideological practice. On this reading, ideology is the fusion of signifier and signified in a 'moment' of hegemonic authority. This does not foreclose struggle as a meaningful practice. On the contrary, struggle is identified as the only way to decouple the chains of articulation that fix identity. Radical politics therefore shifts from the traditional Marxist concern with building unity to the new problematic of constructing solidarity around difference.

This is the main problematic addressed by Hall's writings after the mid 1980s. Laclau and Mouffe break with Althusser's model of ideology as a uniform, ahistorical force and replace it with an approach that recognizes the specificity of conjuncture, infinite semiosis in discourse and the radical contingency of articulation. Their appropriation of Foucault and Lacan prioritizes discourse in the investigation of agency and the imaginary in the analysis of structure. One important consequence is to disempower class analysis. For Laclau and Mouffe, the interpellation of subjects as class formations or class agents is always an effect of discourse and never a reflection of concrete social reality. 'Bourgeois' and 'proletariat' are representations that elucidate some aspects of the social formation, but to attribute reality to them is to assign misplaced concreteness. In fact, Laclau and Mouffe reconceptualize struggle as involving 'the power bloc' and the 'people', a device that Hall himself increasingly employed after the mid 1980s.

Characteristically, Hall goes along with a good deal of the discursive turn without ever becoming a fully paid-up member. In particular, he was troubled by Laclau and Mouffe's notion of the radical contingency of discursive reconfiguration on the grounds that it translates identity and meaning as free-floating categories (Hall 1997a: 32). Hall remained enough of a Marxist to insist on historical specificity in the analysis of politics and culture. His deployment of the discursive turn limited the notion of radical contingency by grounding conjuncture and articulation in broader historical and political narratives. 'I loosen the moorings,' he declared, 'but I won't float. Identity is not fixed, but it's not nothing either. The task is how to think the fact that identities are important to us, and register some continuities along a spectrum, but we're never just what we were' (1997a: 33). This is the perspective that informs Hall's most recent work on the politics of difference, hybridity and hyphenated identity.

Tremors of disquiet: the Centre and the high Althusserian moment

Ideology continues to be a central theme in Hall's analysis of culture. However, in contrast to the high Althusserian moment, the emphasis is now on the point of suture between the discourses and practices that attempt to interpellate us as social subjects, and the processes that produce subjectivities, which construct us as reflexive agents. Arguably an unacknowledged influence here is the tremors of disquiet surrounding the proposition that there is no space outside ideology that emanated from some of Hall's associates in Birmingham in the 1970s and 1980s. John Clarke (1992) notes that there was always an 'uneasy and critical' tension in Birmingham around almost every formulation of ideology, culture and consciousness. He distinguishes two broad fronts of tension. First, the conflict between those who addressed the specificity of cultural orders, most obviously through ethnographic study, and those who sought to elucidate determinate connections between specificity and class. Second, the tension between the culturalist tendency, which regarded culture to be the product of social practice by social agents, and the structuralist tendency, which theorized social practice and agency as informed by structural determinacy. Hall's application of Althusser's model of ideology touched on these tensions at nearly every point. It was interpreted as a decisive move towards structuralism, even though Hall always insisted that his purpose was to synthesize the best elements of culturalism and structuralism.

The Women's Studies Group (WSG), inaugurated in the Centre in 1974, provided a different challenge by attributing negligence in the Centre's treatment of women. They alleged that women constituted an 'underdeveloped theoretical concern' in the CCCS

(Women's Studies Group 1978: 14). By way of evidence, the Editorial Group of *Women Take Issue* pointed to women's 'invisibility' in the collective writing and in 'much' intellectual work conducted in the Centre. Woundingly, they highlighted the 'general tendency' in the Centre towards an *'unself-*conscious use of theoretical language' which was instrumental in 'perpetuating knowledge as a property of the few' (1978: 7–8; emphasis in the original). As we have seen, Hall laboured long and hard to try and enhance the sophistication of theory in the Centre, and there can be no doubt that this comment was aimed squarely at him. On the subjective level, most members of the WSG held Hall in high esteem. Both Charlotte Brundson (1996) and Angela McRobbie (2000) subsequently paid warm tribute to his powers of innovation and general openness. However, the WSG's placing of the remark identified Hall – arguably the Centre's most prominent theorist – as an active, albeit unintended cog of male-stream domination.

In addition, Hall's management of the Centre was also reprimanded. The WSG asserted that: 'we found it extremely difficult to participate in CCCS groups and felt, without being able to articulate it, that it was a case of the masculine domination of both intellectual work and the environment in which it was being carried out' (1978: 11).

The WSG did not seek to split from the Centre. On the contrary, engagement with the general intellectual work conducted in the Centre was identified as the pivotal strategy in raising consciousness of male-stream prominence in the Centre. At the same time, the WSG recognized the urgent requirement to clear a space in the CCCS that would be more sensitive and supportive to women. To this end the Women's Forum (WF) was established in 1976 as a closed woman's space available to all women in CCCS. Its purpose was twofold: first, to raise general feminist issues; and second, to act as a conduit to the Women's Liberation Movement. The establishment of the WF directly challenged the validity of the ethos of accessibility and collaboration cultivated by Hall during his directorship.

In his later work Hall pays tribute to feminism for being an element in recasting his whole approach to culture and theory. But in 1978, as he tried to steer the Centre's major projects on the generation of the law and order society and racism through to publication in *Policing the Crisis* (Hall et al. 1978) and *The Empire Strikes Back* (CCCS 1982), and at a juncture when CCCS was under scrutiny from unsympathetic elements in the university's managerial hierarchy, it was a very uncomfortable moment for him. Throughout the Birmingham years, Hall prided himself on widening access and establishing non-hierarchical relations across the board. The WSG recognized Hall's sincerity in this respect. However, the burden of their criticism was that despite the reflexive, questing spirit nurtured by Hall in the CCCS, women were finally treated as 'absent', and the recognition that women's lives are structured through subjugation was not realized (Women's Studies Group 1978; Brundson 1996). The difficulties of this moment were, perhaps, one factor in Hall's decision to quit Birmingham and accept the Chair of Sociology at the Open University in 1979.

On a different flank within the Centre, both Dick Hebdige (1979; 1988) and Paul Willis (1977; 1978; 1990; 2001), albeit labouring in contrasting intellectual traditions, produced work that challenged many aspects of Hall's involvement with Althusserianism. Hebdige's work draws first on poststructuralist theory, notably the writings of Roland Barthes, and later postmodernism to disconnect style and taste from the imperialism of ideology. He moves from reading style as articulation to exploring it as the free play of indeterminate signifiers rather than what they signify. Structures of taste are analysed as objects rather than 'bearers' of ideology. The Althusserian model of ideology is explicitly rejected as 'monolithic', although the associated concept of interpellation is retained. Hebdige invites us to regard hegemony as a 'precarious moving equilibrium' (1988: 206–7) and to embrace the postmodern emphasis on flux and the absence of anchored subjects. In brief, he emulsifies Gramscianism with postmodernism, a move that Harris judges to be understandable, but also indefensible (1992: 42–4).[15]

If Hebdige used the indeterminacy of the signifier to challenge the proposition that there is no space outside ideology, Willis resorted to more concrete means, based in fieldwork practice. His famous studies of 'the lads' and hippies in the English Midlands (1977; 1978) demonstrate that emplacement and embodiment cannot be satisfactorily explained by ideology. His argument is complex, but at its core is the proposition that what he calls 'sensuous knowing' (2001: 35) is the foundation of the human subject. Sensuous knowing transcends ideology by holding off or invalidating practices of normative coercion. 'The laff', 'the crack', 'the piss-take', 'the put on', and swearing belong to profane culture, but their profanity lies not in being reactively determined, in the last instance, by ideology, but in demarcating a space that ideology cannot reach and therefore does not recognize. Throughout Willis's work human creativity is privileged as an anarchic force that cannot be muzzled or erased by ideology. The proximate conditions of embodiment and emplacement provide us with concrete resources to engage in social signification that are, so to speak, beyond ideology. His analysis of how the commodity form simultaneously fetishizes us and, through the creation of living, moving, thinking and acting communities of consumers, is defetishized through exchange illustrates how meaning is not contained by discourse. As Willis puts it:

> Whereas ideological and official linguistic forms seek to annex all lived meanings to their own powerful constitution of meaning – good citizen, worker, student, etc. – socio-symbolic practices stabilize alternative liminal, uncoded or residually coded identities and meanings. They are held sensuously and practically and therefore relatively *outside* and resistant to dominant linguistic meaning. They refuse to be swallowed whole. 'Integrated circuits' open or reinvent what should have been closed by those who 'take the floor'. New or unseen or differently used 'use values' – smoking and drinking in the case of 'the lads' – open up new avenues for meaning and activity showing practical grounds for autonomy and independence. (2001: 36; emphasis in the original)

Hall, in the high Althusserian moment, would probably have regarded the very idea of 'uncoded' identities and meanings as perverse, which for Willis is part of the problem. Present in his ethnographic work is the implicit criticism that Hall's use of ideology is objectionable because it 'writes over' embodiment and emplacement by phrasing them as a function of ideological positioning. In a revealing footnote, Willis comments on the absence of sensuous and somatic meaningfulness within 'discursive' approaches: 'The "sutures", hybridities and articulations of discourses all point to the "absent presence" of numerous small human sewings of profane material' (2001: 134).[16] What this implies is that Hall's use of ideology and representation is too selective and suggests an implausible totality in the concept of ideology; and further that Hall's conception of cultural agency is unsatisfactory.

After the mid 1980s Cultural Studies abandoned the notion of difference in unity and replaced it with a postmodern concern with diversity and dedifferentiation. Hebdige's work takes over the Barthesian theme of the pleasure of the text, and enlarges it to argue that cultural aesthetics is a neglected category in Birmingham work. Within the Birmingham circle, Willis's socio-symbolic approach constitutes in some ways the most significant critical departure from Hall. He was evidently uncomfortable with the textual reading of ideology and representation that Hall attempted in the 1970s. He showed no interest in following Hall in the discursive turn of the 1980s. His defence of ethnography over theory as the locus of the 'real' work (2001) may be taken as a comment that Birmingham work on ideology and representation in the 1970s, and the shift towards the discursive turn had gone too far in the direction of privileging theory over the concrete. Interestingly, Hall attributed the same error to Laclau and Mouffe (Hall 1997a: 32–4). Certainly, a common criticism of Hall's writings on representation and ideology in the 1970s and 1980s was that they were too abstract.

Yet the work done by Hall in these years was foundational. Through exhaustive theoretical manoeuvres, he established interpellation, overdetermination, articulation and later discourse as axial principles in his approach to Cultural Studies. His utilization of Althusser and Laclau and Mouffe dismounted the traditional socialist emphasis on class as the central influence in ideology. He retained the premise that the capitalist mode of production is the arena in which subjects, meanings and agency are situated. Traditional socialism sought to build unity around class. The new realism recognized that sutures in identity and meaning are the inevitable corollary of overdetermination and representation. The central political task is therefore redefined as the construction of solidarity around difference. In fact, Hall never abandoned the central importance of class. Instead he takes over Gramsci's emphasis on the complex unity of social formations and demonstrates how class is not the only variant of exploitation in play, filling out meanings, articulating the 'common sense' of a conjuncture and representing the 'hard road' from which all political calculation begins. The principal other variants are racism, sexism and imperialism. After the discursive turn, Hall devotes more energy to the task of exploring how they are naturalized in the social formation. However, naturalization is never theorized as stable or fixed. Hall moved towards a position that regarded identity as never fixed or singular, but multiply constructed across different, often intersecting and antagonistic discourses, practices and positions.

3

State and Society

Hall never fully abandoned class, but radically modified its significance in cultural analysis. Likewise, he never evacuated the
Gramscian proposition that hegemony in mass democracies is
reliant on the state. The *May Day Manifesto*, formally edited by
Raymond Williams (1968), included substantial contributions from
Hall and Edward Thompson.[1] It was striking in its attack on 'the
affluent society', 'consensus politics', the inadequate levels of public
provision in education, health and welfare, and the general failure
of the Labour government to seize the initiative for socialist transformation. Interestingly, Hall returned to all of these themes thirty
years later in his condemnation of new Labour as 'the great moving
nowhere show' (1998a).[2] The premise of the *Manifesto* is that the
state is necessarily the central institution in the management and
leadership of society and, as such, constitutes the real lever to socialist transformation. Of course Hall's position has not remained static.
He has praised 'people's events', like Live Aid, Band Aid and Sport
Aid, in challenging the dominance of capital, and social movements
such as feminism, lesbian and gay liberation and environmental-
ism, as innovative contributions to socialist renewal (1988a: 231–67).
The New Times thesis also recognizes the limited room for manoeuvre provided by globalization and the rise of what Castells calls
'the network society' (1996).

For all that, Hall remains stubbornly faithful to the *Manifesto*'s
proposition that control of the state is pivotal. As he puts it:

> Though the state is a contradictory force, it does have a systematic
> tendency to draw together the many lines of force and power in

society and condense them into a particular 'system of rule'. In that sense, the state does continue to organize and orchestrate the space of capital accumulation in its broad societal aspects, and hold a particular, exploitative social order in place. (1988a: 230)

Of course, Hall is not interested in acquiring control of the state as an end in itself. He harbours no illusions about the state's negative propensity to tyrannize social life. However, he also acknowledges that because the state holds a particular (capitalist) exploitative order in place, it is the indispensable instrument for dismantling this order and, eventually, implementing popular initiatives that ensure the passage of power from the state to society. This reasserts Gramsci's premise that a crucial interface in politics and ideology is between the state and civil society. As I noted in the last chapter, Althusser's concept of the ideological state apparatus tends to present civil society as the reflection of state imperatives. For Hall this move indicates unacceptable functionalism, and it is one reason why Althusser's influence ceases to be prominent in his work after the discursive turn.

Like Gramsci, Hall allocates more autonomy to civil society and stresses the contradictions of ideology in complex society. His view of the socialized state envisages a partnership between the state and civil society. This is offered as the prerequisite for the transition to democratization in personal associations and compulsory responsibilities, in the family and the neighbourhood, as well as in the office and workplace. Hall proposes that the socialized state must progressively yield space to the variety of different forms, social movements and initiatives engendered in civil society.

The necessity of transition is an article of faith in Hall's work, as it is for the whole of the New Left project. Effective politics involves the use of political parties and social movements to socialize the state apparatus and transform it to achieve the liberation of human capacities. In Hall's analysis the Labour Party is positioned as the decisive agent. However, Hall's account of postwar politics in Britain constantly returns to the theme that Labour in power has been insufficiently radical. Faced with the choice of socializing the state and the means of production, or tailoring redistributive ideology to the interests of capital, Labour governments have consistently chosen the latter option. Other approaches emphasize the declining significance of the state and political parties, and the rise of 'subpolitics' and active citizenship (Beck 1992; 1999; Castells 1996; 1997; 1998). Hall's work certainly recognizes the significance of active citizenship and social movements in social change. However, it is quite traditional in enjoining the pivotal significance of the state in the transformation of society.

Hegemony and the state: 1880s–1920s

Hall's discussion of the state concentrates on the struggle and counter-struggle to win hegemony. It comprises the most histori-cally detailed analysis in his writing, culminating in what is arguably his most impressive work, *Policing the Crisis* (Hall et al. 1978), and paving the way for his important and high-profile criti-cal engagement with Thatcherism in the 1980s. He argues that the period between the 1880s and 1920s was formative in the construc-tion of modern state and society in Britain (Hall 1984c; Hall and Schwarz 1985). The settlement of 1945 that created the welfare state and extended public ownership was constructed on a constitu-tional, corporatist and welfare framework established between the 1880s and 1920s. In this period the laissez-faire state was replaced by what Hall calls 'the representative-interventionist state'.[3]

Hall portrays this transition as a complex, multilayered process. The context for it was the irreversible decline in Britain's imperial fortunes. After the 1880s, Britain gradually ceased to be 'the work-shop of the world', and was challenged by other national economies, notably Germany and the USA. The First World War accelerated this process, exposing structural vulnerabilities in in-dustry, education and welfare provision. Hall's analysis of the rise of the representative-interventionist state applies classic Gramscian principles. Thus reconstruction is depicted as being correlative with complex tendencies in the social formation that precipitated the construction of a new social bloc intent on winning consent from a significant section of the working class. The transition was accom-plished by a series of calculated coalitions and concessions, a shift-ing 'war of positions', notably in the areas of constitutional reform, redistributive taxation, social reform and trade union rights. The economic climate of falling prices, declining profits and increasing unemployment formed the context for change and reconstruction. But, as might be expected, Hall's analysis eschews economic reduc-tionism in favour of an approach that regards economic change as inflected through a 'complex unity' of social, political and ideologi-cal manoeuvres and alliances. For Hall, the complex unity at issue formed the assumptions, practices and positions of the welfare settlement achieved in 1945. By the same token it is the terrain that the New Right, led by Margaret Thatcher, sought to shatter in the 1980s.

Hall submits that the erosion of the laissez-faire state derived from a range of fissures 'from below' developing along different lines to influence state policy and action (1984c: 25–6). Some of these can best be described in class terms, notably the unrest in some sections of the working class over unemployment, the formation of the Labour Party and the desire of the bourgeois Liberal Party to form an alliance with Labour. Some of the new forces had no evident class character and may be most usefully described as 'social movements'; the suffragettes are a good example. Hall had not yet articulated his New Times thesis, but his analysis here supports the inference that class analysis is too limiting to elucidate the relations of force that elevated the representative-interventionist state into dominance. Class interest and class position are 'useful' in the analysis of ideological formation, but they are 'not sufficient' to explain the 'actual empirical disposition' and 'movement of ideas' (Hall 1988a: 45). The party political system is the key mechanism in which 'democratic forces' are positioned in national policy. By the end of the 1920s, the rudiments of two-party constitutionalism founded on universal suffrage, the prime institutions for corporatist bargaining and a system of public welfare provision were in place. The ideology of collectivism was ascendant over market liberalism, and the elements of the new social order and the consensus politics of social democracy were cemented (Hall and Schwarz 1985: 31).

The postwar settlement drew sustenance from all these elements. In some ways, the Attlee government of 1945 signified continuity rather than change. Hall maintains that the long postwar era of consensus politics was defined by fundamental agreement between Labour and Conservative governments on the necessity for the managed economy and the welfare state. They endorsed and applied a system of corporatist control involving an informal partnership between the state bureaucracy, capital (business and industrial leaders) and organized labour (trade union representatives). This was sustained and strengthened by the long consumer boom of the 1950s that accompanied postwar economic reconstruction.

However, the late 1960s is identified as the start of a crisis in hegemony in which the state gradually abandons consensus politics and adopts the politics of coercion. This is the slide into the disciplinarian 'law and order' society that formed the spine of Hall's analysis in *Policing the Crisis* (Hall et al. 1978) and his controversial lecture

to the Cobden Trust (1979), which criticized the extension of powers
to the police.

Resistance through Rituals

Resistance through Rituals (Hall and Jefferson 1976) rehearses a conceptual model and set of case studies that would be more extensively developed in *Policing the Crisis*. It examines British youth
subculture in terms of a negotiation between the 'hegemonic' dominant culture and the subordinate 'parent' culture. Hegemony is presented in orthodox Gramscian terms as the 'moment' in which a
ruling power bloc imposes a horizon on subordinate agency by
winning consent. The 1950s is described as a classic period of 'hegemonic domination' in Britain in which the ideology of 'consensus'
coupled with 'the affluent society' is deployed to 'dismantle'
working-class resistance and deliver 'spontaneous consent' to the
authority of the dominant class (Hall and Jefferson 1976: 40). The
embourgeoisement thesis is cited as evidence of the 'natural' belief
in consensus society that the conversion of the working class to
middle-class values and lifestyles is inevitable. The spurious, constructed nature of 'consensus' and the overblown premise that technology and 'progressive' mixed economy management inevitably
produce 'the affluent society' and embourgeoisement is cogently
stressed.

As with *Policing the Crisis*, the 1960s and 1970s is portrayed as a
period of increasing class polarization in which hegemony is challenged at many levels. In the 1950s the rising disposable income of
youth and their increasing visibility in the social landscape make
them a symbol of wider social change. To be sure they are a highly
ambivalent symbol. While increasing affluence is widely regarded
as a sign of progress, it also signifies the redefinition of traditional
social, moral and cultural boundaries. 'Movements which disturb
society's normative contours', the authors note, 'mark troubling
times' (Hall and Jefferson 1976: 71).

The concepts of 'moral panic' and 'media spiral' which are
pivotal in the analysis of the rise of 'law and order society' in *Policing the Crisis* debut here. Thus moral panics are portrayed as constructing 'stereotypes' and 'scapegoats', and the media 'amplifies'
the threat to the social order. The police and courts are depicted as
soft agents of control. 'Get tough' policies are demanded as the
antidote to the creeping liberalism of 'the permissive society'. The

closing sentences of the study prefigure the extraordinary confidence and passion exhibited in more mature form in *Policing the Crisis*:

> The dominant culture [sought] to seek and find in 'youth' the folk devils to people its nightmares: the nightmare of a society which, in some fundamental way, had lost its sway and authority over its young, which had failed to win their hearts, minds and consent, a society teetering towards 'anarchy', secreting, at its heart, what Mr Powell so eloquently described as an unseen and nameless 'Enemy'. The whole collapse of hegemonic domination to which this shift from the 1950s to the 1970s bears eloquent witness was written – etched – in youthful lines. (Hall and Jefferson 1976: 74)

Gramsci is already the dominant theoretical influence in *Resistance through Rituals*. But Althusser's theory of ideology is also applied, notably in respect of the analysis of skinhead subculture. Althusser argued that ideology presupposes both a 'real' and imaginary relation between groups and the conditions of their existence. Ideology is an overdetermination of unity between real and imaginary relations. It is frequently expressed through nostalgia. Thus Hall and Jefferson explain the territoriality and the strong sense of solidarity expressed in the shaved heads and fashion of the skinheads as an attempt to represent the sense of locality and place that town-planners and speculators are destroying through urban redevelopment (1976: 48). Interestingly there is no resort to Williams's (1973) concepts of oppositional or alternative cultures in the study. This reflects a concern to present resistance as diffuse, and to pre-empt the inference that it constitutes a counter-hegemonic force.

Although *Resistance through Rituals* strongly reasserts the importance of class in the analysis of youth subculture, it seeks to avoid the implication that resistance signifies nascent class revolution. Hall and Jefferson note that the character of youth subculture is segmented from 'parent' subordinate working-class culture (1976: 69). For example, they maintain that youth work out at an 'imaginary' level a contradiction in their class situation. But this is very different from politically motivated, effective class action. While the emphasis throughout is on a balance of forces challenging hegemonic rule, class struggle is identified as the primary organic contradiction. This emphasis is also stressed in *Policing the Crisis*, which was published two years later.

Policing and the drift towards the law
and order society

Policing the Crisis (Hall et al. 1978) is Hall's most substantial work.
It fuses the Birmingham work on encoding and decoding in the
media, youth subculture, race, crime, representation and ideology
into a richly detailed, coherent and panoramic analysis of the hegemonic crisis in Britain that commenced in the late 1960s and produced Thatcherism. In this study, in which Hall collaborated with
Chas Critcher, Tony Jefferson, John Clarke and Brian Roberts, the
Gramscian insistence on complex unity is powerfully articulated
through a multilevel analysis of the crime of mugging. The crisis in
hegemony is portrayed as an accumulation of contradictions. Hegemonic struggle is represented as a war of position, an incessant
battle to achieve political, moral and intellectual leadership over the
national-popular to present the appearance of mastery over a contradictory and discordant ensemble of relations. Hall's approach
denies the logic of a paradigmatic ideology for each class and
instead concentrates on the contradictory alliances and concessions
made in forging an organic ideology, a construction of the world
through which new collective will is interpellated. The perspective
is resolutely non-teleological, constantly revealing contingency and
unstable equilibria in the ensemble of relations constituted by the
field of force rather than the vulgar Marxist fixation on laws of historical necessity. Nevertheless, organic ideology constitutes the
backdrop to agency and practice.

    In the study the concrete and the theoretical intermesh to demon-
strate how society, or more especially ruling-class alliances between
the state apparatus and the media, responded to public perceptions
of a deepening economic, political and social crisis. Even critics who
rejected many of the study's central arguments acknowledged that
it is a triumphant vindication of the programme of pedagogy and
collaborative labour in Birmingham during Hall's years as Director
of the Centre (Barker 1992; Harris 1992).

    Yet the study also displays the perversity of the attempt to join
Althusser with Gramsci. Structural Marxism is applied to establish
how ideology turns agents into bearers of class positions, but in
doing so it seems to erase consciousness and reflexivity from
agency. At several points in the analysis, most notably in the long
final chapter on 'The politics of "mugging"', a quasi-romantic construction of the mugger emerges. Hall et al.'s typification of the

black school-leaver, confronting a series of 'dead-end jobs' and surviving in conditions of racism and police intimidation, almost portrays the career of mugging as a *fait accompli* (1978: 361). Not unreasonably, David Harris complains that the methodology of biographical typification is inconsistent with the logic of structural Marxism (1992: 101). But leaving that aside for the moment, the application of ideological distinctions 'write over' the sensuous, moral and practical relation with embodiment and emplacement that, other approaches maintain, cannot simply be 'read off' from dominant ideological codings (Willis 2001: 36). John Hartley also criticizes the 'universal power' that *Policing the Crisis* attributes to ideology, pointing out that the study seems to offer no way out of the circle of ideological force (1996: 238–40).

Similarly, the insistence on reading the state as the focus of the crisis in hegemony reflects the presupposition that the state is pivotal in organizing and connecting the national-popular. However, the effect of this is the marginalization of the role of civil society in the political, moral and intellectual struggle over leadership. *Policing the Crisis* exaggerates the importance of statist ideology in the experienced reality of ordinary people. Although it recognizes the vitality of liminal space in culture that the law cannot control, it perhaps fails to represent the prolific fecundity of this space and its chronic tendency to transgress not only capitalist boundaries, but also socialist alternatives. Hall has criticized Foucault for developing a position of difference without elucidating a position of articulation (Hall 1988a: 53). For Hall, the problem is that Foucault's 'micro-politics' demonstrates that power is omnipresent, but fails to locate hegemony. This raises questions about what Hall regards as the political, ideological and moral character of successful socialist leadership which are not addressed in the book. The doubts that Mulgan and Giddens later raise about the political realism of Hall's position are prefigured in the opacity of the book's emancipatory politics (Mulgan 1998; Giddens 2000: 27–8).

The encoding/decoding model was criticized for being unduly selective and overly politicized. Similar criticisms have been made about *Policing the Crisis*. Keith Tester has raised difficulties with the analysis of the mechanics of the moral panic about mugging (1994: 84–5). Firstly, he argues that the Birmingham study produces an inadequate view of the media because it presents media reporting of mugging as 'one-sided', and underplays the role of the media in deconstructing the stereotype of 'the black mugger'. Secondly, he castigates Hall and his associates for failing to analyse the relationship between the media texts alleged to produce moral panics and audience reception. Elsewhere Hall (1993e) acknowledges the latter point to be a relevant criticism of the encoding/decoding model. But Tester's proposition is that it is a general weakness of Hall's approach to cultural analysis and derives from the political a prioris of Hall's position.

Harris also stresses that it is essential to read the study as part of a coherent political project (1992: 99–103). This is presumably why the cautious emphasis in the text on the need to see the work of ideology as partial, rhetorical and uneven is finally overwhelmed by the thesis that political life in Britain in the 1970s experienced a cataclysmic transition from consensus to coercion. It is not simply a difficulty of reconciling this shift with the 'piecemeal' 'gradualism' that Hall et al. otherwise attribute to British governance. Although, incidentally, this returns to the problem that Gramscianism's capacity to maintain mutually contradictory propositions simultaneously makes it impossible to test the adequacy of its arguments. It also suggests that Hall et al. perhaps amplified the crisis in the 'whole way' of British life in the 1970s, and exaggerated the New Right's transformation of popular 'common sense'. I will take this point up in greater detail later in the chapter when I discuss Hall and authoritarian populism.

Nonetheless, despite these reservations, *Policing the Crisis* is unquestionably a major work which, arguably, constitutes the high-water mark of the Birmingham achievement. Hall recalls that the Centre's subcultures group initiated the study (1995c: 669). Interestingly, he remembers them as among the most resistant formations to the Althusserian-Gramscian moment. This is ironic because *Policing the Crisis* is generally regarded as the climax of the Centre's attempt to merge key elements of the Althusserian and Gramscian traditions. The origins of the study were appropriately concrete. What happened was that the subcultures group fastened on the subject of mugging through a local news item. In 1973 three boys of mixed ethnic background were sentenced to between ten and twenty years for attacking, robbing and badly injuring an elderly man in Birmingham. The Birmingham researchers sympathized with the grievance expressed by local community that the sentences were grossly disproportionate to the severity of the crime.

The initial focus of research was the official reaction to the crime and its relation to media portrayals of an escalating crime wave. Stan Cohen's (1972) concept of *moral panic*, which refers to exaggerated, media-amplified responses to acts of social deviance that stereotype the offender as a threat to society, was enlisted to clarify the social reaction to mugging. Hall et al. demonstrated that the moral panic over mugging which peaked in 1972–3 was related to media amplification. Through content analysis of media reports they established clear connections between media encodings of mugging as a new, terrifying trend in the crime rate, and a putative postwar history of so-called 'soft' policies in the courts. A 'get tough' response was the media's solution to this state of affairs. Hall et al.'s comparison of media presentations with an analysis of the official statistics on violent crime and sentencing policy is compelling. They demonstrated that the official statistics did not verify the 'rising crime rate' equation. The incidence of violent crime had been rising since 1915. There was nothing 'unprecedented' about the rate of robberies with violence in 1972. Indeed, statistically speaking, the period of greatest violent crime had *passed* in 1972, and sentences for violent crimes were growing *longer* not shorter. The question, then, is what are the causes of the moral panic over violent crime in the early 1970s?

The moral panic about mugging is explained as a consequence of a shift from a national politics of consensus to one of coercion. The rise of the disciplinary society is presented as a response to the crisis in the hegemony of the state. The postwar settlement, which utilized alliances in the ruling power bloc and institutions of regulation established between the 1880s and 1920s, was constructed around the all-party acceptance of the managed economy and the welfare state. The creation of a representative-interventionist state was believed to be the prerequisite of the modern state formation process.

In the 1950s, consensus politics was reinforced by the consumer boom following the Second World War, and, crucially, by the emergence of the Cold War as a threat to the national interest. Hall et al. are particularly acute in demonstrating how the state span myths of an immemorial 'way of British life', the 'innate common sense of the British people', and the concomitant threat of 'foreigners' and the Soviet bloc, in the defence of nationalist consciousness and continuity.

However, the state-sponsored interpellation of the people around the category of the 'nation' always disguised unresolved class tensions and economic frictions. In the 1960s and 1970s, wage inflation and pressures on public spending exposed the entrenched relative decline of the British economy. The discussion of the 'exhaustion of consent' is one of the best chapters in the book. It identifies four phases in the rise and fall of national-centrist politics and the tilt from consensus towards coercion.

(1) Postwar construction of consensus (1945–61)   During this period
the foundations of postwar consensus were hammered out. Its principal features were the construction of the welfare state; the adaptation of capitalism; the co-option of the labour movement; the
development of the mixed economy 'solution'; and the identification with the 'free society' side of the Cold War. The ruling power
bloc made concessions on full employment and the welfare state
that soothed class conflict. However, these operated to support the
logic of capitalist development rather than to oppose it. The high-
wage, mass-production, domestic-consumer-orientated modern
economy was constructed around Keynesianism and the expanded,
interventionist state. Britain participated in the global capitalist
boom, but with less relative success than its major rivals. Even so,
capital now appeared to enhance rather than exploit labour interests. The phenomenon of 'the affluent worker' and monied youth
subcultures became pronounced in cultural life. Simultaneously,
new technologies and modifications to the labour process, and new
structures in the technical division of labour generated new occu-
pational strata and cultures within the working class. In 1960 a
major balance of payments crisis exposed the depth of Britain's real
economic decline.

(2) Social democratic hegemony (1961–4)   This was a transitional
period in state hegemony. By the end of it the individualist, 'you've
never had it so good'[4] social and political cohesion of British life,
underwritten by the long consumer boom, was over. It was replaced
by a social democratic variant of state hegemony that appealed
more to individualism than the national interest. This centrist strategy called on the people to draw on the traditional British values
of common sense, notably realism, moderation and patience. Social
democracy was constructed around a *corporatist* partnership between the state, capital and labour. The function of the 'neutral'
state was to commit each side to the national interest and to per-
suade each to regulate the share extracted from the common pool
of wealth. Modernization was the ideological watchword of this
period. The 'white heat' of Harold Wilson's 'technological revolution' offered a postindustrial solution to the problem of want and
traditional class tensions.

At the cultural level, the social democratic emphasis on moderation was contradicted by the hedonism of pop culture and the
expectations explosion of upwardly mobile workers. Conspicuous
consumption and the politics of sexual liberation challenged the

culture of restraint produced by the Protestant work ethic. The confrontation between mods and rockers dramatized anxieties for the nation's moral guardians that the relaxation of codes of conduct in youth culture had gone too far. Worries that the affluent society would spawn a contagion of immorality began to surface in the public sphere.

At the economic level, continuing balance of payments difficulties and the run on sterling forced the government to introduce statutory pay restraint, with the consent of the Trades Union Congress. Cuts in public expenditure and the retreat from the 'social package' were made to appease global capitalism's worries about the British economy. When the seamen struck for higher wages the state cast them as a threat to social order and the community, and therefore the national interest. The tactic contributed to settling the strike, but it undermined the credibility of the Labour Party's 'power bloc'.

(3) The descent into dissensus (1964–70) Consensus and the social democratic variant of hegemony had won a measure of liberalization in British cultural life. The laws on homosexuality, censorship, divorce, abortion, licensing and Sunday Observance were all relaxed. But by the mid 1960s the relaxation of restraint produced a moral backlash that discredited the permissive society for opening the floodgates of pornography and violence. The media stereotyped 'wishy-washy liberals' as the ring-masters of general moral decay. The student protests and sit-ins of 1968 produced a moral panic about the imminent collapse of society which led to a search for 'subversive agents'. In a telling passage, Hall et al. remark that

> this reduction of all forms of dissent or protest to the search for agitational cliques bent on violence, coupled with the arithmetic of consensus, in which 'majorities' were continually reckoned up against 'minorities', marks the whole ideological signification of student protest in Britain. It was gradually to become a dominant signification paradigm for the whole gamut of social conflicts and political troubles. (1978: 243)

The themes of conflict, permissiveness, protest and crime began to condense in a homologous 'threat' to the Social Order itself. The emergence of the counterculture symbolized this 'threat' by redefining consensus and liberal tolerance as repressive, and demanding freedom at all levels of social life. The women's movement contributed to this crisis of authority through its attack on patriarchy

State and Society

and the bonds of family life. Towards the end of the period the erup-
tion of violence in Northern Ireland threatened the break-up of the
United Kingdom, which led to British troops entering Derry and
Belfast. Enoch Powell made his notorious 'rivers of blood' speech
which raised the spectre of inter-racial warfare on the streets of
Britain and demanded much tougher immigration quotas. At the
industrial level, wage militancy from the manual working class
pointed to the re-emergence of class tensions.

(4) The rise of the 'law and order' society (1970–8) Against the
backdrop of the structural decline in the British economy, the
Conservatives were elected under Edward Heath in 1970. The Heath
government sought to restore a centrist government of national unity
committed to growth and competitiveness. The national interest
was defined against 'extremists' and the law was used to 'protect'
economic and civil 'liberties'. A 'rational-legal' solution to the class
and separatist tensions that beset Britain was attempted.

At the economic level, the Industrial Relations Act of 1971
restricted workers' rights and introduced the Industrial Relations
Court to manage the 'disciplined' reform of labour. State intervention was replaced by the renaissance of laissez-faire principles, in
which 'lame ducks' were left to fend for themselves. At the level of
civil society, laws against civil disobedience and protest were interpreted liberally by the judiciary, leading to harsher, 'deterrent' sentences against demonstrators, squatters and student activists. The
police regrouped to intensify monitoring and surveillance of 'dan-
gerous areas' or 'threatening elements'. These included heightened
policing of ethnic minorities, who were connoted with crimogenic
tendencies and eventually, the problem of mugging. The attack on
the values of the permissive society sharpened. The Emergency
Powers Act of 1971 was hastily introduced to cap the increasing
rate of unrest and disturbance in Ulster. 'The mobilisation of
legal instruments against labour, political dissent and alternative
lifestyles', declare Hall et al. 'all seemed to be aimed at the same
general purpose: to bring about by *fiat* what could no longer be won
by consent' (1978: 284).

The year 1972 is, of course, 'the moment of the mugger'. *Policing
the Crisis* relates media amplification of violent crime directly to the
gathering climate of coercion produced by the rise of the authoritarian state. The book downplays divisions and schisms in the proletariat caused by changes in the technical division of labour and
the rise of consumerism. Instead it portrays the wave of industrial

unrest between 1972 and 1974 as a triumph of working-class unity. Edward Heath met his Waterloo not once but twice in 1972 and 1974 at the hands of the miners who successfully struck for significant improvements in the terms and conditions of work. The 1972 defeat, coupled with fears about rising levels of general unemployment, precipitated a humiliating U-turn in state economic strategy. Following the 1972 Budget, a new Industry Bill was passed injecting huge sums of public money into industry in a bid to promote competition and investment, while the government granted itself unprecedented powers of direction and regulation to create the 'right' climate for growth. A statutory incomes policy was introduced to control wage militancy and an attempt was made to revive the tripartite structure of corporatism, by inviting union leaders and industrialists to join with government in a partnership to manage the economy in return for voluntary restraint in price increases and a wage freeze.

The state therefore sent out contradictory messages to industrialists and workers. On one side, they encouraged cooperation and dialogue; on the other, they increased the tendency towards coercion by devising unilateral powers of price and wage regulation. The state dealt with the second miners' strike in 1974 by driving distress into every home in the country through the imposition of a fuel-saving three-day week. In a bid to let the nation settle the matter, Heath called a snap election in 1974, fought on the issue of 'who governs the country?' The defeat of the Conservatives paved the way for the conquest of the Tory Party by the New Right. The Labour government struggled to revive corporatism by introducing a 'Social Contract' between labour and capital, designed to control wages and prices. This failed to deliver. The so-called 'winter of discontent' in 1978–9 seemed to reveal the bankruptcy of corporatism and provided the final rationale for the Thatcher adventure.

It has been impossible here to offer anything beyond a schematic account of *Policing the Crisis*. After all, the book is a densely argued study of over 400 pages that utilizes a wealth of interdisciplinary material from Marxism, social history, sociology, criminology, economics, cultural studies, journalism and political science. The book concludes that the moral panic over mugging is one of the principal ideological forms through which the 'silent majority' was won over to support the assumption of coercive powers by the state (Hall et al. 1978: 221). Crucially it was a war of position that sought to command the terrain of civil society *before* seeking to acquire control of the state apparatus. This signals the tension between Gramscianism and Althusserianism in the study. Althusser's position inscribed civil society with limited autonomy because it prioritized the ideological significance of the state. *Policing the Crisis* tends finally to endorse Gramsci's position, which is that civil society possesses relative autonomy from the state and constitutes a terrain on which the battle to command the state apparatus can be meaningfully waged.

As even this schematic account demonstrates, the study attempted much more than a solution to the problem of mugging. It amounted to a full-scale elucidation of the postwar crisis of hegemony in Britain. The study identifies three central dimensions of this crisis. First, and central to the conjunctural turmoil that it surveys, the failure of postwar reconstruction to match the competitiveness and growth of rivals in Western Europe and North America exposed the underlying weakness of the economy. Hall and his associates interpret this as part of the long-term structural decline of British capitalism. The consensus politics of the consumer boom between 1945 and 1961 rode on the back of a global re-gearing of capitalism and disguised the structural vulnerability of the national economy. Without a sound and successful economic base, the state was unable to deliver on ideological promises of redistributive justice and universal welfare cover.

Second, the economy limited room for manoeuvre at the political level. The struggle for hegemony produced power blocs based on unstable class alliances. For Hall et al., the Labour Party never seized the nettle of pursuing deep and lasting socialist change. Instead, it repeatedly cast itself in the role of managing the economic crisis of capitalism. *Policing the Crisis* deplores Labour for adopting a social democratic, rather than a socialist, bearing in government, with damaging fissures in its power base that were to cripple the party's electoral prospects in the 1980s and for most of the 1990s. Hall repeats the argument in his evaluation of New Labour (1998a), which he pillories for reproducing some of the central tenets of Thatcherism.

Third, the ideological neutrality of the state is compromised by the historical tendency for state interventionism to take over more and more of economy and society. The state's capacity to improve the condition of 'the people' is undermined by the successive annual restraints on public expenditure, and interventionism's tendency to support the continued expansion of capital. The hegemonic legitimacy of state functions is contradicted by the intrinsic state attachment to the interests of capital. The resort to law and order is a sign of an increasing lack of tolerance in the ruling bloc towards dissent and liberalism. The struggle to win consent from critical, oppositional and undecided forces is compounded by the state's ultimate identification of the national interest with the logic of capital accumulation.

Policing the Crisis was published as the Social Contract, the last best hope of corporatist hegemony, breathed its death rattle. The winter of 1978–9 was dominated by media reports of strikes by public service workers that left refuse uncollected and the dead unburied. The industrial unrest destroyed the Labour claim to manage organized labour better than the Conservatives and marooned consensus politics as a postwar period piece. The stage was set for a radical shift in political direction. Hall (1983) characterizes Thatcherite populism as a 'particularly rich mix' of 'organic Toryism' (nation, family, duty, authority, standards, traditionalism) with the aggressive revival of neoliberalism (self-interest, competitive individualism, anti-statism) (Hall and Jacques 1989: 29). Margaret Thatcher herself claimed that her policies were based on popular support (1993: 618), otherwise the Conservative Party would have lost the three elections fought under her leadership, not won them. On British nationalism, Britain in Europe and, initially at least, the Falklands War, Thatcher was undeniably populist. But how 'popular' was Thatcherism? And how far did it really change the centrist values produced by the postwar settlement?

Thatcherism: authoritarian populism

Hall's analysis of Thatcherism (1988a) proposed that she possessed advantage in the war of position and manoeuvre during the 1980s but that the power bloc that she headed never acquired hegemony. This position was famously contested by Jessop et al. (1989). They argued that Hall's blitzkrieg in *Marxism Today* against the Thatcher adventure is, in fact, based on the premise of Thatcherite hegemony. Hall flatly denied the charge (1989a). He pointed to the 'yawning gap' between Thatcherism's ideological advance and its economic achievement. His analysis identified 'real limits' to the appeal of neoliberalism, notably in respect of maintaining the quality of public services and managing public protest. Thatcherism, he maintained (1989a), was in 'dominance' during the 1980s, but never hegemonic.

There is good reason to side with Hall in this exchange. For Gramscianism, hegemony consists of a shifting, heterogeneous, contingently related ensemble of elements that constitute a field of force with the capacity to win consent over popular consciousness. As a Gramscian scholar, Hall would never have committed the solecism of treating Thatcherism as an 'uncontradictory monolith'. Yet if Jessop et al. were wrong in literal terms, they accurately represented the spirit of Hall's writings in the 1980s. Hall's writings demonstrably maintained that the 'reactionary common sense' of Thatcherism achieved 'significant headway' in popular opinion (Hall 1983, see Hall and Jacques 1989: 11; Hall 1988a: 8). Privatization, the attack on the rights of organized labour, the revival of nationalism, the use of tough law and order measures and the rationalization of the welfare state appeared to command widespread popular support.

According to Hall (1988a) the long Thatcherite *imperium* rested on three pillars:

1   The revival of a neoliberal power bloc advocating political, moral and intellectual leadership on the basis of free market doctrine and possessive individualism.
2   The rejection of the Keynesian form of corporatism and the consensus politics of the managed economy and welfare state.
3   The restoration of the prerogatives of management, capital and control over working-class power and organized bargaining strength.

By the mid 1980s Hall was arguing that Thatcherism had achieved a shift in the relations of force into a new configuration: Gramsci's 'new reality' (Hall 1988a: 132). This new reality in the Thatcherite version consisted of the replacement of publicly owned industries and utilities with private ownership; a fixation with market value as the ultimate source of all value; the general deregulation of the market; well-rooted social acceptance of the need for strong policing; commitment to a low tax economy; and widespread support for the strict legal control of trade union powers. In Hall's view, its centrepiece was the apparent co-option of popular consciousness to a more legalized, disciplinary regime in economics and civil society.

Hall praised the political sociology of Nicos Poulantzas for recognizing the tendency in social democracy for the state to extend interventionism into every sphere of economic and civil life (Hall 1980b; 1988a: 126–7). Poulantzas (1979) associated this with the decline in the institutions of political democracy and the draconian curtailment of formal liberties. He termed this condition 'authoritarian statism'. This is not equivalent to fascism, nor does it imply that fascism is the inevitable next stage of development. Rather it refers to the tightening up of restraint and, in some cases, the repeal of civil liberties within a democratic framework. What is missing in Poulantzas, argues Hall, is the elucidation of how the tendency of authoritarian statism in social democracy is cemented at the cultural and political levels by winning popular consent to the 'new reality'. Hall's concept of 'authoritarian populism' was designed to fill this lacuna. In the Thatcher variant, authoritarian populism condensed a wide range of popular discontents concerning the postwar economic and political order and mobilized them around a right-wing remedy for the nation's 'ills'. The success of Thatcherism lay not merely in commanding the state apparatus, but also in using 'the trenches and fortifications of civil society as the means of forging a considerable ideological and intellectual *authority* outside the realm of the state proper and, indeed *before* – as a necessary condition to – taking formal power *in* the state, as part of an internal contestation against key elements within the power bloc' (Hall 1988a: 47; emphasis in original). Again the tension with the Althusserian view of the functionalist relation between the state and civil society is evident.

Authoritarian populism dominated Hall's analysis of Thatcherism as a cultural, economic and political phenomenon. He submitted that the paradox of Thatcherism is that its electoral success depended on support from large numbers of the working class with the most to lose from the policies of trade union reform and the rationalization of the welfare state. The concept of authoritarian populism provided a convincing way of solving this paradox by postulating that the 'get tough' policies were part of a many-sided process of condensation in which the rising power bloc adduced the decline of Britain as the defining feature of postwar experience. But not everyone was convinced by the analysis.

Jessop et al. (1989) contended that Hall exaggerated the headway made by Thatcherism over public opinion and misrepresented the ideological success of authoritarian populism. They proposed that the rightward lurch in the balance of forces in the 1980s owed more to strategic errors in the Labour Party's conduct of opposition than popular consent to the values of Thatcherite authoritarian populism. They further maintained that Thatcher's economic policies aggravated frictions within the ruling bloc in respect of the

North/South divide, the needs of manufacturing industry versus the service sector and the orientation towards import or export output, greatly inhibiting the chances of achieving hegemony. Jessop et al. submitted that Thatcherism clearly failed to win popular support for some of its central economic and social policies. In as much as this is so, they concluded that the thesis of authoritarian populism exaggerates the neutralization of centrist, consensus politics by the Thatcherite power bloc.

Interestingly, Williams also questioned whether it is correct to regard Thatcherism as an ideological break (1983; 1989b). He emphasized the continuation of pro-Labour loyalties among union members, the unemployed and manual workers. He also maintained that the scale of Conservative domination was distorted by the 'first past the post' principle of the British electoral system. Popular support for socialism, he argued, was much stronger than the model of authoritarian populism implied. The contrasting response of Hall and Williams to the miners' strike (in 1984–5) is instructive in this regard. As the strike ground to defeat, Hall, rather controversially, proposed that the Greater London Council now constituted the 'most important front' in the struggle against Thatcherism. It is a judgement that was found by Andrew Milner, for one, to raise serious doubts about Hall's political judgement (Milner 1993: 83). Milner notes that Williams held a more ecumenical view about the strike, arguing that the mobilization of socialism must be national rather than metropolitan, and address the conditions in the 'crisis-ridden communities' traumatized by Thatcherism.

What emerges most forcefully is that the social, economic and political consequences of Thatcherism and the popular and academic responses to it were very uneven. The popularity of Thatcher's policies was never as great as she claimed, and the crucial project of remaking common sense in Britain to conform to a reactionary culture was unsuccessful. This is not inconsistent with Hall's view that the Thatcherite power bloc involved an accumulation of contradictions within the same ideological formation. He was careful to give a pronounced reading of the social contradictions other than those of class within Thatcherism (1988a: 7). Thus, Jessop et al.'s point about the regional schisms generated by Thatcherism is compatible with Hall's general position. Nonetheless, Jessop et al. do not exaggerate Hall's argument that the project of Thatcherism was to dismantle the whole postwar formation; to reverse the political culture that had evolved around the postwar settlement – the historic compromise between capital and labour – anchored in the welfare state of 1945. This is indeed what Hall meant by the term 'regressive modernization'. The difference between Jessop et al. and Hall is that the former stress the continuities in postwar culture, politics and economy during and after Thatcherism, while Hall sees the 1980s as a watershed in the English state formation process.

The persistence of continuities is also the picture developed by Heath, Jowell and Curtice (2001) in their study of British social attitudes based on extensive time series data gathered between 1979 and 1997. They maintain that the public accepted Conservative policies of trade union reform and privatization. In this respect Thatcherism changed the institutional face of the country by breaking the high inflation/high tax/high strike mould. Yet significant discontent with high taxation, militant trade unionism and high inflation had been building since the mid 1960s. So it is likely that Thatcher drew on popular sentiment that pre-existed the 1979 election, rather than introduced new moral, political and economic leadership that persuaded the country to break the mould. Whether or not Thatcherism can be credited with the move away from a high inflation/high tax/high strike equation, today's electorate shows no sign of wishing to turn back the clock. Moreover, New Labour has clearly assimilated these precepts in government.

But in other respects the country remained resistant to the Thatcherite mission. Most importantly there was no appreciable electoral support for the policy of reduced public spending on public services, and once the battle against inflation had been won, the electorate wanted a return to full employment. Margaret Thatcher's nationalism, which Hall was not alone in finding abhorrent, condensed a range of issues: strong defence, the protection of British sovereignty, the advocacy of British autonomy in Europe and the maintenance of the Union. But only on Europe were her policies truly popular as well as populist. The electorate did not support her outlook on nuclear defence, nor was there a majority against devolution. The victory in the Falklands was fleetingly popular and populist. Hall described it as a time of 'rampant and virulent patriotism' (1988a: 72–3) and concluded that it symbolized the ascendancy of authoritarian populism. However, the evidence is that, like her victory over inflation, the Falklands issue was regarded equivocally in the country. The victory of the British troops was of course generally welcomed, but there were highly public and damaging criticisms that the government had been derelict in funding defence in the South Atlantic before the Argentinian invasion, and Thatcher's role in the sinking of the *Belgrano* was subject to considerable public disquiet.

The evidence is that the Falklands factor was a declining asset. It helped to win the 1983 election, but it reinforced public worries that Thatcher's style of leadership was too abrasive and overbearing. Margaret Thatcher's nationalism appealed to an older generation with memories of the British Empire, the Battle of Britain and the Second World War. For most people born after 1945 it appeared eccentric and old-fashioned. It became an electoral albatross after the 1983 election, when the euphoria over the Falklands began to wear off and Thatcher's opposition to devolution in Scotland, Wales and Northern Ireland was widely read as uncompromising and condescending.

In none of the three elections won under Thatcher's leadership did the Conservatives secure more than 44.9 per cent of the vote. In the 1983 and 1987 elections there was a slight but clear decline in the Conservatives share of the vote.[5] The electorate's centrist instincts were not uprooted and replaced with 'reactionary common sense' in the Thatcher years. Government spending as a percentage of GNP was not reduced during her decade of dominance. The power and finances of local government were unquestionably eroded. However, despite the rhetoric of 'setting the people free', central government under Thatcher became more interventionist. Similarly, victory in the Falklands may have temporarily revived nationalist sentiment, but the war could not have been conducted, let alone won, without support from the White House. The Conservative domination owed much to strategic errors by the Labour Opposition, tax cuts and the largesse of privatization windfalls for small investors (Ramsden 1998: 451).

Hall (1988a) insists that authoritarian populism is contradictory and composed of a shifting balance of forces. As such, none of the points made by Jessop et al. or Heath, Jowell and Curtice would be seen by him as necessarily falsifying his thesis. As I noted above, it is notoriously difficult to test Gramscian theory since it holds that mutually contradictory tendencies always and already constitute social reality. On this basis there is no satisfactory way of deciding if Hall's thesis of authoritarian populism was right or wrong. But there is reason to believe that he exaggerated the watershed effect of Thatcherism and that the continuities in civil society, particularly in respect of the welfare state and the commitment to full employment, were more profound than his analysis led his readers to believe. Perhaps Cannadine gets it right with his observation that while Thatcher may have been feared, respected and admired by large sections of the population, she was loved and believed in only by a minority (1998: 294). She was 'a populist who was not popular', a judgement which again raises doubts about the validity of the Hall thesis.

New Labour

For his part, Hall has stuck to his guns in maintaining that Thatcherism created a new reality in Britain (1988a; 1988b). His aggravation with New Labour stems from his belief that 'the Blair project, in its overall analysis and key assumptions, is still essentially framed by and moving on the terrain defined by Thatcherism' (1998a: 14). On the economic front he points to New Labour's 'essentially neoliberal' support for the deregulation of the market, the reconstruction of the public sector by the New Managerialism, privatization, low taxation, removing 'inhibitions' to market flexibility and tight trade union regulation. In cultural policy, Hall declares that New Labour promotes self-reliance, family values, competitiveness and entrepreneurial dynamism. He berates Blair for 'ruthlessly emasculating' the Labour Party and replacing real debate with the carefully controlled blandishments of the Millbank public relations machine. New Labour, he concludes pointedly, is in fact a 'species of authoritarian populism' (1998a: 13). Thus his proposition that the Thatcherite solution to the crisis in hegemony fundamentally changed the rules of the game in British society is verified.

Hall's attack on New Labour makes many valid points, notably in respect of the overuse of spin, state underinvestment in transport, health and education, the reduced concept of collectivism, the renewal of Christian moralism to frame ethical questions and the deployment of the tactics of the 'New Managerialism' to construct a bogus national-centrist consensus and impose it on the country. But it is less satisfactory in positing a version of popular socialism capable of replacing New Labour's social democracy.

Blair's historic second election victory in 2001 illustrated the extent to which New Labour had captured the national-centrist ground.[6] The Conservative challenge, led by William Hague, was fought on policies of cutting taxes, defending sterling from European integration and increasing public spending, partly through intensifying the war against scroungers and tax dodgers. What worked for Thatcher in 1979 proved disastrous for Hague in

2001. The voters who returned Blair to power had no immediate memory of violent trade union unrest. They were critical of many aspects of the privatization programme in the 1990s, notably in respect of the performance of the railways. However, there was no appreciable support for a policy of renationalization. While they disapproved of many aspects of New Labour's management of the public services, they judged Health and Education to be in safer hands under New Labour than it would be under the Conservatives. Preserving and improving public services were generally regarded as more important than cuts in direct taxation. The Conservative attack on scroungers misfired because the public had grown used to a stable economy and low inflation. To be sure, disquiet about welfare cheats was still an electoral issue, but it was eclipsed by the desire for a continuation of the sound management of the economy and transparency in government. Hague's anti-Europeanism was regarded as old-fashioned and out of touch, and it never ignited the flames of patriotic popular fervour that it was designed to achieve.

The Major government tilted the balance of forces in the Thatcher inheritance back to the national centre, and, to date, the two Labour administrations under Tony Blair have continued the process. If New Labour really is a variant of authoritarian populism, as Hall suggests, it is generally much less jingoistic and more concerned with striking a balance between the private and public sectors than was the case with the Thatcher power bloc. Hall described Thatcherism as an example of 'regressive modernization' (1988a: 2). By this he meant an attempt to 'educate' and 'discipline' society by dragging it back into an equally regressive version of the past, preserving, for example, traditional symbols of nation and family. In contrast, New Labour has supported more internationalism rather than less. Its record on asylum seekers is equivocal and perhaps, on balance, discouraging. But this is also the government that detained General Pinochet for the contravention of human rights in Chile, much to the consternation of Margaret Thatcher, and expanded British responsibilities in protecting the global environment and international peacekeeping. True, Pinochet was eventually released; and true the first Blair government expanded arms sales on dubious 'ethical' grounds, and bombed Kosovo. Blair's second administration fell into line with American interests after the bombing of the World Trade Center in New York and the Pentagon in Washington by lending military and intelligence support to the war against the Taliban in Afghanistan. Blair's copy-book is far from unblotted.

Yet nobody who lived in Britain through the long night of the Thatcher–Major years can seriously doubt that New Labour better understands global civic responsibilities. Margaret Thatcher held a sectarian view of globalization. She identified it as broadly good for the economy, and particularly the City of London, but disapproved of the rise of multiculturalism in Britain and the transfer of British administrative and economic power to Brussels. Hall is one of the great scourges of the day on the question of British insularity. His writings on nationalism, heritage, white working-class alienation and new ethnicity have done much to lever British introspection into some kind of clear light. He is quite right to suspect that Blair and New Labour share many of Margaret Thatcher's gut instincts (1998a). This, incidentally, is one reason why Blair succeeded in achieving two election victories for Labour where Michael Foot and Neil Kinnock failed in three consecutive elections.

Hall's instincts are for more state management of the economy, restriction of the freedom of global corporations, progressive taxation to redress inequalities in wealth, curtailment of the private sector in education and health, and less spin in government (1998a). The difficulty is that these are substantially the same policies that Labour put to the electorate in 1983 and 1987, resulting in the third successive election defeat. The scale of the defeat in 1987 prompted Neil Kinnock to initiate a thoroughgoing policy review that discarded the most extreme policies, notably in respect of nationalization and unilateral nuclear disarmament. Hall is not making a case for a return to these unpopular policies. On the other hand, the policy turn he advocates for New Labour amounts to the revival of the core programme of traditional socialism, enhancing the role of the state and regulating the market. The evidence of six successive elections in Britain between 1979 and 2001 is that the public does not want these policies.

Now, of course, rejection can be explained by exploring how ideology operates to create the political agenda and shape our sense of reality *à la* Althusser. But this is basically a circular argument that separates itself from the national-popular by denying the validity of popular choice. Hall's long and agonized reflections on the requirements of socialist renewal (1988a; 1988b) concluded that there are real dangers in developing a form of popular politics that is cut off from genuine popular roots. However, his agenda for New Labour is isolationist, and populist only in the elitist sense of affecting to know what is best for the people.

The third space and the social imaginary

Hall would doubtless not accept the charge that his agenda is
isolationist. He regards his work as challenging the boundaries
of neoliberalism, statism and social democracy. 'I am trying to see',
he writes, 'whether it is possible to think about a society which is
not wholly driven back into private, atomized, fragmented individualism but which understands its commitments and solidarities
to forms of mobilized collective action as always conditional,
never complete, always operating through difference' (1989h: 153).
He declares himself to be in favour of radical socialism that occu-
pies the 'third space' (1989h: 150) between statism and social
democracy.

Naturally, this has nothing to do with the 'Third Way' approach
associated with Anthony Giddens and Ulrich Beck, about which
Hall has been nothing but richly sarcastic (1998a: 10). In his view
the claim that the Third Way has transcended the divisions between
Left and Right is a fantasy.[7] Hall finds the Third Way avocation of
social inclusion and global democracy anodyne. In failing to pin-
point convincing measures to curb the excesses of global capitalism,
or to devise a systematic public investment programme for equality, it ends up colluding with capitalism. It overexaggerates the
prospect of meaningful partnership with capital by mitigating the
capitalist imperative to achieve a quasi-monopolistic market position and maximize profit margins. Its worthy sentiments on the
environment and redistributive justice are undermined by a lack of
political realism about the adversarial character of the corporations
and multinationals. For Hall, the Third Way is the latest variant
of the endogenous, limpid tradition of Anglo-Saxon pragmatism.
It fails to address the hard choices of structural transformation that
must be made to achieve a social order based on the mutual benefit
of equal participants.

The clear import of Hall's exhaustive labours to rehabilitate
socialism in the 1980s and 1990s (1988a; 1988b) is that only the Left
has the capacity to make these choices. The Left alone has pursued
a social imaginary which looks forward to the transcendence of
capitalism and the foundation of a social order based on the
mutual benefit of participants. The reason why he concentrated so
single-mindedly on the prospect of socialist renewal is that he
believed that Thatcherism's success in detonating consensus politics
provided the Left with a historic opportunity to seize the ground

from the New Right and colonize it for socialist advance. The concept of the social imaginary is important to Hall. In the Introduction I noted that he regarded it as one of the two principal identifying characteristics of the New Left. But what does it mean to pursue a social imaginary?

Hall's old friend and New Left veteran, the Canadian social philosopher Charles Taylor, clarifies the undertaking and, by extension, the concept, somewhat. He portrays the social imaginary as a collective orientation towards an enriched version of social order represented through fables, myths, poetry, songs, stories and allegories (Taylor 2000). It is an imagined construct that, however, draws on concrete or emerging elements in the present. Roger Bromley has coined the phrase 'narratives for a new belonging' (2000), and this captures the discursive and utopian features of the social imaginary well enough. The relationship between the social imaginary, politics and theory is complex. A vision of an enriched social order may exist for decades or centuries without being concretely realized. For example, Taylor notes that the social imaginary of equality enunciated in seventeenth-century theories of the State of Nature and contract did not pass into political agency until the end of the following century (2000: 371). Thus the social imaginary may bind collectivities to dreams, aspirations and desires long before it becomes politically or theoretically relevant.

The *May Day Manifesto* (Williams 1968) is one of the fullest expressions of the New Left's social imaginary. It was intended as a 'counter-statement' against the Labour government's ethos of consensus in 'the national interest' and policies. It arose from the conviction that Harold Wilson's government 'continually bypassed' the 'substance' of socialism. It demanded the creation of a non-militaristic social order, based on comprehensive social security, full employment, and control of national sources of investment in the banks and insurance companies; the end of the division between private and public provision in health and education; effective public transport and policies; and enhanced internationalism, notably in respect of increased aid to the Third World and opposition to the Cold War. It called on the Left to oppose the power elite of the 'men' in industry, finance and government who ran the country. The power elite in Britain was portrayed as being more cohesive and integrated around education, marriage and therefore class than Wright Mills's famous description of its American counterpart (1956). The *Manifesto* demanded a 'socialist national plan' that would not only tackle necessary economic reforms, but establish the strategy for changing the culture of private competition and possessive individualism (Williams 1968: 137).

Indeed cultural transformation is regarded as the key to socialist advance. The *Manifesto* ends by insisting that communication is the precondition for successful agency. The flow of information and debate necessary to concentrate radical consciousness requires the revitalization of the left-wing press. The *Manifesto* warns of the threat to civil freedoms when the press falls into the control of capitalist proprietors – a prescient, but ironic observation in view of the strides made by Rupert Murdoch, the late Robert Maxwell and Conrad Black in controlling the British press after the 1970s. The emphasis on the need to increase communication and defend the channels of information is characteristic of the ideological formation of the New Left. As is the advocacy of independence in the formulation of political and cultural opinion:

> It is very important that groups retain their own identity, while they feel it to be necessary; even that groups should see (themselves) as in argument and contention with others on the Left, in the necessary process of discussion and dispute; but still recognizing an effective community against a system which suppresses or reduces them, that they should help each other, in practical and immediate ways, so that the socialist and radical culture stays alive and can extend. (Williams 1968: 185)

Underlying the whole document is the presupposition that change will only be accomplished by smashing the illusion of consensus politics. Again, this is very characteristic of the ideological formation of the New Left, and remains a pronounced theme in *Policing the Crisis* and Hall's attack on New Labour. The war against capitalist hegemony is waged not with guns or sabres, but with better arguments that reconstitute the whole culture.

Since the 1990s Hall's writings on hyphenated identity, interrupted identity and multiculturalism have queried the concept of identity. Set against the Thatcherite neoliberal celebration of identity through 'competitive individualism', 'private interest' and 'the nation', this makes some sense. By establishing the argument that identity is no more than a 'temporary attachment' to discourses and practices which attempt to interpellate or 'hail' us into place, he seeks to disrupt the neoliberal credo that society is composed of atomized, stable, independent agents. His use of the postcolonial concepts of hybridity and diaspora reinforce this project by problematizing the purity and autonomy of identity. Identity is now regarded as always and already 'under erasure'. Hall elaborates:

> What we call 'our identities' are probably better conceptualized as the sedimentations over time of those different identifications or positionalities we have taken up and tried to 'live', as it were, from the inside, no doubt inflected by the particular mix of circumstances, feelings, histories and experiences which are unique and peculiar to us as individual subjects. (1997c: 219)

Postnationalism, contingent identity, multilocational cultural space and the politics of difference now form the cornerstones of Hall's version of the social imaginary. This is interrogated along a variety of binary oppositions, notably 'the West and the rest', 'nation and post-nation', 'identity and difference' and 'local and global'. There are continuities here with the Birmingham rejection of the base–superstructure dichotomy. But while this was played out in the context of exposing the defects of vulgar Marxism, the new enquiry is designed to reveal the exhaustion of Western cosmology and binary thought throughout the whole culture.

New Times

Hall positions Thatcherism and his response to it in the context of a seismic transformation in culture, economy and society. The neoliberal response to this structural condition was to renew the ideology of the autonomous, atomized agent. Hall's reaction is to reject this ideology by demonstrating the decentred, hybrid character of identity. Hall and Jacques have called the seismic transformation in question 'New Times' (1989).

According to Hall and Jacques the New Times thesis sought first to take the Left off the defensive back-foot in relation to Thatcherism; and second, to break the Left's doctrinal fixation with certain features of the postwar world that had vanished (1989: 11). The first objective attempted to develop a positive agenda for the Left by insisting that Thatcherite regressive modernization was only one strategy for handling the new economic, social and political conditions. Margaret Thatcher's view that 'there is no alternative' to the neoliberal solution is ideologically motivated and therefore unsound. Hall and Jacques argue that the Left has been remiss in framing New Times in terms of the dilemmas that it poses for socialist advance. Instead they dwell on the opportunities for gaining hegemony.

The second issue is a more complex and sensitive task because it involved converting the Left from its dependency on class analysis. This was sensitive because the Marxist tradition identified class relations as pre-eminent in history and society. To propose that class no longer determines the code of identity as it did in the past may seem unobjectionable today. But for a sizeable number of left-leaning intellectuals, even ten years ago, it was problematic.

The New Times thesis proposed that a general structural change in society, economy and culture had occurred. This involved a many-sided shift away from homogeneity, standardization and regimentation to diversity, differentiation and fragmentation. It held that the Left was wrong to continue to privilege production in the analysis of capitalist society, and emphasized the importance of reproduction and consumption. The effect of this was to bolster the significance of culture to an unprecedented level in the Left's approach to economy and society.

The Left had heard the argument before. In the 1970s and early 1980s Alain Touraine (1971) and André Gorz (1982) each maintained that the new productive regimes associated with new technologies and the new organization of the division of labour reduced the salience of class struggle. Gorz questioned whether in consumer society it still made sense for the Left to regard identity, community and agency as organized around work. For his part, Touraine contended that new social movements were replacing older forms of class struggle. David Harvey (1989) spelled out the theoretical and practical implications for the Left in his richly documented argument that society has moved into the condition of postmodernity. In his view the circumstances demanded that the Left rehabilitate the old modernist concept of socialism by intensive critical interrogation. On the whole, Hall and Jacques (1989) kept faith with Hall's already stated caution about the realization of postmodernity (1986a). But there is no mistaking their full agreement with Harvey that New Times require the Left to drastically overhaul and rehabilitate the concept of socialism.

The concept of New Times was a catch-all for a complex condensation of factors in social change. Hall isolated three central themes in his understanding of the term (1989h; 1991d).

(1) Post-Fordism The centralized, regimented assembly-line system of mass production and mass consumption associated with

Henry Ford's approach to accumulation dominated the first two-thirds of the twentieth century. In the closing third of the century it was replaced by post-Fordism attached to flexible accumulation. Post-Fordism involved a shift in investment to new information technologies and the service sector; the decentralization of the labour process; the decline of old manufacturing centres and the growth of sunrise computer-based industries; the contracting out of functions and services; more emphasis on choice and product differentiation; the targeting of consumers by taste, lifestyle and culture rather than social class; a decline in the size of the skilled male working class; the growth in the number of female workers; the expansion of the service sector and white collar workers; the globalization of production through the multinational division of labour; greater fragmentation and pluralism in the consumer market; and greater governance of the global economy by financial markets.

The rate of replacement was uneven, with some parts of the global economy moving faster to full-scale flexible accumulation than others. But the effect was a profound restructuring in product design, the organization of the division of labour, consumer subcultures and the general types of association linked together under production and consumption.

(2) The return of the subject Flexible accumulation and increased mobility have combined to weaken the sense of the individual as a stable, centred and autonomous 'self'. Under New Times, a more fragmented, incomplete, contingent notion of the self is naturalized. Similarly, the subject is recognized as positioned by different discourses and practices. The boundary between objective and subjective dimensions is redefined. The modernist faith in an inner world that is separate and distinct from the external world is rendered obsolete. Aesthetics and difference play a more significant role in the organization of lifestyle, practice and association. Structuralist analysis is fundamentally challenged by the new emphasis on fragmentation, diversity and multiple selves.

(3) The proliferation of civil society In these New Times the sites of antagonism and resistance proliferate and the sphere of politics is enlarged. New subjects, social movements and collective identities based both inside and outside the formal political system emerge. Political struggles and cultures become more pluralistic. This both reflects and reinforces the tendency towards multiple selves and

fragmented identities. Politics and culture operate around a network of strategies and powers, and their articulation is always positional. They have an unsettling effect on everything once thought of as 'settled'.

Hall and Jacques (1989) are unabashed that New Times are still fundamentally capitalist times. Alongside established inequalities, new social divisions, new types of inequality and disempowerment are emerging. Conversely, they are in no doubt about the novel significance of New Times. 'Identities become detached – disembedded – from specific times, places, histories and traditions and appear "free-floating",' Hall writes. 'We are confronted by a range of different identities, each appealing to us, or rather to different parts of ourselves, from which it seems possible to choose' (1992b: 303). To redeploy the metaphor used in *Resistance through Rituals*, capitalism remains the parent culture for identity just as Hall and Jefferson (1976) argued that class is the parent culture of subculture. But New Times is a significant shift from the conceptual model employed in both *Resistance through Rituals* and *Policing the Crisis*. Hall has already assimilated the postmodern argument that identity is fragmented and contingent. He is moving to embrace and politicize the Derridean procedure of deconstruction by arguing that problematic concepts in the West, such as 'identity', 'nation' and 'race', are not elided when criticism exposes their defects, but are placed 'under erasure'. Problematic concepts cannot be elided because there is no satisfactory alternative to them. The critical intervention therefore consists in subjecting them to reflexivity which captures both their analytic misrepresentations and fallibility.

4

Culture and Civilization

Culture and civilization is an orthodox conceptual pairing in Western thought, although it is of relatively recent historical provenance. The terms *civilité* and *politesse* were used in France in the sixteenth century. The term 'barbarian' was applied to describe people who lacked qualities of courtesy, manners, *finesse* and polite conduct. But it was not until the 1770s that the term 'civilization' acquired its modern meaning. The Dictionary of the French Academy finally recognized it in 1798. Even then the meaning was dualistic and contradictory. Lucien Febvre (1973) noted that it referred, first, to the ethnographic characteristics of collective life that differentiate a group. This is a non-evaluative meaning that simply describes the features of life that obtain in a group. The second meaning was just as strong but altogether more controversial. It referred to qualities of collective life deemed to be superior, thus invoking a value judgement.

The growth of the disciplines of geography and history during the Enlightenment condensed these meanings into a fateful mix. The *philosophes* assimilated data from voyages of discovery to speculate on a universal history of mankind leading from savagery to civilization. As European societies advanced to colonize the globe, the notion of Western superiority became ascendant. The Enlightenment normalized the idea of a universal model of progress based on the West in which all societies 'high' and 'low' could be ranked according to their level of development. Progress was therefore conceptualized as a ladder from the 'lowest rung' (savage society), which was often conceptualized as 'relatively unchanging', to 'the highest', signified by the West, which was inherently 'dynamic' and 'progressive' (Kuper 2000).

Hall's writings on Western colonization are among the most declarative of all his publications (1992b; 1996b; 1997c). The close attention to the shifting balance of forces, uneven contradictions and unstable equilibria that he displays in his analysis of, for example, the state or authoritarian populism seems to be abandoned. Indeed, Hall can hardly bring himself to use the term 'civilization', preferring instead to refer to 'compulsive Eurocentrism' (1996a: 16). The accent on the extractive, dominating aspects of the Western rise to power is inexhaustibly pronounced. Colonization comes to stand for civilization, as if the analytic value of the latter is compromised by the political and cultural presumptions of the former. Given the historic, class-based condescension present in many contributions to the debate on civilization, this response is perhaps understandable. By the same token it suggests a one-sided view of the relationship between civilization and culture which is detrimental to tenable analysis.[1]

What is the reason for this orientation to the concept of civilization? When Hoggart and Hall established the Birmingham Centre there was little or no risk that they might call it the Centre for Contemporary *Civilization* Studies. For anyone on the Left at that time the term civilization was redolent with connotations of class superiority, immovable hierarchy and a monolithic view of human achievement modelled on the West. Civilization was the totem that Matthew Arnold in the nineteenth century and T. S. Eliot in the twentieth used to belittle and marginalize working-class culture. It would be going too far to propose that in the Birmingham Centre, civilization was seen as the enemy. Nonetheless, the strong early emphasis on studying the conditions of life in local class cultures and repressed proletarian traditions in literature and the arts remained faithful to Hoggart's argument (1958) that the civilization defended by Arnold and Eliot was remarkably myopic when it came to recognizing working-class cultural achievement – let alone 'native' accomplishment. The culturalist tradition of socialist humanism represented by Thompson and Williams broadly confirmed this view.

Not surprisingly empirical studies in the Centre under Hall's directorship concentrated on working-class conditions and histories. When Hall championed the structuralist tradition, theoretical and political questions became pre-eminent, but they were typically framed through the experience and interests of the working class.

A critic might observe that it is extraordinary that the Centre never initiated a study of aristocratic conditions of life or histories, and that the concept of 'civilization' constitutes a prominent but massively undertheorized feature in the Birmingham terrain.[2]

Culture and discourse

If culture was king in the Birmingham years, and after 1979 when Hall quit to join the Open University, the terms of its rule underwent a profound change. Between the 1970s and the 1990s the discursive approach to culture became accentuated in Hall's writings, thus reinforcing the proposition that a linguistic or discursive turn has occurred in his work. For example, *Resistance through Rituals* defined culture in the conventional terms of social science:

> We understand the word 'culture' to refer to that level at which social groups develop distinct patterns of life, and give *expressive* form to their social and material life-experience . . . The culture of a group or class is the peculiar and distinctive 'way of life' of institutions, in social relations, in systems of beliefs, in mores and customs, in the uses of objects and material life. Culture is the distinctive shapes in which this material and social organization of life expresses itself.
> (Hall and Jefferson 1976: 11; emphasis in the original)

This is a version of cultural materialism that situates cultural form in material conditions of life. Although it recognizes cultural variation, this is typically defined in class terms. For example, the stylistic repertoires and political objectives of youth subculture are analysed as expressing and inflecting the structure of the more inclusive parent culture to which they are attached. Class is understood as a relation of solidarity that derives from the antagonistic character of class struggle in capitalist society. The form of youth subculture is therefore explained in terms of its relation, first, to the 'parent' culture and, by this means, to the dominant antagonism between dominant and subordinate classes.

By the 1990s cultural materialism takes second place to a perspective that emphasizes the discursive constitution of culture, nation, race and identity. Hall now avows that:

> Culture is nothing but the sum of the different classificatory systems and discursive formations on which language draws in order to give meaning to things. The very term 'discourse' refers to a group of

statements in any domain which provides a language for talking about a topic and a way of producing a particular kind of knowledge about that topic . . . The 'cultural turn' expands this insight about language to social life in general. It argues that because economic and social processes themselves *depend* on meaning and have consequences for our ways of life, for who we are – our identities – and for 'how we live now', they too must be understood as cultural, as discursive practices. (1997c: 222; emphasis in the original)[3]

The discursive approach postulates culture as a system of representation. The materialist aspects of culture are not ignored. Rather they are redefined in language which has unmistakable idealist overtones, as 'constructed *within* representation, *through* culture, not outside of them' (Hall 1997c: 220). The tensions in the Marxist base–superstructure model that perplexed Hall during the Birmingham years are now resolved by maintaining the centrality of discourse in every form of association, identity and practice. The economy is not the base or 'substructure' of culture/religion/ideology, or the 'superstructure', because both base and superstructure are now regarded to be only meaningful through discursive representation. On the other hand, this approach seems to be based on a realist view of language as independent from human speakers.

Althusserianism posited that there is no space outside ideology, but that science objectifies aspects of ideology and permits reflexive analysis. After the linguistic or discursive turn Hall (1997c) submits that there is no space outside culture. This suggests an acceptance of cultural relativism that is, however, moderated by Hall's continued commitment to emancipatory politics. His support for multi-ethnic society, progressive fiscal realignment and public investment to redress inequality suggests that while Hall believes that there is no space outside of culture, he holds that some forms of culture are more reflexive and, hence, preferable to others.

The West and the Rest

This is certainly evident in his critique of 'compulsive Eurocentrism'. Hall maintains that the Enlightenment advocated and consecrated a division between the West and the Rest. The West–Rest binary divide underwrote the 'civilized–rude, developed–backward oppositions of the West and the Rest discourse' (Hall 1992b: 316). The 'West' is a complex condensation that constitutes an organic-epochal field of force. It is a system of representation that signifies automatic superiority. It enables classifications of certain kinds of economic and social development so that different societies are labelled as 'behind' or 'catching up' with the West. This produces a kind of Orwellian double-think: 'The West', writes Hall, '= developed = *good* = desirable; "non-West" = under-developed = *bad* = undesirable' (1992b: 277; emphasis in original).

Hall regards colonization in the sixteenth and seventeenth centuries as a process which perpetuated the assumption that European society is the most advanced on earth. This state of affairs was portrayed as the result of internal factors in European history and culture that were believed to be propitious in the assertion of global leadership. The colonized remain excluded from the Western story except as resources for exploitation and objects for moral 'improvement'. While Hall does not ground his discussion in the exploration of Western 'civilization', it is evident that the internal factors he has in mind are Western science, technology, government, religion, economics, medicine and the arts.

The West therefore sees its relationship with the Rest as paternalistic rather than dialogic. Western science, technology, medicine, government and so forth are donated to the Rest to 'improve' native 'backward' conditions. There is no attempt to engage in dialogue with non-Western cultural, moral or spiritual frameworks. True, anthropology and ethnography develop more dialogic strategies in the second half of the twentieth century. But this comes later. The superiority of the West is the original and unshakeable presupposition behind colonial expansion. Western cosmology is automatically prioritized as superior. This was reinforced by the successive conquest of various types of native people through violence and economic domination.

Hall identifies four discursive strategies in the Western system of representation with 'the Rest' (1992b: 308):

1 *Idealization* This refers to the attribution of characteristics to native people by Western explorers and settlers. Instead of engaging with the complexity of native social organization and civil society on their own terms, Western explorers and settlers tended to attribute characteristics to the places and peoples they 'discovered'. Thus the Tropics were portrayed as an 'earthly paradise' and the people inhabiting them as living 'the simple life', showing more candour about sexuality and the body.
2 *The projection of fantasies of desire and degradation* Hall interprets colonization as mobilizing powerful sexual fantasies of sexual

innocence and experience, sexual domination and submission. Living 'close to nature' meant that natives did not possess the reason of Europeans. Their departure from Western codes of marriage and property distribution was not interpreted as difference, but as evidence of an 'uncivilized' state of being.

3 *The failure to recognize and respect difference* Western expansion operated through the a priori of Western superiority. The Enlightenment proposition of one universal path to progress modelled on the West obliterated diversity. Everything was subjected to the law of the West.

4 *The tendency to impose European categories and norms, to frame difference through the modes of perception and representation of the West* Colonization presented non-European knowledge and systems of classification as inherently faulty. Non-European ways of being were consigned to the dustbin of history. The world was remade in the idealized image of the West.

The discursive strategies interconnect in complex and dynamic ways, but they all operate through principles of stereotyping and splitting. The idealization of 'the West' as the pinnacle of the human race was part of a double-circuit that both romanticized the naturalism of 'savage society' and denigrated the 'unchanging simplicity' of 'primitive peoples'. Western cosmology collapsed and simplified an enormous array of different elements into a tyrannical binary opposition between the West and the Rest, to which, Hall attests (1992b: 308), a range of symbolic reconfirming oppositions were attached: good–bad, us–them, attractive–disgusting and civilized–uncivilized. These oppositions were polarized around fixed relations of subordination and domination. Their stereotypes were positioned around the poles of 'superior' and 'inferior' natural species. This arrangement was represented as a fact of Nature rather than a narrative of History. Through these 'naturalized' discursive strategies, Hall contends:

> The Rest becomes defined as everything that the West is not – its mirror image. It is represented as absolutely, essentially different, *other*: the Other. This Other is then itself split into 'two camps': friendly–hostile, Arawak–Carib, innocent–depraved, noble–ignoble ... Without the Rest ... the West would not have been able to recognize and represent itself as the summit of human history. The figure of 'the Other', banished to the edge of the conceptual world and constructed as the absolute opposite, the negation of everything which the West stood for, reappeared at the very centre of the discourse of civilization. (1992b: 308, 314)

'The West' positioned 'the Other' in a secondary subaltern relation. Its perverse power lay in addressing the Other as a subject to internalize this system of representation as the regime of truth. The result was that the Other began to see and experience subjective existence as 'Other' and to look to the West for 'guidance' and leadership.

At the same time, the Other was part of a double-circuit which powered fantasies of the alleged 'naturalism' of so-called 'primitive life' at the same moment as it denigrated it. 'Otherness', exclusion, fetishism and pathologization were required to fix and consolidate 'difference' within a unified discourse of civilization (Hall 1996b: 252).

Hall concedes that there is 'simplification' in his discussion of the West and the Rest. Thus each category covers enormous historical, cultural and economic distinctions. However, he legitimates this simplification as 'necessary' since it accurately reflects the crude binarism that underpinned the Western system of representation with respect to the discourse of civilization (1992b: 280). But it is questionable if this argument carries water. Within the formation of the West there are significant frictions and tensions concerning the concept of civilization.

Consider David Cannadine's (2001) powerful argument that in the British Empire, status was always more important than race. Unquestionably, white Britons held disparaging views about non-whites conceived of as an abstract *collective*. Cannadine does not deny that racism was a structural characteristic of empire. At the same time he submits that racist views were not necessarily carried over to apply to non-white *individuals*. The British establishment did not claim innate superiority over native cultures. On the contrary, rule by analogy was practised. Native social hierarchies were regarded as parallel ladders to the British titular system. Indeed, there were moments in the nineteenth century when the hierarchies in some countries, notably those organized around the ruling princes in India, the emirs and sheiks in Arabia and the sultans in Malaya, were held to be *superior* to the British system. In the late nineteenth century, as the British establishment contemplated the spread of the new unionism, the campaign for electoral reform and the rise of the suffragette movement at home, they looked to India, Arabia and Malaya and saw more stable hierarchical systems in which authority and deference appeared to obey the immemorial 'natural' order. This may have been myopic on the part of the British. For half a century later the movements for national independence in these and other colonies seem to have taken the British colonialists and the chain of command in London by surprise. But it was also more heartfelt and politically significant than Hall's account of the West and the Rest allows.

Within classical sociology the debate between the ghosts of Marx and Weber is often portrayed as turning on the distinctions between class and status. To be clear, Marx is held to place emphasis on class in the analysis of power, while Weber's sociology is regarded as assigning greater significance to status. In this debate Hall plainly sides with Marx, albeit a Marx refracted through the colonial terror sanctioned through some aspects of Enlightenment thought. This leads Hall to underestimate the significance of relations of interdependence and mutuality in human relations in favour of an approach that prefigures conflict and ideology. One important example of this is the concept of civilization. In Hall's work civilization is virtually indistinguishable from ideology.

Kultur and the civilizing process

Hall does not mention the work of Norbert Elias on the civilizing process (1978; 1982). This is a major and troubling omission, since Elias's work identifies significant cleavages in the meaning of the term civilization in Western nations.[4] His work suggests that 'Eurocentrism' is a dubious concept because it ignores national distinctions in seventeenth- and eighteenth-century Europe that produced fateful rivalries that limit the universalism of the concept of civilization and therefore compromise the West/Rest dichotomy. For the French-speaking German ruling class and the English in the eighteenth and early nineteenth centuries, Elias argued, civilization is a universal category expressing 'the self-consciousness of the West' (1978: 3–4). It represented everything in Western society that is regarded as superior to earlier societies and 'more primitive' contemporary ones. As examples Elias noted the self-attribution of pre-eminence with respect to Western science, government, technology and the arts. For the French and English, Western civilization constituted the summit of human achievement. This is the picture of 'compulsive Eurocentrism' that Hall conveys in his work.

However, Elias notes that the seventeenth- and eighteenth-century German middle class held a contrasting view of civilization. For them, the term signified the second rank, expressing qualities that are desirable and useful but subordinate to the possession of *Kultur*, which is recognized as the apex of human attainment. The term *Kultur* signified high levels of learning, artistic cultivation and religious devotion. It accentuated the specific and distinctive, and was therefore incommensurate with binarism organized around abstract collectivity. The West and the Rest distinction possessed resonance for some strata in France, England, Belgium, Portugal and Spain. But for the Germans it was generally an invalid polarity, and the German national recognition of it as such was to have great consequences for the pattern of European and world history.

For Elias the cleavage between civilization and *Kultur* produces many tensions. By belonging to a caste, high class or estate in society, or possessing national citizenship in a 'developed' society vis-à-vis an 'underdeveloped' society, one has leave to call oneself 'civilized'. In contrast *Kultur* is more particularistic and refers to achieved status. One might belong to a high class or estate in society, but breeding and belonging are no guarantee of *Kultur*. *Kultur* is the result of *bildung*, a personal progression towards spiritual perfection. For Germans the spread of civilization was not an unqualified benefit because it threatened the specific qualities of *Kultur*. In their view *Kultur* and civilization expressed the antithesis between depth and superficiality. While they participated in the scramble for colonies in the nineteenth and twentieth centuries, they did so as late-comers and were massively disunited before 1871. Their stance and policies were different from, and partly dismissive of, the French, English, Spanish, Belgian and Portuguese paths to colonial power.

The tension was dramatized in Germany because the standards of civilization had become established in the French and Francophile German courts, resulting in considerable friction with the native tradition of *Kultur*. German intellectuals regarded themselves as under pain of colonization. Louis XIV and Napoleon both invaded Germany, inscribing 'foreign' values and mores on native practices and institutions. Thus German intellectuals defined themselves in opposition to the 'civilized' values of court society. They cultivated the qualities of personal integrity in order to preserve and enhance *Kultur* against what they saw as the meretricious, 'inauthentic' values of 'civilized' men and women. As Elias observes, this meaning of *Kultur* contained 'the gesture of isolation' (1978: 21). Additionally, it suggested asceticism and restraint. The university, not the court, was the theatre in which superior forms of human attainment were nurtured.

Elias was a student of Karl Mannheim and therefore understood well enough the ideological dimension of civilization and *Kultur*.

The terms were mobilized politically to signify national and group identity and difference. In part, the Great War had been waged between France and Germany in the name of civilization. After the defeat of the Germans, the concept of *Kultur* was revitalized as an ideological weapon to represent national integrity and destiny. The conflict between *Kultur* and civilization was the ideological representation of the national rivalry between Germany and France. It symbolized the spiritual, moral, artistic and religious values that divided them. The ideological mobilization of *Kultur* as the distinctive quality of the German nation had malign consequences. Kaiser Wilhelm II and Adolf Hitler both pronounced the independence of the German nation and stereotyped the Western Allies as suffering from obvious deformations of culture.

Like Mannheim, Elias regarded civilization and *Kultur* as inherently ideological constructs. However, unlike Mannheim, he held that 'the civilizing process' is a descriptive social development that is non-ideological. For Elias, the civilizing process is therefore independent of the charge of inherent ideologism to which Hall and postcolonial critics subject the concept of civilization. Nor would Elias have accepted the postcolonial argument that Western cosmology is so tainted with Western domination that the concepts of civilization and *Kultur* are no longer tenable. Instead he maintained that through methods of comparative and historical analysis it is possible to demonstrate that some forms of human behaviour and types of normative institution exhibit higher standards of utility, greater tolerance for others and more control over desire than others. For example, although he was aware of, and sensitive to, the counter-arguments, Elias believed that Western science possessed greater truth value than folklore or magic. He developed a variety of concepts to investigate what the civilizing process consisted of. Among the most important were increasing 'thresholds of repugnance' with respect to violence, higher 'standards of embarrassment' with regard to aggression and public nudity, and the changing, contingent 'tension balance' between desire and restraint.

Hall follows Saussure, Lacan and Derrida in regarding identity to be a set of positions, as opposed to an integrated entity. Elias would have approved of the notion of positioning, but he did not follow the line in structuralism that argues that meaning is arbitrary. Nor did he accept the poststructuralist argument that meaning cannot be contained. Elias's sociology sought to investigate history and culture to produce a better alignment between the human condition and the management of human affairs. In as much as this is so, he believed that an accurate understanding of the civilizing process offered humankind the possibility of reintegrating cultural and historical identity at a more adequate level. He was not averse to regarding identity as a set of positions. Indeed 'process sociology' is partly designed to 'naturalize' this idea in social and cultural enquiry. However, one of the points in studying the civilizing process was to gain accurate knowledge about human interdependence and development in order to make life better for humanity.[5]

Elias was cognizant of the connotations of ethnocentricity and superiority in the term civilizing process but maintained that they were misplaced. For him the civilizing process is a technical term to describe a series of demonstrable changes in human behaviour and social interrelations. Indeed his painstaking analysis of *Kultur* is partly designed to invalidate the claims of superiority and universalism that Western cosmology claimed for itself. Nor did he believe Western civilization to be inherently progressive or superior except in the sense of being more powerful, largely because of its social fund of relatively reality-congruent knowledge. Hall's later work has done much to popularize the proposition that identity, nation, race and culture are processes not objects, and that regarding them as such is a prerequisite for an emancipatory understanding of politics. Elias held the same view, although he would have regarded Hall's left-wing convictions as evidence of unacceptable political 'involvement' because they ideologically prejudge the object and purpose of investigation.

Elias always inclined to the argument that one important purpose of sociological analysis is to destroy myths and so produce an orientation to society and nature that might make life more pleasant and fulfilling. But he is certainly at one with Hall in rejecting binarism and static conceptual formations that present 'identity', 'race', 'nation' and 'civilization' as fixed, solid, stable and polarized phenomena. In fact Elias (1971; 1984a; 1984b) proposed that *Zustandsreduktion*, the tendency to conceptually reduce processes to states, is one of the central defects of Western thought. *Zustandsreduktion* produces unchanging 'false conceptual dichotomies' that are unable to embrace or explain observable changes in human behaviour. Western science, technology and government have all produced profoundly negative outcomes as well as positive ones. The civilizing process is never finished and a review of its history reveals regression or 'downswings' as well as advance.

Hall (1996b) assigns to postcolonialism the lion's share in subverting the old binarism between the colonizing powers and the colonized. Postcolonialism is associated both with the political and cultural transition from colonial rule to formal independence, and the writings of Frantz Fanon, Edward Said, Homi Bhabha and Gayatri Spivak. It is usually understood to mean the set of discursive and non-discursive practices involving resistance to colonialism and colonialist legacies. The radical, perhaps one should say 'prefigurative' contribution of Elias is to posit that this resistance was not merely a reaction of the colonized to European colonialism. It was front-loaded in the European quest to colonize. Hall (1992b: 279–80) acknowledges 'many internal differences' in eighteenth- and nineteenth-century Eurocentrism: the divisions between Eastern and Western Europe, the Germanic Northern and the Latin Southern cultures, the Iberian, Nordic and Mediterranean peoples, and the ambiguous place of women, Jews, gays and lesbians in the European 'formation'. This is appropriate. But it does not begin to convey the significance of the inherent and deep schism in the Western modernizing/colonizing process between civilization and *Kultur*. This is perhaps reason to suggest that, for all its penetrating insights, it is, in crucial respects, a limited reading of Western colonial hegemony.

Postcolonialism

Hall follows the postcolonial line that demarcations between inside and outside, them and us, home and abroad are disrupted by the emergence of a transnational, transcultural, diasporic, decentred rewriting of earlier nation-centred, imperial grand narratives. The closure of Western binarism is exposed as arbitrary. There has been a move from 'difference' to *'différance'*. To some degree this parallels the shift from politics to the 'war of position' identified long ago by Gramsci. But postcolonialism goes much further in 'rephrasing modernity' and interrupting the entire grand historical narrative shared by liberal and Marxist historiography (Hall 1996b: 250).

Hall's account of postcolonialism deploys Derrida's concept of 'double inscription'. This involves treating postcolonialism as an *'episteme* in formation'. The essentialism of Western binarism is theorized as operating 'under erasure'. Its internal contradictions have weakened its authority. Postcolonial critics have of course exploited and developed these contradictions. But politically, economically and socially, binarism has not been abolished. In lieu of a different, more accurate network of concepts, a new language that can express the integral character of hybridity, contingency and decentring in agency and practice, it remains the only way to think about the present, but only if it is applied in its deconstructed form. The double inscription of binarism consists in the representation of difference, and in certain junctures the erasure of the authority that binary representation conveys.

Hall (1996b) borrows Derrida's phrase, 'thinking at the limit', to describe this difficult analytic task. The difficulty is twofold. First, it lies in operating with instruments of analysis that are acknowledged to be faulty, but under the awareness that they cannot be replaced currently or in the foreseeable future. This means occupying the awkward hiatus between deconstruction and reconstruction. It is awkward because, while there is widespread agreement that binarism is disintegrating, the new emerging condition is obscure and involves unfamiliar and challenging ways of thinking about agency, practice and power. Second, it consists in the critical obligation to pursue these faults rigorously until they cease to be pertinent. In Hall's mind the latter renews the traditional objectives of the organic intellectual, namely the pursuit of the most advanced and relevant ideas and the public dissemination of these ideas in order to engage politically with the present conjuncture.

Hall's account of postcolonialism connects up in many places with the New Times thesis. Thus it holds that we are in the midst of an epochal transition in which the centre of gravity of society and culture has moved decisively in a new direction. It recognizes that this shift is uneven and that there is no reason to believe that the disturbed particles of the old order and the rising fragments of the new will settle down into some kind of stable rapprochement.

Above all, the shift in perspective is evident in the question of identity. It has become inadmissible to conceptualize the subject as a centred, stable ego or autonomous rational self. The 'self' is deposed, fragmented and repositioned as a hybrid, multiple, processual agent. To some extent Hall hangs on to his Gramscian and Althusserian past by continuing to maintain that the placing or positioning of the subject occurs historically and contemporaneously in relation to different discourses, and that the stamp of these discourses is capitalist. He never followed Foucault down the path of micro-politics and discursive relativism. He repudiates these traits in Foucault's work, and in uncharacteristic polemical vein declares Foucault to hold a 'proto-anarchist' position (Hall 1986a:

48). This derives from Hall's view that Foucault is 'evasive' on the question of ideology. Foucault gives you a world of micro-politics, and for Hall the questions are where are the power blocs? How is resistance interpellated? What politics of transformation can be extracted from this conjuncture?

Whether or not this is an acceptable reading of Foucault is debatable.[6] However, it underlines Hall's continuing commitment to political intervention in a socialist direction. For Hall, New Times equals the end of one important kind of left-wing orientation and the beginning of new opportunities for socialist renewal. Significantly, while he recognizes that postcolonialism is another nail in the coffin of 'economistic', 'teleological' and 'ultimately reductionist' Marxism (1996b: 258–9), he submits that decentring should not be mistaken for the disavowal of the importance of the economic. Only die-hard Althusserians still believe that history is determined 'in the last instance' by the economy. But this provides no licence either to discount the importance of economic relations or to stop treating the social, economic and cultural formation as decisively capitalist. This is not tantamount to a call for postcolonial theorists to read Althusser again. But it is perhaps a grapeshot from Hall that the textual approach in postcolonialism comes perilously close to idealist relativism by failing to engage with the concrete level of capitalist accumulation. Hall refuses to accept that there is an 'unbridgeable incompatibility' between the postfoundationalism of postcolonialism and the 'serious investigation' of the local and global 'complex articulations' of capitalism (1996b: 258).

Hall rejects the postmodernist thesis that the self is merely a kind of perpetual signifier. He does not wish to discard the notion of identity, since it is a prerequisite for agency and cultural and political intervention. Derrida's notion of *différance* is important to him, but he recognizes that 'if we are concerned to maintain a politics, it cannot be defined exclusively in terms of an infinite sliding of the signifier' (1992a: 257). Elsewhere, he warns that 'it is only too tempting to fall into the trap of assuming that because essentialism has been deconstructed *theoretically*, therefore it has been displaced *politically*' (1996b: 249; emphasis in original). Hall remains a consistent New Leftist in holding that cultural and political strategies can make a difference and that they always involve a struggle with established interests.

The repositioning of identity and the process of enunciation were prominent themes in *Policing the Crisis*, and they remain central to Hall's approach. Positioning in terms of class, gender or ethnic roots is necessary for the purposes of cultural and political engagement. However, an accurate reading of culture and politics must recognize that our position in relation to them is culturally and politically constructed. Identity is therefore stripped of any essentialist connotations and redefined as part of a narrative, always connected to representation. Hall conceives of representation as multidiscursive and therefore abounding in contradictions. Identity is written over the Other and part of the analytic task is to engage in a process of 'cultural recovery' (1989c: 19). That is what Hall means by the argument that it is now necessary to operate under and with 'erasure'. The overwritten character of both English national identity and the old Left's faith in class were major themes in Hall's criticism of Thatcherism. This criticism was partly concerned to demonstrate how splitting and closure failed to contain meaning. It sought to treat identity not as a fixed point but an unfolding, ambivalent process.

Postcolonialism utilizes the same arguments to unpick the Western notion of identity with its strong connotations of solidity, integration and independence. One reason why Hall's later work has concentrated so much on questions of ethnicity is that the poverty of the Western concept of identity is most clearly expressed in the subject of race. This is because it cannot avoid confronting the issues of memory, silences, displacement, migration, inclusion and exclusion. As Hall puts it:

> In black popular culture, strictly speaking, there are no pure forms at all. Always these forms are the product of partial synchronization, of engagement across cultural boundaries, of the confluence of more than one cultural tradition, of the negotiations of dominant and subordinate positions, of the subterranean strategies of recoding and transcoding, of critical signification, of signifying. (1996d: 471)

Although race is the subject of this passage, it is apparent that Hall regards the decentring of racial essentialism as bound up with a much wider set of challenges in rethinking association, identity and practice. Because the construct of 'black race' intertwines and interpenetrates with the 'Other', disrupting the articulation of 'black' destabilizes the entire representational system and field of power of binarism. The postcolonial decentring of race becomes a metaphor for the exhaustion of the entire Western cultural, social, political and economic *episteme*. It exposes the closure in Western notions of being, and therefore expedites creative thinking and agency about new forms of belonging.

'Identity Politics One', 'new ethnicities' and 'the politics of difference'

Hall's work on race rejects biological racism and offers a discursive reading of race as part of a system of representation. '"Black"', writes Hall, 'is essentially a politically and culturally *constructed* category, which cannot be grounded in a set of fixed trans-cultural or transcendental racial categories and which therefore has no guarantees in Nature' (1992a: 254; emphasis in original). Ethnicity is a question of cultural positioning, not biological essentialism.

Hall illustrates this by a series of reflections on the postwar history of black immigration in Britain (1970; 1991b; 1992b; 1996d). He detects a major shift in the stance of the black diaspora both to the host culture and to their own formation. In part this reflects what Hall calls 'multicultural drift' (2000c: 1), namely the unplanned, unintentional increase in the profile of non-white, ethnic influence in British public life. The greater visibility of the ethnic diaspora is a reflection of postwar immigration and the participation of first, and now second and third generation non-white migrants in the school system, the labour market and the general public sphere. The first wave of black immigrants developed what Hall refers to as 'Identity Politics One' (1991b: 52). This consisted of a singular and unifying framework based on articulating identity across ethnic and cultural difference. For Hall it is a moment of 'profound historical reversal' (2000c: 7), the juncture in which black became beautiful and anti-racism began to confront politically the Western system of representation. Identity Politics One was part of a counter-hegemonic war of manoeuvre designed to reposition blacks from the margins where they had been cast by the white host society. It produced many successful anti-racist initiatives and increased the awareness of multiculturalism in Britain.

Incidentally, Hall is somewhat dismissive of multiculturalism (1991b: 55; 2000c: 2–3), believing it to be tainted with traditional Western connotations of 'the exotica of difference' and not the axial processes of inequality and oppression central to racism.[7] The Parekh Report favoured multi-ethnic society as the presiding concept to describe social and cultural relations in Britain. Nonetheless, Hall recognizes that 'multiculturalism' has made considerable headway in colloquial conceptions of race and ethnicity (2000c), and for this reason seems resigned to deploying it in his writings. Its profile in the postwar period has been raised through the combination of a number of factors, the most important of which are the process of decolonization, the collapse of the Soviet Union and the increasing significance of globalization in national and local practices.

Of course, Hall does not believe that the nirvana of racial and ethnic brotherhood has arrived. On the contrary, he insists that the politics of anti-racism is far from being played out (1992a; 1992b). The material and symbolic features of racial inequality require the rhetorical, and on occasions practical, counterposing of black identity against white identity in order to achieve redistributive justice. Identity Politics One operated to challenge, resist and, wherever possible, transform the dominant regimes of representation. It worked on many fronts, at first through music and style and later literature, photography and film. It exploited the dialectic between denigration and desire that partly phrased the relation of the West to the Other. Identity Politics One was and remains a necessary war of manoeuvre. It established repertoires of black popular culture that engendered important forms of 'camaraderie and community' among blacks occupying 'an alien social space' (Hall 1996d: 471). But these repertoires were doubly overdetermined. First, by the inheritance of 'Africa' and 'roots' as signifiers of belonging; and second, by the eclectic and partial synchronization of 'black' idiom and character. Hall is careful to insist that this inheritance and synchronization were necessary counter-hegemonic strategies (1991b: 56–8; 1996d: 461). Equally, he submits that Identity Politics One tended to essentialize both the past and ethnic integrity. Identity is always a matter of positionality and process. It is always a matter of narrativizing the past and collective unity, rather than directly and literally appropriating them.

The implication, although Hall does not spell it out, is that Identity Politics One confused the two issues. The discourse of identity cannot be reversed simply by assigning a plus sign instead of a minus to the black side of the binary racial dichotomy. Nor can we solidify our identity by journeying back into the past. There is no original, imaginary space insulated from the fire and soot of modernity to which the ethnic minorities of the West can be 'restored'. Nor do white Westerners, those inhabitants of 'the imagined communities' of nation-states, possess a privileged relationship to the past. Heritage is an imagined construct, part of a system of representation that has real political, cultural and economic consequences in the present, but to which we have pre-eminently a narrative, partly fictive relationship (Hall 1999: 13–15). Our relationship to the past, to 'roots', is always and already an imaginative relationship which must ever be 'retold, rediscovered and reinvented' (Hall 1991b: 58).

The problem of essentialism in Identity Politics One was expressed vividly by the sense that many Asians and blacks had of being estranged from the formation. Identity Politics One did not necessarily speak to the interests, needs and histories of an Indian shopkeeper trying to build up a business in Bradford, or to a Ugandan teacher working in an inner city school. In forming itself in reaction to white domination it erased multi-ethnic distinctions and hence isolated itself from many of the people it wanted to embrace.

Difference is the watchword of Hall's writing on ethnicity and culture since the 1990s. The 'new ethnicities' which he contends are supplanting Identity Politics One practise 'the politics of living identity through difference. It is the politics of recognizing that all of us are composed of multiple social identities, not of one' (Hall 1991b: 57). Note that there are two aspects to difference identified in this sentence. First, the differences in values, lifestyles, beliefs and family networks which differentiate one ethnic group form another. Second, the differences in being that derive from recognizing that each person is composed of 'multiple social identities'.

This involves a shift from a struggle over the relations of representation to a politics of representation itself (Hall 1992a: 253). It is no longer a question of trying to reverse one discourse of identity by counterposing another. Rather it is a question of investigating the diversity of black experience and *all* experience in relation to place, position and process. This involves a substantial revision of the concept of ethnicity. Hall is concerned to retain the concreteness of ethnic difference, but to pre-empt the implication that ethnicity is bounded or essentialized. As he puts it:

> This marks a real shift in the politics of contestation, since it is no longer between antiracism and multiculturalism but inside the notion of ethnicity itself. What is involved is the splitting of the notion of ethnicity between on the one hand the dominant notion which connects it to nation and 'race', and on the other hand what I think is the beginning of a new, positive conception of the ethnicity of the margins, of the periphery. That is to say, the recognition that we all speak from a particular place, out of a particular history, out of a particular experience, a particular culture, without being contained by that position as 'ethnic artists' or film makers. (1992a: 258)

The emphasis on particularity is deliberate. The function of ethnicity in 'new ethnicity' is to position, demarginalize and validate ethnic forms in the experiences of the ethnic communities from which it draws its strength. Its axis is local despite the fact that it necessarily mediates with global forces. It addresses people through the multiple identities that they possess via the groundings and contingencies of family, work, leisure, region and religion. It respects difference and diversity. Its social imaginary is unity through difference. At the same time, Hall is disarmingly frank in admitting that he cannot yet see how a politics can be constructed that works with and through difference to build unity without suppressing the real heterogeneity of experience and interests or reifying them (1992a: 254–5).

Hall's account bids yet another farewell to the traditional politics of socialism. He maintains that the politics of difference is not a variation on the familiar Marxist war of manoeuvre in which all of the locals around the world will fuse into a grand movement of liberation to roll back global capital (1991b: 59). Globalization works through and upon particularity and locality. The opposition to its repressive and brutalizing consequences must perforce be conducted at the local level and through particular associations and practices. Hall reminds his readers that the Thatcher–Reagan era demonstrated that cultural racism and ethnic absolutism are not dead (1996d: 468–9). The turning back of the canon of Western civilization as the privileged 'regime of truth' from which all arguments, debates and interventions are positioned arouses the entrenched interests of 'old ethnicities'. The concept of new ethnicities replenishes Hall's social imaginary of a social order based on the mutual benefit of participants. But it insists that abandoning the logic of struggle against established interests would be premature.

The Parekh Report

What does it mean to wage ethnic struggle against established interests in order to achieve redistributive justice? For Hall, one of the most hopeful strategies is to revise, through education and debate, what it means to be British. He contends that 'the question of Britishness is a timebomb which is ticking away at the centre of society' (2001: 19). Increasingly since the 1990s his work has seized upon Benedict Anderson's (1991) proposition that nations should be considered as imagined communities. Once the fictive character of nationhood is recognized, the visceral fiat of nationalism is exposed as a delusion. One way of reading Hall's work on nationalism and race today is that it maintains that 'we are all hybrid now.' Traditionally, hybridity has been associated with racial enervation and the dilution of power. Hall wishes to invert this association. The recognition that we are all hybrid produces strength because it ends the futile quest for purity in race or nation.

Although Hall develops this line of thought in interesting ways in his theoretical writings (1993c; 1993d; 1996d), perhaps its most powerful evocation is to be found in the Parekh Report (2000), which examines the policy implications of hybridity and racism in multi-ethnic Britain. The report is a multi-authored work by the Committee on the Future of Multi-Ethnic Britain set up by the Runnymede Trust in 1998 to promote the cause of racial justice in Britain.[8] Hall is a major signatory to the report, and while he did not head the commission, the influence of his ideas on race and identity permeate many of the central recommendations.

When it was published, some sections of the tabloid press ridiculed the report for purporting to demand the erasure of British history. In fact something more subtle, and truer to Hall's convictions about hybridity, interrupted identity and the rise of new ethnicities, was attempted. The Parekh Report (2000) demanded a rethinking of national history and identity. The purpose was not to erase British achievements or to deny British identity. Rather it sought to demonstrate the original hybrid character of British history and identity. The nation was always more ethnically diverse than it was popularly imagined to be. Britain is now reconceptualized as 'the community of communities' (Parekh Report 2000: 3). The unified consciousness of Britishness has long been disputed by sections of the Welsh, Scottish and Irish communities. But in the postwar years, and especially since the 1970s, the imagined character of the British nation has been thrown into sharper relief. This is the result of a combination of several tendencies. The most important are globalization, the British entry into the European Community, devolution, the end of empire and the growth of 'social pluralism'.

Several factors are condensed into the latter term, including the rise of post-Fordism, the decline of traditional industries, the casualization of the labour market, the feminization of the workforce, the decomposition of traditional class hierarchies, the comparative decline of marriage, the shifting of gender and sexual norms, the resurgence of individualism, the decline of the public service ethos, the increase of moral relativism and the emergence of a more personalized ethics. All of these factors are prominent in Hall's examination of 'New Times' (Hall and Jacques 1989). However, while they have contributed significantly to the destabilization of national identity by demonstrating the hybrid character of British history and the porous form of the British nation-state, they have not swept away racism. The Parekh Report follows the Macpherson Report (1999) in holding that racism and institutional racism are widespread in Britain.

Parekh proposes a variety of policy initiatives in education, policing, employment, immigration and asylum, health and welfare, and arts, media and sport to combat racism and uproot discrimination. All are built around an interlocking triangle of principles of cohesion, equality and difference. The realization of these principles is predicated in a twin strategy of government leadership and legislation, and enforcement. Parekh makes a number of recommendations for active government leadership and legislation designed to eliminate racial discrimination and to promote equality with respect to sex, race, colour and ethnic or national origin. The introduction of an Equality Act and an Equality Commission is recommended. Parekh proposes that every organization should be called on to audit its workforce by ethnicity and set action plans and performance targets. The Equality Commission must have powers to ensure that organizations comply with these measures. In cases where compliance is deemed to be faulty, the issue should be subject to judicial review. It also proposes a Declaration on Cultural Diversity to preserve the heritage and promote the equality of all members of society.

Some readers may identify tensions between these recommendations and Hall's view of multiple identities, increasing flexibility and New Times. For this view suggests increasing pluralism and fragmentation, making society and culture less amenable to centralized, state control. At the levels of legislation and organization, Parekh identifies a substantial increase in bureaucratization, and the reference to 'action plans' and 'performance targets' smacks of the 'new managerialism' that Hall (1998a) abhors in New Labour. Interestingly, the state is identified as the primary instrument of change. Other approaches, notably the 'Third Way' associated with the writings of Anthony Giddens (1998: 2000), tend to give a more pronounced significance to partnership between the state and the corporation. Despite all the obvious arguments to the contrary, globalization requires multinationals to adopt new responsibilities in respect of the workforce and the environment, and it pressurizes governments and nation-state power blocs to intervene in global business practices. Parekh accepts that globalization has changed the parameters of racism and anti-racism. International human rights declarations are indeed recognized as providing the ground rules for protecting minimum standards, negotiating conflicts of interest and enjoining ethical standards of practice. Even so, the nation-state is presented as the fulcrum of anti-racist strategy and action.

However, the politics of difference suggests a much looser relationship between citizens and the state. The state no longer 'stands over' the citizen and uses education, policing and welfare policy to attempt to impose cultural homogeneity within the territorial boundaries where it claims a monopoly of jurisdiction. Instead the state acts as the guarantor that the rights of citizenship are applied to cultural heterogeneity, and that the one is a condition of the other. Hall has characterized the modern nation-state formation process as a system of representation dedicated to fusing the ethnic diversity of modern nationality into the 'primordial unity of "one people"' (1993c). He goes on to elaborate that this system of representation operates to project 'the ruptures and conquests' of 'real history' backwards into an 'apparently seamless and unbroken continuity towards pure, mythic time'. It is this system of representation that Parekh maintains is now evidently coming to an end. Cultural diversity is 'the fate of the modern world' (Hall 1993c: 349). Living in and with difference will be the defining experience of civil society in the twenty-first century. As Hall writes, for once resorting to a stereotype to press home the point:

> It should not be necessary to look, walk, feel, think, speak exactly like a paid-up member of the buttoned-up, stiff-upper-lipped, fully corseted 'free born Englishman' *culturally* to be accorded either the informal courtesy and respect of civilized social intercourse or the rights of entitlement and citizenship. (1993c; emphasis in the original)

The margins have not quite become the centre. Hall's writings on aesthetics and ethnicity (1992g; 2000a), notably the photography of black migration to Britain and the cinema of 'new ethnicities', takes great delight in the capacity of art from the margins to poleaxe culture into vital unrepressed configurations of recognition. But notwithstanding this there is a long way to go before the margins shed their status and relate to the centre on equal terms. On the other hand, the positioning of those in the diaspora on the margins of society has given them a head start in living in and with the culture of hybridity. It is this culture that Hall proclaims is destined to be 'truly representative' of 'late modern experience' (1993c).

Conclusion: 'The Future Belongs to the Impure'

The palimpsest in Hall's thought is anti-essentialism. It is evident in his family of origin, torn between brown, country and Anglophile loyalties and frictions. The backcloth to this is the chequered identity of the Caribbean which Hall has characterized as divided between three conflicting currents: *Presence Africaine, Presence Europeanne* and *Presence Americain* (1989g). Schooled in Jamaica College to revere the values of elite culture in England, he migrated, over fifty years ago, to find the English coldly haughty in their assumption of innate superiority and blankly indifferent to colonial 'difference'. Hall's involvement with the New Left presupposed and harnessed an attachment to class politics. But Hall's Marxism was always conditional. He never supported the rhetoric of class revolution and he rejected the productivist bent in the base–super-structure model. His approach to culture was always sensitive to difference, diversity and process. This inhibited him from identifying with traditional Marxist models of class struggle and historical determinism. The Birmingham approach always regarded itself to be a *selective* tradition within the study of culture. According to Johnson its distinctive coherence ultimately derived from seeking to systematically link the question of culture with a critique of forms of power and the recognition of differences in power and identity formation (2001: 264).

Hall's inveterate anti-essentialism produced a resilient independence in his cast of thought. There is a burning need in him to interrogate every 'obvious' feature of the present to prove that nothing is 'natural' or 'transparent' in culture. Signification, ideology and representation are central for him because they are the means through which the absence and presence of the past and the location of meaning in the present are positioned and repositioned. Power is understood as always a state of balance in a field of forces. The purpose of decoding and disrupting taken-for-granted meaning and practice is to reveal the sinews of power which 'phrase' or interpellate identity, association and agency.

For Hall, politics is first and foremost a struggle over representation. He was captivated by the ideas of Gramsci and Althusser because they argued that culture and history position us not simply as 'facts' but as subjects constructed through memory, fantasy, narrative and myth. Cultural identities are the unstable, shifting points produced within the discourses of culture and history. They are not essences, but positioned processes. He regards this as contributing decisively to emancipatory politics because it recognizes, first, that identities and positions are not immutable, and second, that 'origins' are inextricably mixed or hybrid.

But what kind of politics flows from the premise that all origins are mixed or hybrid? Henry Giroux has highlighted the connection between politics and critical pedagogy in Hall's work (Giroux 2000: 157–72). Hall's conception of intellectual labour envisages critical engagement with a variety of public sites by working within dominant institutions to expose and challenge their authority and cultural practices. Critical pedagogy is attached to public spaces in which culture operates to secure identity. It is rooted in issues of compassion and social responsibility and seeks to reveal the hand of power in shaping identity, association and practice. In Hall's work, critical pedagogy pursues the task of resisting hegemony and engaging in intertextual negotiations across different, interdisciplinary sites of cultural production. A major objective of this process is to learn to live with difference. Hall's later writings return repeatedly to a positive reading of hybridity and contrast it pointedly with the various forms of cultural purity that Hall believes are inherently bogus. But it is not easy to extrapolate solidarity from this position. Can difference be the basis for effective political agency? This is the question that Hall's later writings pose most forcefully. It raises the ancillary issue of what kind of politics Hall believes to be effective.

Before coming to these matters I want first to contextualize Hall's thinking in terms of the history of ideas. I have already referred to him as an eclectic thinker. But he is not undisciplined in his eclecticism. Hall has not provided a detailed account of his place in the history of ideas. Where he has attempted to compare and contrast his work with others it has typically been done *en passant*. These writings are not without interest. His paper on ideology and the science of knowledge (1978d) is one of the best secondary accounts available. It is surprising that it has not been anthologized more often. True to his anti-essentialist credentials, Hall regards late twentieth-century and early twenty-first century thought to be galvanized around the issue of the decentring of power/knowledge. But the roots of this process reach back to the end of the nineteenth century. He has produced an interesting, albeit schematic, account of the development of decentring (1989c: 10–12). It is interesting because it demonstrates how far Hall sees himself working with a sort of semi-detached sympathy for the Marxist tradition. He distinguishes four ground-breaking intellectual developments that combined to destabilize power/knowledge in Western thought:

1   *Marx* destabilized the bourgeois 'common-sense' perspective on identity by revealing the *situated* character of agency and practice. Men and women make their own histories but not under conditions of their own making or choosing. There is no such thing as a free or independent agent. Capitalism is the context in which agency and practice are located and agents are ineluctably entwined in relations of power.

2   *Freud* decentred the association between identity and fully self-reflective agency by introducing the concept of the unconscious. Once it is accepted that agency reflects unconscious processes, the traditional Western notion of the autonomous, rational actor is problematized. Agency here must be interpreted in its broadest sense as referring not only to the actions of the individual but to the development of culture and society. Freud's later writings, notably *The Future of an Illusion* (1927) and *Civilization and its Discontents* (1930) were clearly moving towards a deeper understanding of the role of the unconscious in the construction of culture.

3   *Saussure* decentred traditional concepts of meaning by arguing that discourse and enunciation itself are located within the relationships of language. Intentional meaning therefore bears the traces of these wider relationships, so that it carries unintended connotations and consequences. Saussure also introduced the distinction between the signifier (the written or acoustic form of the term) and the signified (the concept or form of the term), and maintained that the relationship between the two is arbitrary. In the study of culture this structuralist approach shifted the

emphasis decisively from the meaning and value of discrete cultural products to the system and conventions through which particular texts are produced and consumed.

4 *The end of Truth*, which Hall associates with many writings, notably the work of Nietzsche, Foucault and Derrida, results in the 'relativization of the Western world'. The collapse of the Western *episteme* as the universal authority reveals Foucault's link between knowledge and power. The Western *episteme* is just another 'regime of truth'. This recognition opens up 'the discovery of other worlds, other peoples, other cultures and other languages' (Hall 1989c: 12).

This focus on mental life does not expose Hall as having been a closet idealist all along. Throughout he is clear that decentring at the level of ideas both reflects and reinforces material processes. He neither attributes independence to ideas, nor proposes that they are the fruit of the material level. For Hall, Cultural Studies treats discursive frameworks as constitutive of 'reality' and not merely reflexive, in the sense of occurring 'after the event'. This does not preclude the proposition that material forces have real effects. Rather it submits that only through discursive regimes, and subject to the normative rendering of representation, are these effects intelligible. But it does show that Hall consciously places the emergence of Cultural Studies in a crisis in the Western *episteme* that partly reflected the deliberation of Western thought in taking itself to be an object of study. For all Hall's criticism of the 'West' as a socio-economic and political power bloc, his work exploits and extends the Western tradition of self-interrogation and reflexivity.

Post-Cartesianism, cultural relativism and the 'incomplete horizon': Hallmarks of the organic intellectual

Since 1989, Hall's writings have returned repeatedly to the argument that we are living in a moment of profound cultural change. Traditional postwar notions of place, nation, race and work have been disturbed by globalization, the rise of multicultural society, hybridity and post-Fordism. Old notions of stability in identity and transparency in history and territory are no longer tenable. It is a moment when all the positive drives and destabilizing tensions of anti-essentialism have come home to roost. We might characterize the principal features of this new juncture as involving three dominant features: post-Cartesianism, cultural relativism and what Ernesto Laclau has called the politics of the 'incomplete horizon'.

To elaborate, other post-Cartesian approaches have speculated on the challenge to Cartesian concepts of body and society posed by bio-engineering and transplant surgery (Haraway 1991; Featherstone 2000). The concepts of cloning, replacement surgery and genetic modification have tangible consequences for the Cartesian model of the body because they possess the capacity to revolutionize traditional concepts of the life-cycle, genetic determination and the relationship between body and society. Hall does not necessarily discount this approach, although he has not commented on it in detail. Instead his version of post-Cartesianism concentrates on the fragmented, multiple, processual character of identity. In the New Times thesis it is precisely the failure of the Cartesian mind–body dualism to achieve genuine integrity or stable fusion that dominates his writing on agency and meaning. The significance of this is not merely practical in that one must learn to look at the categories of agency and meaning in unfamiliar ways; it is also philosophical. Cartesianism articulated the notion of the self as an absolute presence. It either reduces the Other, by the attribution of the universal category of Reason, to a state of equivalence, or denigrates it as residing outside the realm of humanity.

Both processes are pronounced in Hall's critical account of the West and the Rest (1992b). Each stands at the gates of difference, repelling notions of Otherness and *différance* as chimeras. Thus the exposure of the Cartesian conception of absolute presence as a metaphysical construct disrupts the entire intricate scaffolding of power and coherence on which the authority of the West is based. Hall now refers to 'diasporic identities' that constantly produce and reproduce themselves anew through transformation and difference (1989c; 1993c). The unfinished, contingent and processual character of diasporic identity is paramount in Hall's most recent work. There is no going back to the solid Cartesian world of identity as absolute presence.

Turning now to the question of cultural relativism, Hall submits that multicultural drift and the emergence of multi-ethnic Britain present new challenges for the governance of diverse societies and disrupt traditional common-sense categories, theories and assumptions of belonging and solidarity (2000c: 4). Hybridity and diaspora are no longer confined to the margins of political economy and the study of culture. Instead they must be harnessed as the core conceptions of how agency, association and practice operate. Of course, the dragon of cultural absolutism has not been slain. Witness the euphoria among different cultural groups in Britain following victory in the Falklands War (1982) and in Britain and the US after the Gulf War (1991); the race riots in Oldham and Bradford in 2001; the racism of both Western and Muslim groups following the terrorist destruction of the World Trade Center and attack at the Pentagon, and the Anglo-American blitzkrieg on the Taliban in Afghanistan in the autumn and winter of 2001. However, the attribution of cultural superiority is now deeply problematic. One can no longer automatically say, for example, that 'white British is best', because the fictive and imagined character of nation is now popularly understood, if not always popularly observed. Even the concept of 'white British' is widely appreciated to be a hybrid construct. Hence Hall's preference for the term 'hyphenated identity' to represent not merely the conditional character of identity, but the hybrid nature of roots.

Cultural relativism is partly a reflection of the penetration of globalization into national and local conditions. The deregulation of markets, the rise of the weightless economy, the growth of multinationals and the expansion of the global mass media are at the vanguard of multicultural drift, heightening popular awareness of cultural diversity and cultural relativism.

Hall argues that globalization cannot be understood as a homogeneous, standardizing process (2000c: 4). Although it does create cultural, economic, political and technological homologies, it simultaneously generates what Hall calls 'the subaltern proliferation of difference'. Cultural relativism opposes the thesis that globalization results in the triumph of the West. After all, the proliferation of subaltern difference is a symptom that Cartesian modernity and the old West and Rest dichotomy are no longer 'in ascendance'. Hall wants to capture the disintegration of Western modernity as a universal model of progress, without assigning subaltern difference to the category of the recrudescence of the 'primitive'. Western modernization has inevitably influenced the character and form of subaltern difference. By positioning it as the Other it created the basis for 'the Empire to strike back'.[1] The 'bearers' of the West's 'panoptic aspirations to global culture' are ethnic minority populations (Hall 2000c: 5). Upon them the contradictory inscriptions of exclusion, racial disadvantage, denigration and institutional racism are most deeply etched. Their presence and participation in society negate the traditional notion of primordial unity in nation and culture.

Physically and symbolically they represent the limits of the West to Westerners.

Cultural relativism involves the recognition of difference and hybridity. Hall speaks of 'vernacular modernities' to describe the situation (2000c: 5). By this term he means the diverse and various ways in which Western cosmology and modernity have been challenged, opposed, inflected and reconstituted through the engagement of ethnicity, class and gender. But Hall is careful to pre-empt the inference that this recognition will be the trigger to a new level of hyper-integration. Something different is involved. As he puts it, hybridity

> insists on displaying the pluralities and the dissonances that have to be crossed over despite the relations of proximity. It insists on marking the disjunctures of power and position that have to be contested; the values, ethical and aesthetic, that have to be translated but which refuse to be seamlessly transcended. (2000c: 6)

Hybridity and cultural relativism connect up with the turn towards post-Cartesianism by emphasizing that the individual is fundamentally dialogic.[2] He or she is always and already constituted in the Other, and is only meaningful in terms of what he or she excludes, only by his or her 'radical insufficiency'.

Hybridity and cultural relativism demand the practice of a politics of difference. Of course, this politics possesses no guarantees. It cannot operate through the affirmation of 'exclusive particularism', which was the road followed by both Western modernity and Identity Politics One. In multi-ethnic society every particular must be negotiated with other particulars in a wider multi-ethnic frame. Hall maintains that this framework must be based around a contradictory demand for greater equality and social justice and a demand for the recognition of difference and cultural diversity (2000c: 10). He acknowledges that these demands are 'incommensurate', at least in terms of the traditional language of governance and political economy. But the point about cultural relativism is that it takes us into a 'new political space' in which our traditional political conceptions and vocabularies are no longer adequate. It is necessary to rethink agency and solidarity in the conditions set by multi-ethnic society, rather than the imagined communities and territorial imperatives of classical governance and political economy. The tensions between relative particularities have to be debated and negotiated in a new *modus vivendi*. This *modus* must recognize particularity but also enjoin universal rights and responsibilities. Hall elaborates:

> I follow Ernesto Laclau here in thinking this qualified return of universalism in terms of what he calls an 'incomplete horizon'. Laclau argues that universalism does not arise from outside all particularities, it arises from within the particular, but it is a particular which is obliged to take account of the others because it acknowledges the old radical insufficiency. All identities are radically insufficient because they require the existence of the other. In acknowledging their own radical insufficiency they don't desert what makes them particular, but they recognize that this relativizes the degree to which they can, as it were, affirm difference. It expands the horizon within which the demands of others must be recognized. (2000c: 11)

This is in tune with the intellectual spirit of the times, which is not to belittle it. If Hall's sentiments fit flush with contemporary critical opinion, he and the New Left have done much to make them *au courant*.

Other approaches have explored the notion of cosmopolitan citizenship as the response to deterritorialization, post-Cartesianism, cultural relativism and the recognition of radical insufficiency (Giddens 1998; 2000; Linklater 1998; Turner 1998; 1999; Turner and Rojek 2001). They have emphasized irony as a strategy to achieve reflexive distance from one's own culture and history, and nomadism in the sense of never being fully at home in cultural categories or geopolitical boundaries. Although Hall does not dismiss these accounts, he is more traditional in focusing on the transformation of the national-popular through the state apparatus. To some extent, post-Cartesianism, cultural relativism and the acknowledgement of radical insufficiency are the corollaries of multicultural drift. But the *naturalization* and legitimation of these characteristics in civil society are, Hall maintains, the task of the state apparatus through policies of redistributive justice, education, empowerment, and reform of the labour market and the criminal justice system. It is a surprisingly centrist solution to the difficult questions raised by decentring and hybridity.

The politics of hybridity

Hall's politics favours widening access, exercising compassion, encouraging collaboration and achieving social inclusion. But there is a curious lack of precision about the ends of transformative politics. To make living with and through difference the central plank of cultural revisionism is laudable. But it begs the question of what *kinds* of difference Hall wants to flourish. Certainly, we are aware of some kinds of difference of which he disapproves. Hall's standpoint on some aspects of popular culture is often censorious. In common with the New Left he abhors the idea of high culture, but is rather priggish in his dislike of commercialism and commodification in popular culture. This was nicely expressed in an embarrassing moment during Hall's appearance as a castaway on the BBC Radio 4 programme *Desert Island Discs* (13 Feb. 2000). (In parenthesis one should note that it is highly unusual for a social scientist, let alone a radical of Hall's stature, to be invited on to this flagship for middle England.)[3] Despite Hall's oft-repeated, querulous observation that he feels an outsider in British culture, his appearance on *Desert Island Discs* perhaps proves that he has been more accepted and honoured by the establishment than he would wish to recognize. Be that as it may, Hall seized the opportunity to discuss with great eloquence questions of his own relationship to 'Britishness', the meaning of Cultural Studies and his aspirations for multicultural/multi-ethnic society. But at one telling moment his eloquence deserts him and he comes close to being tongue-tied on air. The host, Sue Lawley (SL), asks him:

SL: Do you watch *Who Wants to be a Millionaire?*?
SH: Well, um, I knew you would find the limit point . . . the breaking point . . . I can't watch that.
SL: Why not? It's great!
SH: If you ask me do I watch soaps, I do.
SL: But, I mean again, it's exactly what you are talking about . . . It's what . . . It's what turns people on, it's what shows all kinds of things about human nature.
SH: Oh yes, I think that's quite true.
SL: It's got it all!
SH: You asked me whether I watch it, and you know, there are limits to my taste. But if you ask me whether we should study it? I think we should study it! I mean it is, it comes right out of – well – everything that has happened in economic life in Britain and the Western world in the last ten years. It's kind of . . . It's the *ur* story of the free market.

The ascription of *ur* status to a show like *Who Wants to be a Millionaire?* is, I think, portentous. It invests the programme with a cultural significance that it does not possess, and it misses the reflexive character of both the agent and the audience. There is in Hall something of the Old Testament prophet who fumes at popular culture's tendency to worship at the feet of the golden calf.

If Hall is uneasy about commodification and commercialism, he has not supplied a convincing politics to transcend them.[4] The labour of the organic intellectual must be judged finally on its effect in *socializing* society and culture through critical pedagogy and engagement with the public sphere. Ioan Davies ventured the proposition that one of the paradoxes of British Cultural Studies is that it has not changed the logic of everyday life very much (1993: 154). Hall and his associates would doubtless see this as a heretical statement. Cultural Studies has unquestionably inspired genera-tions of students to become more reflexive about power and to engage critically with the public sphere. These students are now employed as cultural intermediaries in schools, universities, the media, social work agencies, the information industry and trade unions. The transformative politics that Hall's work is designed to ignite has a long fuse. By contributing to serious public under-standing of the authoritarianism of Western cosmology, the shifting configuration of hegemony, and the ubiquity of hybridity, multi-culturalism and hyphenated identity, Hall's work has unquestion-ably 'loosened the moorings'. It has helped to contribute to a climate in which ordinary political debate looks beyond the nation-state, beyond the attribution of fixed identity, and beyond the presuppo-sition that agency is independent of culture. To this extent Davies's observation may be judged excessive.

Be that as it may, the fulcrum of Cultural Studies and Hall's own position in culture remains the Academy, and here Davies's obser-vation bites hard. When Hall joined Hoggart in Birmingham it was realistic to conceive of the universities and the student movement as occupying the vanguard of opposition.[5] This ethos was certainly cultivated in the Birmingham Centre. Hall partly conceived of his project there as a collective enterprise to transform the national-popular. His work on the crisis of hegemony, the selectivity of media reporting, the drift towards more draconian policing and the rise of authoritarian populism directly engaged with the public sphere, in the manner envisaged by Gramsci. It enabled students to engage intellectually and at the level of practical politics with a project of revising the national-popular that identified the state as the decisive agent of change. *Policing the Crisis* was an exemplary work in this respect, for it sprang from a news item that clearly demonstrated the unselfconscious depth of institutionalized racism and authoritarianism in British society. The book is a brilliant account of how identity is ordered and how political extremism can be rendered palatable as 'common sense'. The vital political engagement of the book paved the way to Hall's highly public, decade-long critical interrogation of Thatcherism. Through the pages of *Marxism Today* he played a politically significant role in marshalling the case against the hubris of the New Right. His involvement with the Parekh Report (2000) built on this experience. It is a landmark contribution to the debate on multicultural/multi-ethnic society, and is unusual in Hall's oeuvre in setting forth a detailed set of policy proposals.

But Hall's principal audience remains overwhelmingly situated in the Academy. This has wide implications for the political consequences of his work. For it is surely fair to submit that the radical moment of the University and the student movement has now passed and, for the forseeable future, will not return. Few students who enroll on Cultural Studies courses today regard themselves to be engaged in a struggle to transform the national-popular. Of course, academics and students continue to pursue work in theory and practice that explicitly challenges hegemony. Cultural Studies retains an attachment to critical pedagogy that is designed to change individuals through learning and debate and, by this means, to change society. But there is no genuine sense of a collective project.

Without a formulation of the political ends of Cultural Studies the basis for solidarity is weak. Difference signifies a contrasting position in the distribution of scarcity with respect to cultural and material resources. There are real difficulties in envisaging how solidarity can be extrapolated from distinctions of scarcity in relation to cultural and material resources. The political challenge for the politics of hybridity rests in establishing what different agents hold in common and building a strategy of transformation around binding political ends. The Parekh Report is a major contribution to this task, notably in respect of the new rights and responsibilities of citizenship that it identifies. But in terms of the revision of society and culture around dialogic relations of mutuality and the redistribution of cultural and material resources it is still no more than a beginning.

The political challenge for Cultural Studies remains the old one of classical political economy of constructing solidarity from the twin condition of material scarcity and unequal access to material and cultural resources. But this is now compounded by globalization, which requires the struggle for solidarity to be waged along many different boundaries, involving players that exhibit considerable cultural, ethnic and economic diversity. Hall's approach has contributed to the exposure of the sinews of normative coercion, revealing them to be either arbitrary or serving the social interests of determinate formations of power. It has resisted a Foucaultian take on power that privileges micro-politics, on the grounds that to do so dissipates effective agency. But it is unreasonable to suppose that the acknowledgement of the right to difference will spontaneously generate effective political agency. Indeed, within Cultural Studies there is a danger that the focus on the aetiology and form of cultural relativism will neutralize political activism. Hall (1992f) himself has lamented the tendency towards depoliticization in American Cultural Studies. Exposing cultural conditioning is easier than building and maintaining dialogic cultures in which mutuality and respect for difference are naturalized parts of civil society. Hall's work is a contribution to the task of erasing myth, dismantling barriers, learning to live with difference and understanding power as a condition of balance within a field of forces.

Ultimately, as doubtless Hall would wish, it will be judged on its capacity to constitute classes and individuals as an effective popular democratic cultural force. 'The people', he wrote over twenty years ago, 'versus the power bloc: this, rather than "class-against-class", is the central line of contradiction around which the terrain of culture is polarised' (1981b: 238). During the last twenty years the centrality of class in his analysis has waned and the politics of difference has waxed. In as much as the agent of social transformation has become more nebulous and dissipated there has been a marked decentring in Hall's position. The status of the power bloc in his analysis has changed too. It has shifted from a primary focus on capital and the state apparatus in the national framework to a more pronounced recognition of the dialectic between the nation-state and global nodes of power; although in Hall this shift is made with many caveats and reservations. On the global level, it is as difficult as it ever was to conceive how the politics of difference will be transformed into effective popular democratic cultural agency, or how the liquid network of capital can be forced to relinquish power. If Hall's version of Cultural Studies is intrinsically and irredeemably political, the balance facing it would appear to be stark. Either it will act as one active element in triumphantly reconciling the people into an effective popular democratic cultural force from the midst of liquid hybridity – a prospect that other intellectual traditions hold to be remote – or it will be hoist by its own petard.

Notes

Introduction

1 *Verstehen* is the German word for 'understanding'. The term is primarily associated with the sociology of Max Weber. Weber distinguished between *aktuelles Verstehen* and *erklarendes Verstehen* (1947: 94). 'Aktuell' refers to the possibility of deriving the meaning of an act or symbolic expression from immediate observation without reference to the wider context. *Erklarendes Verstehen* involves deriving the meaning of a particular act from the broader context of meaning, pertaining to facts that are not immediately 'given' through observation.

2 In a letter of 22 June 1960, written to Ralph Miliband, Mills outlines several publishing plans for the future, one of which is *The Cultural Apparatus* (Mills 2000: 291). Earlier, in *The Power Elite* (1956) Mills took a leaf from Veblen's (1899) book and drew attention to the emulatory significance of the celebrity elite. Mills was singular in 1950s sociology for treating culture as a significant field of enquiry. When Mills died in 1962, the manuscript of *The Cultural Apparatus* was unfinished, although he did publish an essay of that name in the *Listener* (no. 1565, 20 Mar. 1959).

3 Broadly speaking the socialist humanism of Edward Thompson was ascendant until 1961. The position owed much to the Historians Group founded under the auspices of the British Communist Party in 1946, which numbered Maurice Dobb, Eric Hobsbawm, Rodney Hilton, John Saville, Christopher Hill and Thompson himself among its members. This group, with its emphasis on the deep roots of English popular radicalism and the 'experience' of 'the people', was a seminal influence in what Hall later called English 'culturalism' (1980a).

After 1961 the socialist humanism came under increasing fire from the younger generation. They argued that socialist humanism is vulnerable to charges of empiricism and essentialism because it neglects the ideological dimension of experience. For this generation the question of agency was decisive. Their rise was symbolized by Perry Anderson's accession to the editorship of the journal and the restructuring of the editorial board. Anderson and his circle saw struggle in terms of the effective vanguard leadership of a progressive political cadre over the working class, rather than the spontaneous transcendence of capitalism through class contradiction. An altogether bleaker picture of the popular was sustained, one that rested on the postulate of working-class incorporation into consumer culture and the dominant ideology. In many ways this 'new' New Left represented a return to the classical considerations of Marxism with a pronounced accent on the centrality of class struggle and the reconstruction of the socialist agenda around revolution rather than reform. By 1968 Trotskyism was clearly a significant influence.

4 For Hall, 'the state of nature' is an inherently problematic concept since it posits an essentialist foundation to human evolution and existence. Even as a metaphor, he would find the term unhelpful since it is loaded with Enlightenment presuppositions about universalism and rationalism. If there is a 'state of nature' in Hall's view of humankind, it is one which emphasizes the 'hybrid', 'mongrel' form as the human condition.

5 Bourdieu's sociology of distinction (1986) makes the same point. His approach bears traces of Durkheimian epistemology in its concentration on the character of cultural reproduction and the persistence of knowledge classifications. However, in as much as Bourdieu conceptualizes pedagogic practice through the formalized education system as reinforcing the general tendency towards repression, he radicalizes Durkheim. In Bourdieu, formalized cultural reproduction is equivalent to symbolic violence, thus reviving the Marxist emphasis on the importance of alienation and estrangement in capitalist culture.

6 Structuralism argues that the reproduction and adaptation of cultures is a manifestation of an unconscious and universal rule system that is integral to cognition. Thus, irrespective of varieties of expression across space ('the synchronic') and time ('the diachronic'), cultures have ubiquitous characteristics which reflect the universal mechanics of the human mind. Hall was drawn to the totalizing aspect of structuralism which he regarded as more useful than the localism and particularism of culturalism. However, the essentialism in the arguments of Lévi-Strauss and Mauss inhibited the development of structuralism in Hall's work. Nonetheless, through the incorporation of Althusser's work on ideology and Lacan's psychoanalytic model of split identity, Hall's mature work clearly bears traces of neo-structuralism.

Chapter 1 The 'Absolute Cultural Hybrid'

The title of this chapter is drawn from Stuart Hall's description of himself in an interview with Roger Bromley (1995c: 661).

1 United Fruit was a major economic, political and cultural influence in Jamaican society. Interestingly, the leadership of the nationalist movement was drawn from the upper middle class, mostly urban professional groups and independent landowners, hostile to United Fruit's land and price-fixing monopolies.

2 Hall describes the house, as 'a big house in Port Antonio (now owned by the singer Eartha Kitt) with a palm-fringed drive by the sea. This gave her peculiar airs and graces, as the adopted owner of a landowner, whereas my father was more an aspiring local boy. It was a continuous source of tension in our family. He could never earn enough to guarantee her the status she thought she deserved' (Jaggi 2000: 8).

3 The early editorial board of *NLR* included a large number of people who lived and worked outside London and the Oxbridge axis: Ken Alexander and D. G. Arnott in Scotland, Alan Hall in Staffordshire, Alasdair MacIntyre and John Rex in Leeds, John Saville in Hull, Edward and Dorothy Thompson in Halifax, Peter Worsley in Manchester and Raymond Williams in Sussex.

4 Richard Hoggart taught adult education in the University of Hull; from 1948 to 1965, Edward Thompson was extra-mural Lecturer at Leeds University in the West Riding; and Williams worked in Workers' Educational Associations and extra-mural departments in East Sussex.

5 Chelsea College appointed Hall to a lectureship in Complementary Studies, a now extinct nomenclature, which perhaps reinforces the novelty of Hall's enterprise. As he recalls: 'I may have been one of the first full-time appointments teaching film and media studies. The head of department there was in conventional literary studies, but nevertheless, was sensitive to these cultural debates going on and opened a space, within the framework of complementary studies, for what, in fact, we would now call "cultural studies", work on the media, and British culture and so on, and we used to teach the stuff, unexamined, to dentists' (1995c: 665).

6 In his autobiography Hoggart recalls that Allen Lane was fond of observing that it cost him only sixpence in the pound to be generous (Hoggart 1992: 89). At the time, the top rate of taxation was nineteen shillings and sixpence (97.5p). The Inland Revenue therefore provided well over 90 per cent of the funds to support the Centre.

7 The M.A. by thesis required students to spend one academic year in full-time study or two in part-time study. The thesis was approximately 50,000 words. The M.Litt. by thesis required a one-year period

of full-time study or a two-year period of part-time study. The thesis was approximately 80,000 words.

8 As noted, Hall rejected the central features in the Leavisite tradition while still at Oxford. However, he declares that he rated Leavis's analysis of cultural relationships as more complex and accurate than the base–superstructure reductionism of classical Marxism.

9 Neither Gramsci nor Hall was the first to make this point. The *methodenstreit* debate in late nineteenth-century German philosophy, involving Wilhelm Dilthey, Heinrich Rickert and Wilhelm Windelband, addressed the questions of value judgements in academic study and the proper means of interpreting the cultural worldview of social strata.

10 Fordism is the method of organizing production in advanced industrial society introduced by Henry Ford in the mass production of automobiles. Most people know that Fordism combines mass production with mass consumption. However, the concept is in fact somewhat complex and refers, *inter alia*, to rigid, hierarchical management structures, large-scale capital intensive plant, standardized systems of production, the recruitment of semi-skilled labour performing repetitive, routinized tasks, a tendency towards strong unionization and the protectionism of national markets.

11 The Women's Studies Group in the Centre published *Women Take Issue: Aspects of Women's Subordination* in 1978. In the Introduction they noted:

> We (the Women's Studies Group) found it extremely difficult to participate in CCCS groups, and felt, without being able to articulate it, that it was a case of masculine domination of both intellectual work and the environment in which it was carried out.

Hall recalls that the book initiated 'a quarrel' (1992f: 282), but also recognizes that, despite welcoming feminism, there were 'unsuspected' residual aspects of patriarchal power at the Centre which mobilized both before and after the book was published.

12 Interestingly, when Tony Bennett returned to a Chair in Sociology at the Open University after many years at Griffith University in Australia, one of his first acts was to launch The National Everyday Cultures Programme. The programme utilizes the OU's unparalleled network of associate lecturers in the social sciences to research the relations between everyday cultures and contemporary social life throughout Britain and Ireland. The strengths of the national network are augmented by the participation of affiliate researchers from other institutions. This is a very good idea and all credit should be given to Bennett for seizing the day. But the theoretical inspiration behind the project, as Bennett is the first to acknowledge, is Raymond Williams's observation that 'culture is ordinary'. Williams's insistence that pedagogy must connect with the everyday social practices of people is also prominent in the Programme.

13 A feature of syncretic fusion is the bold way in which it bolts elements

of contrasting and, in some cases, incompatible theory together. Just as in the 1970s, Hall felt no inhibition in trying to fuse Althusserian structuralism with Gramsci's interpretive, process approach, in the 1980s and 1990s he mixed elements of Lacanian psychoanalysis, Derrida's philosophy, Judith Butler's feminist theory, Laclau and Mouffe's Marxist revisionism and Foucault's perspective on regimes of power and discourse with a commitment to socialist transformation. This restless and voracious appetite testifies to an unusual generosity of intellect, especially for someone who has been so closely associated with left-wing traditions. However, for some critics it reveals too much interest in intellectual fashion. Hall himself sees no contradiction in practising syncretic fusion in theory and method. As he puts it:

> The construction of a new political will must be grounded, if it is to be concrete and strategic, in an analysis of the present which is neither ritualistic nor celebratory and which avoids the spurious oscillations of optimism and pessimism, or the triumphalism which so often passes for thought on the traditional left . . . I believe, with Gramsci, that we must first attend 'violently' to things as they are, without illusions or false hopes, if we are to transcend the present. (1988a: 13–14)

14   According to Giddens, the central plank of Hall's political formulae is the centralized correction of inequalities and instabilities produced by the market. This implies increasing the role of the state in the management of the economy and civil society, and curbing the powers of business corporations through a combination of fiscal and legal provisions. Giddens criticizes Hall for not following through the logic of the New Times thesis and sheltering behind old Left shibboleths of class inequality and a strong socialist state. It should be noted that the criticism exists in some tension with Hall's self-image of being a scourge of socialist traditionalism in the 1980s and 1990s.
15   The phrase was originally coined by Romain Rolland and appropriated by Gramsci.

Chapter 2   Representation and Ideology

1   Hall's conflation of behaviourism with the Leicester School is arguably unfair. Although James Halloran and his colleagues were influenced by the behaviourist tradition in American media research, they were always more critical about the notion of transparent communication and the 'scientism' of media research than perhaps Hall allows. In a later contribution to ideology and communication theory, Hall (1989d) clarifies his position by arguing that the individualism and naturalism of behaviourist research in media and communication are most fully exemplified in the American tradition.
2   Although Hall does not refer directly to the work of Harold Garfinkel and his associates, he would have been aware of its significance. The

influence of semiotics is more overt. In an interview published twenty
years after the encoding/decoding paper, Hall cites the work of the
early Barthes, notably *Elements of Semiology* and *S/Z*, and also Marx's
1857 Introduction to the *Grundrisse* as formative influences (1993e:
254). Umberto Eco is also clearly standing in the shadows. Althusser
is another influence. Indeed, Hall observes that the paper is 'founded
on the Althusserian notion of the overdetermined, complex totality'
(1993e: 261).

The aetiology of the encoding/decoding paper is interesting. The
level of analysis is far more sophisticated than Hall's paper on 'Innovation and decline in cultural programming on television' (1971),
which he prepared as part of a report to UNESCO on Innovation and
Decline in the Treatment of Culture on British Television. Hall may
have felt hamstrung in the latter paper by the need to write in a style
suitable for an official report. Certainly the discussion is largely
descriptive, with little of the theoretical risks and inspiration demonstrated in the encoding/decoding paper. Hall's citation of Marx's 1857
Introduction is significant. The importance that Hall attaches to the
1857 Introduction is evidence of a major shift in his engagement with
the Marxist tradition. It freed him from the base–superstructure
dilemma in Marxism, a dilemma from which his anti-essentialist soul
would recoil. The liberation that Hall feels in finding consumption and
culture taken seriously by Marx is evident in the theoretical range and
confidence exemplified in the encoding/decoding paper.

3   His work with Ian Connell and Lidia Curti (1976) at the Birmingham
Centre on the construction of current affairs programmes related
power and signification at the heart of the broadcasting process. Hall
and his associates argued that broadcasters gather, select and pre-
arrange topics by mobilizing a variety of verbal and visual codes.
Programme transmission is defined as an 'audio-visual discourse'
involving systems of signification which encode 'preferred readings'.
The broadcaster's professional encoding practices are geared to bringing the encoding and decoding moments into alignment in order to
establish ideological closure and, *ipso facto*, to achieve a preferred
reading of the topic. At the same time, polysemy means that absolute
closure in the construction and reception of messages is impossible.
Audiences are reflexive and decode meaning as an ordinary condition
of the viewing process. The parameters of decoding are defined in
fairly conventional sociological terms, as relating to class, status,
gender, race and generation. Privileged access refers to the availabil-
ity of politicians, business leaders and celebrities to the media. Hall's
point is that media professionals move easily in elite circles and therefore have a higher risk of contamination with elite ideology. However,
this point is not empirically developed in Hall's work. One profitable
area of research might be to compare patterns of recruitment into
the media and key elite institutions focusing on factors of class

background, education, marital alliances and leisure practice. But this is not examined in Hall's work.

4 Achievement here is a double-edged sword. It refers to the unreflexive assimilation of the preferred reading, a condition that Hall describes as 'harmony' between the encoding and reception 'moments'. However, achievement also refers to the decoding of the encoded reading by working through the negotiated or oppositional codes to disable ideology.

5 The term bears a characteristically Gramscian inflection. Gramsci distinguished between 'common sense' and 'good sense'. Because he regarded common sense to be saturated with bourgeois values, he tended to scorn it. Good sense refers to the working-class conscious-ness that the mode of production in which they are enmeshed is limiting. As Hall puts it: 'Working people have known that their ways of being in the world would always be different and would find forms of cultural expression, kinds of relationships, ways of building values into the day-to-day, which set limits to the degrees to which the logic of capital could impose itself. That is good sense. It is the sense of what Lenin called "the class instincts" without which no political and intel-lectual work can be done' (1978e: 10).

6 Marx argues that Hegel did understand production and labour. However, he could not extricate it from the labour of the mind. For Hegel, the historical production of the world is nothing but a 'moment' in the realization of the Idea. Against this, Marx situates production and labour in real, concrete relations of 'many determinations'.

7 Gramsci hailed from a poor Sardinian family. In 1911 he won a schol-arship to the University of Turin to study linguistics, but abandoned the university for political activism. Unlike Hall, Gramsci's adult career was spent outside of an academic setting. Following his impri-sonment in 1926, he worked on the *Prison Notebooks* until he died in 1937.

8 Tony Crosland declared in a famous phrase in the 1970s that 'the party's over', and his speech climaxed in a sober plea for a new realism in the Labour Party's management of the public sector. With hindsight, this was one of the first significant political recognitions of globaliza-tion, and the role of global interdependence in national affairs. In pointing to the economic 'realities' of Britain's position, Crosland was exposing the lack of autonomy of the Labour government in socialist construction. That the criteria of autonomy were ultimately defined by the International Monetary Fund cruelly exposed the reliance of the conduct of British socialism on the logic of capital.

9 Hall takes over this emphasis, with the result that the business cor-poration is strangely absent in his analysis of capitalism. For Hall the state is the central change agent since it alone possesses a monopoly over the legitimate means of national-popular leadership through the election system and its governance of the central institutions of

normative coercion. Interestingly, Hall rejects the view that globalization fatefully limits state power. His chief criticism of the first Blair government (1998a) is that Labour capitulated to the tight controls on public spending introduced by the Thatcher–Major governments. For Hall, the socialist challenge is to redress economic, social and cultural inequality. This necessarily means increasing public spending, boosting the welfare state and extending progressive taxation. Hall interprets Labour's view that this runs counter to general, current trends in the global economy, and as such will damage Britain's position, as evidence of the bad faith of the Blair leadership.

10 Several aspects of Hall's analysis do appear to lend themselves to a structuralist interpretation. Examples include the causal relationship between ideology and subjectivity and the argument that there is no space outside ideology. Classical structuralism, in the manner of Lévi-Strauss's analysis of myth, posits a timeless universalism for the effects of structure. Hall's appropriation of the dialectical method prevents him from siding with the classical structuralist approach. On the contrary, from Gramsci he regards the elucidation of change at the epochal and concrete levels to be crucial.

11 Although Saussure (language), Lévi-Strauss (myth) and Althusser (ideology) adopted foci of theory and research that might, retrospectively, be said to illuminate culture, they did not directly and systematically adopt culture as their central problematic. Properly speaking, Hall applied them as *generative influences* in constructing a structuralist position in cultural analysis.

12 Although I hold that the relationship between the Althusserian and Gramscian traditions was decisive for Hall's work, and the intellectual labour in the Centre during the 1970s, I stop short of attributing to it a universal influence. Birmingham was always a broad church, much broader in fact than has been generally recognized in secondary accounts, which tend to suggest that nearly all intellectual labour occurred under the canopy of Marxism. In fact, culturalism, feminism, linguistics, psychoanalytic theory and poststructuralism were vigorous influences on the Birmingham scene throughout the 1970s. That said, however, I think that it is correct to identify the interface between Althusser and Gramsci as the central nodal point, a proposition supported by what is arguably the Centre's most significant collaborative publication, *Policing the Crisis* (Hall et al. 1978).

13 The late Cornelius Castoriadis (1987) was one of the most formidable critics. He makes two main points. First, Lacan's argument that the subject enters the world of the imaginary at the mirror stage misconstrues the nature of the imaginary in social life. For Castoriadis the imaginary precedes the mirror stage because it is a creation *ex nihilo*. Indeed, misrecognition is only conceivable if one accepts that the infant *already* possesses the imaginary capacities of identification and representation. Second, Castoriadis argues that Lacan's approach is

fatalistic since it proposes that misrecognition is the universal state of affairs. The approach does not allow for reflexivity or corrective insight, thus undermining the wider claim of psychoanalysis to undo psychological knots.

A sociological objection to the arguments of both Lacan and Castoriadis is that they deal with insoluble questions that belong finally to the area of philosophical speculation rather than testable argument and explanation. The attribution of misrecognition to an entire culture or civilization is a rhetorical device that can only be validated by extensive and intensive empirical research and theoretical debate. In Lacan and Castoriadis, one might say, the empirical level is submerged under the rhetorical level. This is legitimated by the general attack against empiricism, but it leaves observers with no means to test the propositions advanced by either theorist.

14 Overdetermination, of course, raises the question of whether a scientific understanding of the complex social whole is possible. For if cultural and ideological categories fix experience, how can science elude the pull of these categories? Althusser, of course, maintained that Marxism possessed the investigative and reflexive capacities to do just this, and this is why he regarded it to be a genuine science. Conversely, Michel Foucault and others argued that truth is bound up with discourse, a relation of existence that science cannot escape. The manner of Hall's analysis, especially in *On Ideology* (Hall, Lumley and McLennan 1978) and *Policing the Crisis* (Hall et al. 1978), suggest agreement with Althusser's position, although Hall is never so bold in ascribing unambiguous scientific status to Marxism. Nonetheless, in a barb against Foucault, he remarks that it is objectionable 'to say that all knowledge is simply the product of the will-to-power; there may be some ideological categories which give us a more adequate or more profound knowledge of particular relations than others' (1985a: 105). Note that Marxism is still identified with ideology in this passage, as it is in Althusser's broader framework. The crucial caveat is that 'more adequate/more profound' knowledge of particular relations is implicitly attributed to it. The questions of the criteria of adequacy and the designation of profundity themselves raise difficult questions of epistemology.

15 Harris accepts that Gramscian concepts can be 'deployed tactically' in postmodernism, but he asks the pertinent question, 'why should anyone want to?' (1992: 44). For Harris the ambiguity of Gramscian concepts means that they can be endlessly redeployed. It is not clear what is gained by reinventing Gramsci's notion of struggle as postmodern 'play'. If Hebdige's analysis means anything, it means that play is a more appropriate way to read resistance and conflict under postmodernity than struggle and solidarity. The reinvention of the concept does not demonstrate the flexibility but a lack of precision and circularity. Harris extends this criticism to the whole of Gramscianism and, by the same token, to the Birmingham project.

16 Willis was a student and research fellow at the Birmingham Centre between 1968 and 1981. To begin with he was supervised by Hoggart, but when Hoggart left to take up his post at UNESCO, Hall took over. Willis, like so many other students before and since, was hugely impressed by Hall's moral seriousness and clearly acknowledges Hall as a formative influence. However, if my interpretation is correct, the socio-symbolic approach that he developed in his ethnographic work privileged *from the outset* the interaction of sensuous human activity with concrete materials bearing symbolic form, and existed in considerable tension with Hall's more 'discursive', theoretical approach.

Chapter 3   State and Society

1 The first *May Day Manifesto* was published by the May Day Manifesto Committee in 1967 and was basically written by Williams. Penguin Books suggested a paperback version. As Williams recollected:

> This time I was made editor, but actually Edward (Thompson) and Stuart (Hall) contributed more to the second *Manifesto*, although they weren't formally editors, than to the first. Several new people came in to write certain parts of it: a group used to meet (at) week-ends, drafting different chapters. Eventually I then edited all these into a single text, as a rewriting job. The final chapters were done by all three of us in my house at the very last minute, to get the *Manifesto* out by May 1967. (1979: 373)

2 Thirty years separate the criticisms in the *Manifesto* and 'The great moving nowhere show', but there is a remarkable consistency between the complaints and the solutions. Both documents argue that the Labour government has failed to seize the initiative for socialist transformation. They demand dramatically increased public provision in health, education and welfare. They excoriate the deadening sense of consensus and spin that permeates national politics. However, there are also significant differences. The *Manifesto*'s attack on Americanization and call for a general shift from private to public ownership is replaced in the 1998 document by an insistence that the privatizing effects of globalization are not inevitable and a plea for Britain to pursue a more independent strategy of public investment and management. The dilemmas facing the Left in the two publications are remarkably constant, leaving one with a depressing feeling of *plus ça change* with respect to the Wilson and Blair years of government.

3 Hall submits that the term 'representative-interventionist state' best applies to the Wilson, Heath and Callaghan governments of the 1960s and 1970s when the corporatist management of the economy (involving public officials, business leaders and trade union bosses) reached its apogee. However, the roots of corporatism reach back to the constitutional and regulative reforms of the 1880s to 1920s.

4 The Conservative leader, Harold Macmillan, used this phrase to legitimate consensus hegemony built around economic prosperity and full
   employment.
5 Heath, Jowell and Curtice (2001: 4) report that in 1979 the Conservatives won 44.9%, in 1983 43.5%, and in 1987 42.8%. In 1979 55.1% cast
   their votes against Thatcher, in 1983, 56.5%, and in 1987, 56.7%.
6 In reality Blair owes an immense debt to Neil Kinnock, who led the
   Labour Party between 1983 and 1992. It was Kinnock who took on the
   difficult job of expelling the far-left Militant Tendency from the party.
   In addition, after the third successive electoral defeat in 1987, Kinnock
   initiated a policy review that discarded most of the policies that
   were regarded as extreme by the electorate, notably the commitments
   to nationalize the banks and unilateral nuclear disarmament. More
   subtly, he softened Labour's opposition to Europe, a disastrous stance
   for a party with strong internationalist leanings to occupy.
7 Hall is very hostile to the Third Way approach (1998a: 10). He contends that it is unable to decide whether its aim is to capture 'the
   radical centre' or to modernize 'the centre left'. He argues that it envisages 'a politics without adversaries'. He questions whether a project
   to transform and modernize society in a radical direction that does not
   antagonize established interests and make new enemies is 'a serious
   political enterprise'. Not surprisingly, Giddens has responded in kind
   by categorizing Hall as a relic of 'old Labour' who is out of touch with
   the 'new times' that he (Hall) claims to recognize (Giddens 2000: 28).
   Doubtless, there is a degree of caricature on both sides. But Giddens
   does have a point when he complains that at least Third Way policies
   are specified whereas Hall's own political formulae are 'hardly
   spelled out at all' (2000: 28).

Chapter 4 Culture and Civilization

1 Hall's account does little to convey the notion that civilization created
   a space for criticism as well as colonization. Gandhi was one of the
   first anti-colonial leaders to use the colonial arguments of the sanctity
   of individualism and liberty against the colonizers. The concept and
   practice of civilization was always more mixed than Hall's account
   allows.
2 David Cannadine, Birmingham born but with no formal connection to
   the Centre, filled the gap for a history of the British aristocracy with
   his magnificent *The Decline and Fall of the British Aristocracy* (1990).
3 Hall's position here owes much to Benedict Anderson's (1991)
   emphasis on 'imagined communities' in nation-state formation and
   colonial expansion. The 'imagined community' of the New Right in
   Britain, consisting of white, accumulative, Anglo-Saxon 'warrior-
   entrepreneurs', was, of course, a major target of Hall's writings in the
   1980s.

4 For example, in the sixteenth century the German lands were not a
   'nation-state in the making', unlike early modern Britain, France,
   Spain or Sweden. The lands forming the ancient Reich from the
   Middle Ages to the French Revolution and Napoleon were never
   clearly defined. Before the Treaty of Westphalia they stretched into
   Swiss cantons and Dutch provinces. They were an elastic confedera-
   tion of petty principalities, free cities, ecclesiastical republics and small
   rulers that always exceeded the emperor's control. This made the
   ancient Reich vulnerable to external attack. By the end of the Thirty
   Years' War in 1648, two out of three inhabitants of the German lands
   were dead and the economy was shattered. Out of this grew the
   appetite for a strong state, fully exploited by Bismarck after 1871
   (Stürmer 2000: 23–5). In Elias's sociology this historical context produced quite distinct meanings of '*Kultur*' and 'civilization' in Germany
   in comparison with France or England.
5 Of course, from the standpoint of the 'organic intellectual', the Achilles
   heel of Elias's position is his failure to confront values. Making life
   better for humanity is a goal to which Left and Right can subscribe.
   But as soon as the ends of life are discussed, and the means by which
   superior ends might be realized are raised, the discord between Left
   and Right is thrown into sharp relief. For an 'organic intellectual',
   Elias's reliance on the concept of 'detachment' in the civilizing process
   is a vapid shibboleth, redolent of the functionalist cast of thought.
6 Chen submits that Hall's reading of Foucault is 'not so much incorrect
   as unproductive: it misses Foucault's formulation in accounting for the
   non-discursive (non-ideological) forms of power, and it fails to understand that indeed, with Foucault, "there are different regimes of truth
   in the social formation" (Hall 1986a: 48) of which the ideological is only
   one' (Morley and Chen 1996: 313–14). Elsewhere Hall (1997a) argues
   that a major defect in Foucault's position is that it fails to develop a
   theory of the role of the state in securing a discursive configuration.
7 Hall remembers this moment of 'multi-culturalism in Britain as ges-
   tural. It was a moment of "International Evenings" when people from
   ethnic minorities would "come and cook our native dishes, sing our
   own native songs, and appear in our native costume" . . . I had been de-
   racinated for four hundred years. The last thing I am going to do is to
   dress up in some native Jamaican costume and appear in the spectacle
   of multi-culturalism' (1991b: 55). In his later work Hall prefers to use
   the concepts of the 'difference and diversity' to denote the new ethnicity that he believes to be emerging. Although in the Parekh Report
   (2000) he also lends his support to the concept of 'multi-ethnic Britain'.
8 The commission was headed by Bhikhu Parekh, Emeritus Professor
   of Political Theory at the University of Hull. Included among its
   members were journalists, academics, a police chief constable, the
   chair of a London health authority, a QC, a social worker and the
   former chair of the Commission for Racial Equality.

Conclusion 'The Future Belongs to the Impure'

The title of this chapter comes from Hall (Hall 1998b: 299).

1 This is of course a reference to one of the most famous studies initiated under Hall's term as Director of the Birmingham Centre (CCCS 1982).
2 Hall (2000c: 8) attributes this insight to Charles Taylor.
3 Among Hall's desert island discs were *Sid's Ahead* / Miles Davis; *Redemption Song* / Bob Marley; Bach's Brandenberg Concerto No. 2 in F Major / English Chamber Orchestra; *I Cover the Waterfront* / Billie Holliday; *Caravan* / Wynton Marsalis Quartet; *I Waited for You* / Miles Davis; *Madame Butterfly* / Puccini. The book that he chose to take with him was *Portrait of a Lady* by Henry James. His luxury was a piano.
4 Paul Willis provides a more accurate approach to commodification in culture (2001: 58–64). It argues that commodities are simultaneously subject to commodity fetishism and defetishizing tendencies. The latter derive from the commodity's position as an object for communicative and cultural exchange.
5 Marcuse (1978) also regarded the student movement as a potentially radicalizing force. It was not a view shared by Adorno (1992; 2000), who regarded the movement as too undisciplined and hedonistic to achieve genuine change. Adorno believed that the necessary material/structural conditions for the transcendence of capitalism were not in place in the 1960s. Unfashionably, he called for 'resignation' among the Left.

References

Adorno, T. (1992) *The Culture Industry*. London: Routledge.

Adorno, T. (2000) *Introduction to Sociology*. Cambridge: Polity.

Alexander, J. (ed.) (2001) *Mainstream and Critical Social Theory*. 8 vols, London: Sage.

Althusser, L. (1971) *Lenin and Philosophy and Other Essays*. London: New Left Books.

Althusser, L. (1977) *For Marx*. London: Verso.

Anderson, B. (1990) *Language and Power: Exploring Political Cultures in Indonesia*. Ithaca: Cornell University Press.

Anderson, B. (1991) *Imagined Communities*. London: Verso.

Anderson, P. (1990) 'A culture in contraflow'. *New Left Review*, no. 180: 41–57.

Aylmer, G. (1986) *Reason and Revolution*. Oxford: Oxford University Press.

Barker, M. (1992) 'Stuart Hall, policing the crisis'. In *Reading into Cultural Studies*, ed. M. Barker and A. Beezer, London: Routledge: 81–100.

Baudrillard, J. (1993) 'Afterword: Amor fati (a letter from Baudrillard)'. In *Baudrillard Live: Selected Interviews*, ed. M. Gane, London and New York: Routledge: 208–9.

Bauman, Z. (1992) *Intimations of Postmodernity*. London: Routledge.

Bauman, Z. (1993) *Postmodern Ethics*. Cambridge: Polity.

Bauman, Z. (1998) *Work, Consumption and the New Poor*. Buckingham: Open University Press.

Beck, U. (1992) *Risk Society*. London: Sage.

Beck, U. (1999) *World Risk Society*. Cambridge: Polity.

Beck, U., Giddens, A. and Lash, S. (1994) *Reflexive Modernization.* Cambridge: Polity.

Bell, D. (1971) *The Coming of Post-Industrial Society.* Harmondsworth: Penguin.

Bhabha, H. (1990) 'The third space: interview with Homi Bhabha'. In *Identity: Community, Culture, Difference*, ed. J. Rutherford, London: Lawrence and Wishart: 207–21.

Bhabha, H. (1994) *The Location of Culture.* London: Routledge.

Bourdieu, P. (1986) *Distinction.* London: Routledge.

Bromley, R. (2000) *Narratives for a New Belonging.* Edinburgh: Edinburgh University Press.

Brundson, C. (1996) 'A thief in the night: stories of feminism in the 1970s at CCCS'. In *Stuart Hall: Critical Dialogues in Cultural Studies*, ed. D. Morley and K.-H. Chen, London: Routledge: 276–86.

Butler, J. (1990) *Gender Trouble.* London: Routledge.

Butler, J. (1993) *Bodies that Matter.* London: Routledge.

Callinicos, A. (1989) *Against Postmodernism.* Cambridge: Polity.

Cannadine, D. (1990) *The Decline and Fall of the British Aristocracy.* Basingstoke: Papermac.

Cannadine, D. (1998) *History in our Time.* New Haven: Yale University Press.

Cannadine, D. (2001) *Ornamentalism: How the British Saw their Empire.* London: Penguin.

Castells, M. (1996) *The Rise of the Network Society.* Oxford: Blackwell.

Castells, M. (1997) *The Power of Identity.* Oxford: Blackwell.

Castells, M. (1998) *The End of the Millennium.* Oxford: Blackwell.

Castoriadis, C. (1987) *The Imaginary Institution of Society.* Cambridge: Polity.

CCCS (Centre for Contemporary Cultural Studies, Birmingham) (1982) *The Empire Strikes Back: Race and Racism in Seventies Britain.* London: Hutchinson.

Clarke, J. (1992) *New Times and Old Enemies.* London: HarperCollins.

Cohen, S. (1972) *Folk Devils and Moral Panics.* London: McGibbon and Kee.

Corrigan, P. and Sayer, D. (1985) *The Great Arch.* Oxford: Blackwell.

Coward, B. (1991) *Cromwell.* London: Longman.

Coward, R. (1977). 'Class, "culture" and social formation'. *Screen*, no. 18: 75–105.

Coward, R. and Ellis, J. (1978) *Language and Materialism.* London: Routledge and Kegan Paul.

Davies, I. (1993) 'Cultural theory in Britain: narrative and episteme'. *Theory, Culture & Society*, 10, no. 3: 115–54.

214 References

Davies, I. (1995) *Cultural Studies and Beyond: Fragments of Empire*. London and New York: Routledge.

Denney, D. (1995) 'Hall'. In *Modern Thinkers on Welfare*, ed. V. Gough and R. Page, London: Prentice Hall/Harvester Wheatsheaf: 313–29.

Denzin, N. and Lincoln, Y. (eds) (2001) *The American Tradition in Qualitative Research*. 4 vols, London: Sage.

Derrida, J. (1980) *Writing and Difference*. Chicago: Chicago University Press.

Durkheim, E. (1895) *New Rules of Sociological Method*. New York: Free Press.

Durkheim, E. (1912) *The Elementary Forms of Religious Life*. New York: Free Press.

Eagleton, T. (1996) 'The hippest'. *London Review of Books*, Mar., pp. 3–6.

Easthope, A. (1991) *British Post-structuralism since 1968*. London: Routledge.

Elias, N. (1956). 'Some problems of involvement and detachment'. *British Journal of Sociology*, 7, no. 3: 226–52.

Elias, N. (1971) 'Sociology of knowledge: new perspectives'. *Sociology*, 5, nos 2 and 3: 149–68 and 355–70.

Elias, N. (1978) *The Civilizing Process*, vol. 1: *The History of Manners*. Oxford: Blackwell.

Elias, N. (1982) *State Formation and Civilization*. Oxford: Blackwell.

Elias, N. (1984a) 'Knowledge and power: an interview by Peter Ludes'. In *Society and Knowledge*, ed. N. Stehr and V. Meja, London: Transaction: 251–91.

Elias, N. (1984b) 'Scientific establishments'. In *Scientific Establishments and Hierarchies*, ed. N. Elias, R. Whitley and H. Martins, Dordrecht: Reidel: 3–69.

Elliott, A. (1999) *Social Theory and Pscyhoanalysis in Transition*. London: Free Association Books.

Featherstone, M. (2000) *Body Modification*. London: Sage.

Febvre, L. (1973) *A New Kind of History: From the Writings of Febvre*. London: Routledge and Kegan Paul.

Ferguson, M. and Golding, P. (eds) (1997) *Cultural Studies in Question*. London: Sage.

Freud, S. (1927) *The Future of an Illusion*. London: Hogarth.

Freud, S. (1930) *Civilization and its Discontents*. London: Hogarth.

Gane, M. (ed.) (1993) *Baudrillard Live: Selected Interviews*. London and New York: Routledge.

Geertz, C. (1973) *The Interpretation of Cultures*. New York: Basic Books.

Gellner, E. (1988) *Plough, Sword and Book: The Structure of Human History*. Chicago: Chicago University Press.

Gellner, E. (1992) *Postmodernism, Reason and Religion*. London: Routledge.

Gellner, E. (1997) *Nationalism*. London: Phoenix.

Gibson, M. and Hartley, J. (1998) 'Forty years of Cultural Studies: an interview with Richard Hoggart'. *International Journal of Cultural Studies*, 1, no. 1: 11–24.

Giddens, A. (1998) *The Third Way*. Cambridge: Polity.

Giddens, A. (2000) *The Third Way and its Critics*. Cambridge: Polity.

Gilroy, P. (1987) *There Ain't No Black in the Union Jack*. London: Hutchinson.

Gilroy, P., Grossberg, L. and McRobbie, A. (eds) (2000) *Without Guarantees: In Honour of Stuart Hall*. London: Verso.

Giroux, H. (2000) *Stealing Innocence: Corporate Culture's War on Children*. New York: Palgrave.

Gorz, A. (1982) *Farewell to the Working Class*. London: Pluto.

Gramsci, A. (1971) *Selections from Prison Notebooks*. London: Lawrence and Wishart.

Green, J. (1999) *All Dressed Up: The Sixties and the Counterculture*. London: Pimlico.

Grossberg, L. (1993) 'The formation of Cultural Studies: an American in Birmingham'. In *Relocating Cultural Studies: Developments in Theory and Research*, ed. V. Blundell, J. Shepherd and I. Taylor, London and New York: Routledge: 21–66.

Grossberg, L. (1997) *Bringing It All Back Home*. Durham: Duke University Press.

Grossberg, L. (2000) 'History, imagination and the politics of belonging'. In *Without Guarantees: In Honour of Stuart Hall*, ed. P. Gilroy, L. Grossberg and A. McRobbie, London: Verso: 148–64.

Habermas, J. (1976) *Legitimation Crisis*. London: Heinemann.

Hall, S. (1970) 'Black Britons'. *Community*, 1, no. 2: 3–5.

Hall, S. (1971) 'Innovation and decline in cultural programming on television'. Paper for UNESCO report.

Hall, S. (1973a) 'Encoding and decoding in the television discourse'. Stencilled Occasional Paper, Birmingham Centre for Contemporary Cultural Studies.

Hall, S. (1973b) 'A "reading" of Marx's 1857 Introduction to the *Grundrisse*'. *CCCS Occasional Papers* (Birmingham): 1–70.

Hall, S. (1974) 'Media power: the double bind'. *Journal of Communication*, 24, no. 4: 19–26.

Hall, S. (1976) 'A critical survey of the theoretical and practical achievements of the last ten years'. Paper for Literature, Society and the Sociology of Literature conference, Colchester: University of Essex.

Hall, S. (1977a) 'Culture, media and the "ideological effect"'. In *Mass Communication and Society*, ed. J. Curran, M. Gurevitch and J. Woollacott, London: Edward Arnold: 315–48.

Hall, S. (1977b) 'The "political" and the "economic" in Marx's theory of class'. In *Class and Class Structure*, ed. A. Hunt, London: Lawrence and Wishart: 15–60.

Hall, S. (1978a) 'Psychology, ideology and the human subject'. *Ideology and Consciousness*, no. 3: 113–21.

Hall, S. (1978b) 'Politics and ideology: Gramsci'. In *On Ideology*, ed. S. Hall, B. Lumley and G. McLennan, London: Hutchinson: 45–76.

Hall, S. (1978c) 'Pluralism, race and class in Caribbean society'. In *Race and Class in Colonial Society*, Paris: UNESCO.

Hall, S. (1978d) 'The hinterland of science: ideology and the "sociology of knowledge"'. In *On Ideology*, ed. S. Hall, B. Lumley and G. McLennan, London: Hutchinson: 9–31.

Hall, S. (1978e) 'Marxism and culture'. *Radical History Review*, no. 18: 5–14.

Hall, S. (1979) *Drifting into a Law and Order Society*. London: Cobden Trust.

Hall, S. (1980a) 'Cultural Studies: two paradigms'. *Media, Culture & Society*, 2: 57–72.

Hall, S. (1980b) 'Nicos Poulantzas: state, power, socialism'. *New Left Review*, no. 119: 60–9.

Hall, S. (1980c) 'Recent developments in theories of language and ideology'. In *Culture, Media, Language*, ed. S. Hall et al., London: Unwin Hyman: 157–62.

Hall, S. (1981a) 'Racist ideologies and the media'. In *Silver Linings: Some Strategies for the 80s*, ed. G. Bridges and R. Brunt, London: Lawrence and Wishart: 28–52.

Hall, S. (1981b) 'Notes on deconstructing "the popular"'. In *People's History and Socialist Theory*, ed. R. Samuel, London: Routledge and Kegan Paul: 227–40.

Hall, S. (1982) 'The rediscovery of "ideology": return of the repressed in media studies'. In *Culture, Society and the Media*, ed. M. B. Gurevitch, T. Curran and J. Woollacott, London: Methuen: 56–90.

Hall, S. (1983) 'Thatcherism: rolling back the welfare state'. *Thesis 11*, 7: 6–19.

Hall, S. (1984a) 'The narrative construction of reality: an interview with Stuart Hall'. *Southern Review*, 17, no. 1: 3–17.

Hall, S. (1984b) 'Conjuring Leviathan: Orwell on the state'. In *Inside the Myth – Orwell: Views from the Left*, ed. C. Norris, London: Lawrence and Wishart: 217–41.

Hall, S. (1984c) 'The rise of the representative/interventionist state, 1880s–1920s'. In *State and Society in Contemporary Britain*, ed. G. McLennan, D. Held and S. Hall, Cambridge: Polity: 7–49.

Hall, S. (1984d) 'Reconstruction work'. *Ten-8*, 16: 2–9.

Hall, S. (1985a) 'Signification, representation, ideology: Althusser and the post-structuralist debates'. *Critical Studies in Mass Communication*, 2, no. 2: 91–114.

Hall, S. (1985b) 'Authoritarian populism: a reply to Jessop et al.' *New Left Review*, no. 151: 115–24.

Hall, S. (1985c) 'Religious ideologies and social movements in Jamaica'. In *Religion and Ideology*, ed. R. Bocock and K. Thompson, Manchester: Manchester University Press in association with the Open University: 269–96.

Hall, S. (1985d) 'The role of the intellectuals is to produce crisis' (interview with U. Eco). *The Listener*, pp. 14–16.

Hall, S. (1986a) 'On postmodernism and articulation: an interview with Stuart Hall', ed. Lawrence Grossberg. *Journal of Communication Inquiry*, 10, no. 2: 45–60.

Hall, S. (1986b) 'Gramsci's relevance for the study of race and ethnicity'. *Journal of Communication Inquiry*, 10, no. 2: 5–27.

Hall, S. (1986c) 'The problem of ideology: Marxism without guarantees'. *Journal of Communication Inquiry*, 10, no. 2: 28–44.

Hall, S. (1986d) 'Popular culture and the state'. In *Popular Culture and Social Relations*, ed. T. Bennett, C. Mercer and J. Woollacott, Milton Keynes: Open University Press.

Hall, S. (1988a) *The Hard Road to Renewal: Thatcherism and the Crisis of the Left*. London: Verso.

Hall, S. (1988b) 'The toad in the garden'. In *Marxism and the Interpretation of Culture*, ed. C. Nelson and L. Grossberg, London: Macmillan: 58–74.

Hall, S. (1989a) 'Authoritarian populism'. In *Thatcherism: A Tale of Two Nations*, ed. B. Jessop et al., Cambridge: Polity: 99–107.

Hall, S. (1989b) 'The emergence of Cultural Studies and the crisis in the humanities'. *October*, 53: 11–23.

Hall, S. (1989c) 'Ethnicity: identities and difference'. *Radical America*, 23, no. 4: 9–20.

Hall, S. (1989d) 'Ideology and communication theory'. In *Rethinking Communication*, vol. 1: *Paradigm Issues*, ed. B. Dervin, London and Thousand Oaks: Sage: 40–52.

Hall, S. (1989e) 'New Times'. *Irish Times*, 30 Dec.

Hall, S. (1989f) 'The "first" New Left: life and times'. In *Out of Apathy: Voices of the New Left Thirty Years On*, ed. R. Archer, London: Verso: 11–38.

Hall, S. (1989g) 'Cultural identity and cinematic representation'. *Framework*, no. 36: 68–82.

Hall, S. (1989h) 'Then and now: a re-evaluation of the New Left'. In *Out of Apathy: Voices of the New Left Thirty Years On*, ed. R. Archer, London: Verso: 143–70.

Hall, S. (1991a) 'The local and the global: globalization and ethnicity'. In *Culture, Globalization and the World System*, ed. A. King, Basingstoke: Macmillan.

Hall, S. (1991b) 'Old and new identities, old and new ethnicities'. In *Culture, Globalization and the World System*, ed. A. King, Basingstoke: Macmillan: 41–68.

Hall, S. (1991c) 'Reading Gramsci'. In *Gramsci's Political Thought*, ed. R. Simon, London: Lawrence and Wishart: 7–10.

Hall, S. (1991d) 'Brave New World'. *Socialist Review*, 21, no. 1: 57–64.

Hall, S. (1991e) 'Reconstruction work: images of post-war black settlement'. In *Family Snaps: The Meaning of Domestic Photography*, ed. P. Holland, London: Virago: 152–64.

Hall, S. (1992a) 'New ethnicities'. In *'Race', Culture and Difference*, ed. J. Donald and A. Rattansi, London: Sage.

Hall, S. (1992b) 'The West and the Rest: discourses and power'. In *Formations of Modernity*, ed. S. Hall and B. Gieben, Cambridge: Polity: 275–332.

Hall, S. (1992c) 'Race, culture and communication: looking backward at Cultural Studies'. *Rethinking Marxism*, 5, no. 1: 11–18.

Hall, S. (1992d) 'Identity and the black photographic image'. *Ten-8*, 20: 24–31.

Hall, S. (1992e) 'Introduction'. In *Formations of Modernity*, ed. S. Hall and B. Gieben, Cambridge: Polity: 1–16.

Hall, S. (1992f) 'Cultural Studies and its theoretical legacies'. In *Cultural Studies*, ed. L. Grossberg et al., London: Routledge: 277–86. Reprinted in Morley and Chen 1996.

Hall, S. (1992g) 'Reconstruction work'. *Ten-8*, 2, no. 3: 106–13.

Hall, S. (1993a) 'The Williams interviews'. In *The Screen Education Reader*, ed. A. Alvardo, E. Buscombe and R. Collins, Basingstoke: Macmillan.

Hall, S. (1993b) 'Deviance, politics and the media'. In *The Lesbian and Gay Studies Reader*, ed. H. Abelove, M. Brale and F. Halpern, New York and London: Routledge: 62–90.

Hall, S. (1993c) 'Cultural identity and diaspora'. In *Colonial Discourse and Post-Colonial Theory*, ed. P. Williams and L. Chrisman, London: Harvester Wheatsheaf: 392–403.

Hall, S. (1993d) 'Minimal selves'. In *Studying Culture*, ed. A. Gray and J. McGuigan, London: Arnold: 134–8.

Hall, S. (1993e) 'Reflections upon the encoding/decoding model: an interview with Stuart Hall'. In *Viewing, Reading, Listening: Audiences and Cultural Reception*, ed. J. Cruz and J. Lewis, Boulder: Westview: 253–74.

Hall, S. (1995a) 'Fantasy, identity, politics'. In *Cultural Remix*, ed. E. Carter, J. Donald and J. Squires, London: Lawrence and Wishart: 63–9.

Hall, S. (1995b) 'Negotiating Caribbean identities'. *New Left Review*, no. 209: 3–14.

Hall, S. (1995c) 'Interview with Roger Bromley'. In *A Cultural Studies Reader*, ed. J. Munns, G. Rajan and R. Bromley, London: Longman.

Hall, S. (1996a) 'Introduction: who needs "Identity"?' In *Questions of Cultural Identity*, ed. S. Hall and P. du Gay, London and Thousand Oaks: Sage.

Hall, S. (1996b) 'When was the "post colonial"? Thinking at the limit'. In *The Post-Colonial Question*, ed. I. Chambers and L. Curti, London and New York: Routledge: 242–60.

Hall, S. (1996c) 'Response to Saba Mahmood'. *Cultural Studies*, 10, no. 1: 12–15.

Hall, S. (1996d) 'What is this "black" in black popular culture?' In *Stuart Hall: Critical Dialogues in Cultural Studies*, ed. D. Morley and K.-H. Chen, London: Routledge: 465–75.

Hall, S. (1996e) 'The formation of a diasporic intellectual: interview with Kuan-Hsing Chen'. In *Stuart Hall: Critical Dialogues in Cultural Studies*, ed. D. Morley and K.-H. Chen, London: Routledge: 484–503.

Hall, S. (1997a) 'Culture and power: an interview by Peter Osborne and Lynne Segal'. *Radical Philosophy*, no. 86: 24–41.

Hall, S. (1997b) 'Raphael Samuel 1934–1996'. *New Left Review*, no. 121: 119–27.

Hall, S. (ed.) (1997c) *Representation: Cultural Representations and Signifying Practices*. London: Sage.

Hall, S. (1997d) 'The centrality of culture: notes on the cultural revolutions of our time'. In *Media and Cultural Regulation*, ed. K. Thompson, London: Sage: 208–38.

Hall, S. (1998a) 'The great moving nowhere show'. *Marxism Today*, Nov.–Dec.: 9–14.

Hall, S. (1998b) 'Subjects in history: making diasporic identities'. In *The House that Race Built*, ed. L. Lubiano, New York: Vintage.

Hall, S. (1998c) 'Breaking bread with history: C. L. R. James and the

Black Jacobins', an interview with Bill Schwarz. *History Workshop Journal*, 46: 17–31.

Hall, S. (1999) 'Unsettling "the heritage": re-imagining the post-nation'. Paper for Whose Heritage? conference, North West Arts Board, Arts Council of England.

Hall, S. (2000a) 'A rage in Harlesden'. *Sight and Sound*, 8, no. 9: 24–6.

Hall, S. (2000b) 'From Scarman to Macpherson'. *Society* (Open University), 3: 8–9.

Hall, S. (2000c) 'The multicultural question'. Political Economy Research Centre Annual Lecture, University of Sheffield, at www.sheff.ac.uk/uni/academic/N-Q/lectures/htm.

Hall, S. (2001) 'Occupying Britishness and entrenching change'. *The Runnymede Bulletin*, no. 325: 17–19.

Hall, S. and Jacques, M. (eds) (1989) *New Times*. London: Lawrence and Wishart.

Hall, S. and Jefferson, T. (eds) (1976) *Resistance through Rituals*. London: Hutchinson.

Hall, S. and Schwarz, B. (1985) 'State and society, 1880–1930'. In *Crises in the British State, 1880–1930*, ed. S. Hall, M. Langan and B. Schwarz, London: Hutchinson.

Hall, S., Connell, I. and Curti, L. (1976) 'The "unity" of current affairs television'. Working Papers in Cultural Studies 9, Birmingham.

Hall, S., Lumley, B. and McLennan, G. (eds) (1978) *On Ideology*. London: Hutchinson.

Hall, S., Critcher, C., Jefferson, T., Clarke, J. and Roberts, R. (1978) *Policing the Crisis*. London: Macmillan.

Hall, S., Hobson, D., Lowe, A. and Willis, P. (eds) (1980) *Culture, Media, Language*. London: Unwin Hyman.

Halloran, J. (1970) *The Effects of Television*. London: Panther.

Hannerz, U. (1990) 'Cosmopolitans and locals in world culture'. In *Global Culture*, ed. M. Featherstone, London and Thousand Oaks: Sage: 237–51.

Haraway, D. (1991) *Simians, Cyborgs and Women*. London: Free Association Books.

Harris, D. (1992) *From Class Struggle to the Politics of Pleasure*. London: Routledge.

Hartley, J. (1996) *Popular Reality: Journalism, Modernity and Popular Culture*. London: Arnold.

Harvey, D. (1989) *Condition of Postmodernity*. Oxford: Blackwell.

Heath A. F., Jowell, R. M. and Curtice, J. K. (2001) *The Rise of New Labour*. Oxford: Oxford University Press.

Hebdige, D. (1979) *Subculture: The Meaning of Style*. London: Routledge.

Hebdige, D. (1988) *Cut 'n' Mix: Culture, Identity and Caribbean Music*. London: Routledge.

Hill, C. (1970) *God's Englishman*. Harmondsworth: Penguin.

Hill, C. (1975) *The World Turned Upside Down*. London: Penguin.

Hill, C. (1996) *Liberty against the Law*. London: Penguin.

Hobson, D. (1982) *Crossroads: The Drama of a Soap Opera*. London: Methuen.

Hoggart, R. (1958) *The Uses of Literacy*. London: Penguin.

Hoggart, R. (1970) *Speaking to Each Other*. London: Chatto and Windus.

Hoggart, R. (1992) *An Imagined Life: Life and Times 1959–91*. London: Chatto and Windus.

Horkheimer, M. and Adorno, T. (1997) *Dialectic of Enlightenment* (1944). London: Verso.

Jacoby, R. (1987) *The Last Intellectuals*. New York: Basic.

Jaggi, M. (2000) 'Prophet at the margins' (profile Stuart Hall). *The Guardian*, 8 July, pp. 8–9.

James, C. L. R. (1932) *The Case for West-Indian Self-Government*. London: Hogarth.

James, C. L. R. (1938) *The Black Jacobins: Toussaint L'Ouverture and the San Domingo Revolution*. London: Allison and Busby.

Jessop, B., Bonnett, K., Bromley, S. and Ling, T. (eds) (1989) *Thatcherism: A Tale of Two Nations*. Cambridge: Polity.

Johnson, R. (1983) 'What is Cultural Studies anyway?' Occasional Paper 74, Birmingham Centre for Contemporary Cultural Studies.

Johnson, R. (2001) 'Historical returns: transdisciplinarity, Cultural Studies and History'. *European Journal of Cultural Studies*, 4, no. 3: 261–88.

Jordin, M. and Brunt, R. (1988) 'Constituting the television audience – a problem of method'. In *Television and its Audience*, ed. P. Drummond and R. Paterson, London: British Film Institute.

Klein, N. (2000) *No Logo*. London: Flamingo.

Kuper, A. (2000) *Culture: The Anthropologists' Account*. Cambridge, Mass.: Harvard University Press.

Lacan, J. (1977) *Écrits*. London: Tavistock.

Laclau, E. (1977) *Politics and Ideology in Marxist Theory*. London: New Left Books.

Laclau, E. and Mouffe, C. (1985) *Hegemony and Socialist Strategy*. London: Verso.

Laclau, E. and Mouffe, C. (2001) *Hegemony and Socialist Strategy*, 2nd edn. London: Verso.

Laing, S. (1991) 'Raymond Williams and the cultural analysis of television'. *Media, Culture & Society*, 13: 145–69.

Lévi-Strauss, C. (1952) *Race and History*. Paris: UNESCO.

Levinas, E. (1989) *The Levinas Reader*. Oxford: Blackwell.

Lewis, J. (1983) 'The encoding/decoding model: criticisms and redevelopments for research on decoding'. *Media, Culture & Society*, 5: 211–32.

Linklater, A. (1998) *The Transformation of Political Community*. Cambridge: Polity.

McGuigan, J. (1992) *Cultural Populism*. London: Routledge.

McGuigan, J. (1996) *Culture and the Public Sphere*. London: Routledge.

McGuigan, J. (1999) *Modernity and Postmodern Culture*. Buckingham: Open University.

McLaren, P. (1997) *Revolutionary Multiculturalism*. Boulder: Westview.

Macpherson Report (1999) *The Stephen Lawrence Inquiry*, chaired by Sir William Macpherson. London: HMSO.

McRobbie, A. (1978) 'Working class girls and the culture of femininity'. In *Women Take Issue; Aspects of Women's Subordination*, London: Hutchinson: 96–108.

McRobbie, A. (2000) 'Stuart Hall: the universities and the "hurly-burly"'. In *Without Guarantees: In Honour of Stuart Hall*, ed. P. Gilroy, L. Grossberg and A. McRobbie, London: Verso: 212–24.

Mahmood, S. (1996) 'Cultural Studies and ethnic absolutism: comments on Stuart Hall's "Culture, Community, Nation"'. *Cultural Studies*, 10, no. 1: 1–11.

Marcuse, H. (1978) *The Aesthetic Dimension*. London: Macmillan.

Marx, K. (1971) *Grundrisse* (1857), ed. D. McLellan. New York: Harper and Row.

Marx, K. and Engels, R. (1965) *The German Ideology*. London: Lawrence and Wishart.

Miliband, R. (1983) *Class Power and State Power*. London: Verso.

Mills, C. W. (1956) *The Power Elite*. New York: Oxford University Press.

Mills, C. W. (1959) *The Sociological Imagination*. Harmondsworth: Penguin.

Mills, C. W. (2000) *Letters and Autobiographical Writings*, ed. K. Mills and P. Mills. Berkeley: University of California Press.

Milner, A. (1993) *Cultural Materialism*. Melbourne: Melbourne University Press.

Morley, D. (1980) *The 'Nationwide' Audience*. London: British Film Institute.

Morley, D. (1986) *Family Television*. London: Routledge.

Morley, D. (1992) *Television, Audiences and Cultural Studies*. London: Routledge.

Morley, D. and Chen, K.-H. (eds) (1996) *Stuart Hall: Critical Dialogues in Cultural Studies*. London and New York: Routledge.

Mulgan, G. (1998) 'Whinge and a prayer'. *Marxism Today*, Nov.–Dec.: 15–16.

Parekh Report (2000) *The Future of Multi-Ethnic Britain*. London: Runnymede Trust.

Poulantzas, N. (1973) *Political Power and Social Classes*. London: Verso.

Poulantzas, N. (1979) *State, Power, Socialism*. London: New Left Books.

Ramsden, J. (1998) *An Appetite for Power: A History of the Conservative Party since 1830*. London: HarperCollins.

Ricoeur, P. (1992) *Oneself as Another*. Chicago: University of Chicago Press.

Robotham, D. (1980) 'Pluralism as an ideology'. *Social and Economic Studies*, 29, no. 1: 69–89.

Rojek, C. (1995) *Decentring Leisure*. London and Thousand Oaks: Sage.

Said, E. (1994) *Representations of the Intellectual*. London: Vintage.

Schwarz, B. and Mercer, C. (1981) 'Popular politics and Marxist theory in Britain'. In *Silver Linings*, ed. R. Bridges and R. Brunt, London: Lawrence and Wishart: 143–65.

Scott, D. (2000) 'The permanence of pluralism'. In *Without Guarantees*, ed. P. Gilroy, L. Grossberg and A. McRobbie, London: Verso: 282–301.

Shilling, C. (1993) *The Body and Social Theory*. London and Thousand Oaks: Sage.

Smith, M. G. (1965) *The Plural Society in the British West Indies*. Berkeley: University of California Press.

Sparks, C. (1996) 'Stuart Hall, Cultural Studies and Marxism'. In *Stuart Hall: Critical Dialogues in Cultural Studies*, ed. D. Morley and K.-H. Chen, London: Routledge: 71–101.

Stürmer, M. (2000) *The German Empire: 1871–1919*. London: Weidenfeld and Nicolson.

Taylor, C. (2000) 'Modernity and difference'. In *Without Guarantees: In Honour of Stuart Hall*, ed. P. Gilroy, L. Grossberg and A. McRobbie, London: Verso: 364–74.

Tester, K. (1992) *Civil Society*. London: Routledge.

Tester, K. (1994) *Media, Culture and Morality*. London: Routledge.

Tester, K. (1997) *Moral Culture*. London: Sage.

Tester, K. (2001) *Compassion, Morality and the Media*. Buckingham: Open University Press.

Thatcher, M. (1993) *The Downing Street Years*. London: HarperCollins.

Thompson, E. P. (1963) *The Making of the English Working Class*. Harmondsworth: Penguin.

Thompson, E. P. (ed.) (1970) *Warwick University Ltd: Management and the Universities*. Harmondsworth: Penguin.

Thompson, E. P. (1978) *The Poverty of Theory*. London: Merlin Press.

Thompson, E. P. (1991) *Customs in Common*. London: Penguin.

Thompson, E. P. (1993) *Witness against the Beast: William Blake and the Moral Law*. Cambridge: Cambridge University Press.

Thompson, K. (1982) *Émile Durkheim*. London and New York: Tavistock/Ellis Horwood.

Tomlinson, J. (1999) *Globalization and Culture*. Cambridge: Polity.

Touraine, A. (1971) *The Post-Industrial Society*. New York: Random House.

Tudor, A. (1999) *Decoding Culture*. London: Sage.

Turner, B. (1984) *Body and Society*. Oxford: Blackwell.

Turner, B. (1992) 'Ideology and utopia in the formation of an intelligentsia: reflections on the English cultural conduit'. *Theory, Culture & Society*, 9, no. 1: 183–210.

Turner, B. (1998) 'Postmodernization of political identities'. In *Sociology and Social Transformation*, ed. B. Isenberg, Lund: Lund University: 65–79.

Turner, B. (1999) 'McCitizens: risk, coolness and irony in contemporary politics'. In *Resisting McDonaldization*, ed. B. Smart, London: Sage: 83–100.

Turner, B. and Rojek, C. (2001) *Society and Culture: Principles of Scarcity and Solidarity*. London: Sage.

Turner, G. (1990) *British Cultural Studies*. London: Routledge.

Veblen, T. (1899) *The Theory of the Leisure Class*. London: Allen and Unwin.

Venn, C. (2000) *Occidentalism: Modernity and Subjectivity*. London: Sage.

Volosinov, V. N. (1973) *Marxism and the Philosophy of Language*. New York: Seminar Press.

Walton, P. and Hall, S. (eds) (1973) *Situating Marx: Evaluations and Departures*. London: Human Context Books.

Weber, M. (1947) *The Theory of Social and Economic Organization*. New York: Free Press.

Williams, R. (1958) *Culture and Society*. London: Chatto and Windus.

Williams, R. (1961) *The Long Revolution*. London: Chatto and Windus.

Williams, R. (1968) *The May Day Manifesto*. Harmondsworth: Penguin.

Williams, R. (1973) 'Base and superstructure in Marxist cultural theory'. *New Left Review*, no. 82: 3–16.

Williams, R. (1979) *Politics and Letters*. London: New Left Books.

Williams, R. (1983) *Towards 2000*. London: Chatto and Windus.

Williams, R. (1989a) *The Politics of Modernism*. London: Verso.

Williams, R. (1989b) *Resources of Hope: Culture, Democracy, Socialism.* London: Verso.

Williams, R. (1990) *What I Came to Say.* London: Hutchinson.

Willis, P. (1977) *Learning To Labour.* London: Saxon House.

Willis, P. (1978) *Profane Culture.* London: Routledge and Kegan Paul.

Willis, P. (1990) *Common Culture.* Milton Keynes: Open University Press.

Willis, P. (2001) *The Ethnographic Imagination.* Cambridge: Polity.

Women's Studies Group (CCCS) (1978) *Women Take Issue: Aspects of Women's Subordination.* London: Hutchinson.

Wood, B. (1998) 'Stuart Hall's cultural studies and the problem of hegemony'. *British Journal of Sociology*, 49, no. 3: 399–412

Index